The Georgia Conservancy's
Guide To The North Georgia Mountains

Edited by Fred Brown and Nell Jones

Preface by Jimmy Carter

Charles Wharton, Ph.D., Science Advisor

Published by
THE GEORGIA CONSERVANCY
781 Marietta Street
Atlanta, Georgia 30318

Distributed by
LONGSTREET PRESS, INC.
2150 Newmarket Parkway
Suite 102
Marietta, Georgia 30067

Printed in the United States of America

1st printing 1990

Library of Congress Catalog Number 90-082706

ISBN 0-929264-81-9

This book was printed by Eerdmans Printing Company, Grand Rapids, Michigan.
The text type was set in Times Roman by The Georgia Conservancy, Atlanta, Georgia.
Design by Robert H. Clark, Jr.
Cover photo by Peter Beney.
Illustrations by Mozelle Funderburk, Sheila Ward, Alyce Graham, Mary Jane Warren Stone
and James DeSana.
Maps by Frank Drago, Inc.

Dedication

Dedicated to all who have worked before us and beside us in stewardship of Georgia's mountains, and to our readers in the hope they will gain a new understanding and commitment to the wise use and protection of our magnificent natural resources.

The Georgia Conservancy

Table of Contents

Preface

Looking out from our little log cabin on Turniptown Creek, which flows out of the Rich Mountain Wilderness, Rosalynn and I behold the breathtaking beauty of another Georgia mountain spring. The mountain laurel -- which locals call "ivy" -- is bursting forth with its delicate, pale pink blossoms. The waterfalls outside my window are brimming with spring's fresh rains, rapidly rushing downstream to their rendezvous with the Ellijay River. The hardwood forest surrounding us is clothed in nature's fresh green habit, and the cool spring air is sweet and clean. Phoebes are building a nest nearby in anticipation of the new life soon to appear. In the stream, rainbow trout chase stoneflies emerging to begin their brief mating flights. Everywhere there is evidence of the renewal of life.

Here in this natural setting Rosalynn and I have found peace and serenity we seldom enjoyed in our earlier years. For us, Washington, D.C. was an extraordinary center of temporal power, international politics and human sophistication. These mountains are the antithesis of the political and military power embodied in the statehouses of man's government. Here in the Georgia mountains we enter an earth-centered consciousness where nature's laws are in charge. Here, we return to the physical source of our nurturing -- nature's management of our air, water and soil, without which our civilization could not survive. We return also to a great spiritual resource, amidst God's handiwork.

Our cabin in the Cohutta Mountains has been a refuge from the press of civic duties. Here, the rumble of thunder over our mountain hideaway has replaced the 21-gun salute in some foreign port of call, and the water music of a trout stream, the sound of public ovation.

Both Hernando DeSoto, in the sixteenth century, and William Bartram, in the late eighteenth century, found these Georgia mountains clothed with verdant forests and crystal streams and peopled with the proud Cherokee. Later, Americans of European origin settled far back in the mountain coves, treasuring the solitude and the ability to sustain themselves on the rich mountain soils and forests. Today, our citizens crave these qualities that gave the early Americans spiritual strength and fierce independence. We steal back to the mountains at every opportunity to revel in the pure air and water and untrammelled wildness. This closeness to nature restores us in body and soul. We sit once again by an eternal pool and stare in wonder at the diversity of a forest that has endured the great ice ages -- a forest that remembers the howl of the wolf, the bugle of the elk, the thunder of the bison and perhaps even the cautious footfall of the first humans many years ago.

For over two centuries we have wrested from our mountains the wealth that made our nation strong -- mica, corundum, coal, iron, gold and timber. Our cities have flourished on the water from mountain rivers, filtered and purified by mountain soils. Now is the time for us to acknowledge that we can no longer live without respecting and understanding our mountain forests and the other great ecosystems of the earth which have for millennia supported the habitat of man.

This guide, painstakingly produced by many volunteers of The Georgia Conservancy, opens the door to adventure in a cherished part of our natural heritage. In addition, it introduces the remarkable diversity of mountain environments whose vital functions are powered only by the sun. Here, we stand in awe of divine forces that have shaped our planet. In a remote cove or on a high wind-swept ridge, thoughts and cares of the modern world drop away, letting us for a little while become children of the earth.

Having known the fine work of The Georgia Conservancy for over twenty years, Rosalynn and I are not surprised that this strong conservation organization has produced another excellent publication for those who enjoy nature's wonders. As one of the Conservancy's founding members in 1967, I recall very favorably participating in its annual conferences in the early seventies. Rosalynn joins me in recommending this valuable guide to all those who seek to discover the natural treasures awaiting them in the Georgia mountains.

Jimmy Carter

Foreword

What you have in your hands is the best single guide ever assembled for anyone who wants to explore, really explore, and understand the Georgia mountains.

I say that after living in Georgia for 48 years and spending a good part of that time involved somehow with the northern part of the state—driving it or walking it, or writing about it, or editing the material that others had written about it.

The year-long process of helping compile and edit this book has shown me plenty I didn't know about the mountains, and I promise that reading and using it will do the same for you.

The book looks at the mountains the way everyone should, but few people do: as two separate and distinct mountain ranges—the Cumberlands in the west and the Blue Ridge in the east—separated by three regions of valleys and ridges. This geology is what accounts for the tremendous diversity of terrain from one side of the state to the other and for the intense interest in the area by botanists and geologists. Those readers who come to terms with the mountains' geology, botany and wildlife as described and illustrated throughout the book will know more about the basic structure and the natural environments of the Georgia mountains than most people ever do.

In addition, the exploration of the Georgia mountains in this book follows "nature's organization" rather than political boundaries; it doesn't stop at the state line, but follows the natural terrain where it leads, be that into Alabama, Tennessee, North Carolina or South Carolina. As a result, readers who drive the Lookout Mountain Parkway from Gadsden, Alabama, across the northwestern tip of Georgia to Chattanooga will gain a clearer perspective of the dramatic 100-mile sweep of this flat-topped mountain. Likewise, visitors who discover the corundum deposits of Rabun County can trace them to Franklin, North Carolina, and see the mines that have produced some of the world's finest rubies and sapphires. This guidebook contains much "new" information never before assembled in one place. This happened because a large number of very knowledgeable and dedicated people contributed research, articles, maps and notes about trails, rivers, vistas or waterfalls that they have collected personally over the years or, in some cases, specifically for this book. Al Tate, for example, is a professional ecologist who, in these pages, leads readers on several hikes in the Raven Cliffs area. Mildred and Philip Greear, both recognized experts on the geology, botany, history and wildlife of the area, tell readers where to find fossils in northwest Georgia. Botanists Hugh and Carole Nourse share wonderfully detailed information about exploring the escarpment gorges, an area they have hiked for many years. Few people know more about Georgia's rivers or write about them with more feeling than Reece Turrentine, long-time canoeing editor of Brown's Guide to Georgia. In this book, Reece's guide to Lakes Rabun, Seed, Burton and Tallulah is a gem of guidebook journalism.

Chief among those contributing to this book is Charles Wharton, for 20 years professor of biology at Georgia State University and author of The Natural Environments of Georgia. I believe Charlie knows more about Georgia's Mountains, their geology, trails, trees, flowers, wildlife, rivers and vistas than any single person alive. Much of the new information in this volume was until now in his files, library and brain—it was Charlie's private stash—and he has now generously and lovingly shared it with all of us. Many of the others who contributed bits and pieces of hard-earned information from their personal data bank or did original research specifically for this book are listed in the acknowledgements.

The most gratifying thing for an editor is to witness the pooling of information from a variety of sources into something that is bigger than any one of the contributors could have done on his or her own. I have never been associated with a project that did that more successfully than this one. This book has been compiled and designed for both the casual reader and for those committed to more serious explorations. It is not a guide to the more obvious tourist attractions of the mountains, although some of those attractions are included when they add to our understanding of the natural development, history or culture of the region. It is a book filled with detail, directions and maps. There are no color pictures. To some readers it may appear at first somewhat intimidating. But I promise you that no matter how well or how little you know the mountains, whether you are taking a Sunday drive, introducing young children to their first hiking trail or setting off on a week-long backpacking trek, if you read and use this guide, it will open up a world of mountain experience that will surprise and amaze you.

Fred Brown
Editor

Acknowledgements

Any project attempting to cover an area as expansive and complex as the Georgia mountains requires a great deal of effort and cooperation from many sources. This mountain guidebook is certainly no exception. So many individuals gave of their time and talents to make the guidebook a reality that it would be impossible to recount every contribution. Without certain dedicated Georgia Conservancy volunteers, however, the guide could not have been published.

Foremost among these was Dr. Charles Wharton, research associate at the University of Georgia's Institute of Ecology, and acknowledged expert in the field of natural environments in the Southeast. We are most grateful for his unflagging dedication and support, which were an inspiration to all who worked with him.

Other steering committee members worked over a two-year period to shepherd the guide on its perilous passage from planning to publication. Committee members Donna Wear, Frank McCamey and Jack Byrne served tirelessly as team leaders of more than one hundred volunteers who went enthusiastically into the field to obtain much of the basic data used in the book. Priscilla Golley spent months organizing, further researching, consolidating and writing text from reports as they were received. Tom Perrie displayed infinite patience in setting up computer forms and formatting graphs, memos and agendas. Other invaluable committee members included Steve Bowling and Bob Kerr, who initiated the project and was instrumental in every aspect of the book's development.

The Georgia Conservancy is especially grateful to Mildred and Philip Greear, who diligently reviewed site selections and data and wrote and rewrote several portions of the text. Other volunteers contributed reports and graphics, wrote and proofread text, and carried out numerous special assignments. These included Miriam Talmadge, Chick Gaddy, Judy Alderman, Edwin Dale, Jim Renner of Wapora, Inc., Tracy Battle of Gainesville Whiteprint, Jim Mackay, Kathy Mackay, George McGee, Pat Marcellino, Bill Mitchell, Lisa Davis, Sherri Smith and Bob Humphries.

Mozelle Funderburk, Sheila Ward, Alyce Graham, Mary Jane Warren Stone and Jim DeSana provided the outstanding illustrations for the guidebook, and Bob Clark created its beautiful cover and layout with production assistance by Endra Widjanarko of Osgood and Associates and Martha O'Kelley. Peter Beney searched out and photographed the scene on our cover.

Acknowledgements are also made to the Georgia Department of Industry, Trade and Tourism; the Northwest Georgia Travel Association; the Georgia Department of Natural Resources; Georgia Power Company and the U.S. Forest Service, Chattahoochee-Oconee District, for providing and testing key information. Special thanks are due the law firm of Perrie, Buker, Stagg & McCord, particularly staffers Debra Lee and Pat Axsiom, for administrative assistance.

Without the generosity and commitment of many others to the recognition, protection and enjoyment of Georgia's natural environment, this mountain guidebook would have remained a great idea waiting to be realized. Many thanks to volunteers Cary Aiken, Walter Allen, John Ambrose, Joseph Biesbrock, Cina Smith, Andy Smith, Bud Elsea, and Peter Kirby.

To all other volunteers who helped take our mountain guidebook project from concept to culmination, The Georgia Conservancy and I offer sincere thanks for countless jobs well done: Toby Blalock, Polly Boggess, Gary Breece, John M. Brown, J. Marion Brown, Jr., Elmer Butler, Larry Caldwell, Chris Canalos, Terry Centner, Linda Chafin, Linda Cobb, Nancy Coile, Taylor Crockett, Tony Darnell, Chris deForest, Jeanne DeSana, Harriett DiGioia, Mary Lou Dixon, Marty Dominy, Frank Drago, Diana Durden, Lisha Duvaritanea, Bo Edwards, Lamar Edwards, Betty Fairley, Willard Fairley, Larry Farist, Elaine Fatora, Pat Fincher, Henry Finkbeiner, Dave Funderburk, Jerry German, Frank Golley, David Gomez, Norma Gordon, Vernon Gordon, Tom Govus, Delbert Greear, Fran Hallahan, Jane Harrell, Baker Harrison, Mahala Harrison, Anne Heath, Maryann Herbermann, Linda Hinton, Jan Holland, Amy Horne, Carol Howel-Gomez, Dick Hurd, Janet Hurlburt, Mary Ann Johnson, Bill Kaliher, Lorraine Kaliher, Eleanor Kelly, Carolyn Kidd, Jim Kidd, Reggie Kimsey, Mark Kinzer, Tom Knight, Christy Lambert, Anthony Lampros, Bobby Ledford, Holly Markwalter, Brian Markwalter, Terry McCallum, Jerry McFalls, Ed McGowin, Lucia McGowin, Marie Mellinger, Michelle Moran, Ed Morgan, Marilou Morgan, Sharon Nelson, Steve Nix, Hugh Nourse, Carolyn Nourse, Mark Ogilvie, Steven Pagano, Ray Pierotti, Scott Ranger, Annette Ranger, Ted Reissing, Ann Rhea, Rope Roberts, Carol Schneier, Diana Shadday, Ed Shanahan, Sandy Shobe, Nancy Shofner, Judy Silverman, Bob Slack, Betty Smithgall, Brian Smithgall, Lloyd Snyder, Annice Snyder, Marvin Sowder, Rosalie Splitter, Kathryn Stout, Allen Stovall, Al Tate, Alice Taylor, Claude Terry, Bill Timpone, Dawn Townsend, Ann Vanderbeek, Glen Vanderbeek, Richard Ware, Kristin Williams, Sue Worley, Janie Yearwood, Glenda Zahner and Bob Zahner.

Nell H. Jones
Steering Committee Chair
Editor

Figure 1   NORTH GEORGIA MOUNTAINS

Figure 1   NORTH GEORGIA MOUNTAINS

Guide to Maps

The Cumberland Plateau and Chickamauga Valley

The Cumberland Plateau in the western part of the north Georgia mountains is quite different from the Blue Ridge Mountains in the east (see Eastern Blue Ridge), both in geology, the way the mountains were formed millions of years ago and in physiography, the actual above-ground shape of the mountains. Largely because the Plateau is composed of so much carbonate rock and lies so far to the northwest, many of its plants and animals are found nowhere else in Georgia. Its caves, springs, sinkholes and lifeforms such as cottonmouths are not what one would expect to find in the northern part of the state. It is therefore more closely allied with southwest Georgia than with the Blue Ridge.

The folding and fusing process that formed the Blue Ridge Mountains did not extend as far west as what we know today as the Cumberland Plateau, and the metamorphic process of melting and fusing did not occur in the Cumberland to the extent that it did to the east. What we see today in the Cumberland Plateau are long "flat mountains" like Lookout Mountain. In contrast to the familiar peaks of the Blue Ridge, the rocks -- sandstone and limestone -- are much softer and have been carved and sculpted for millions of years by flowing rivers, wind and weather. The results are the fascinating boulder formations visible throughout the region, especially in places like Rocktown and the Zahnd Tract. In addition, there is a vast network of caves that makes this region of Georgia, together with parts of Alabama and Tennessee (a region referred to by cavers as TAG), one of the caving capitals of the world.

Rugged and isolated, this is a region with its own geography, color and personality. The landscape is dominated not only by the 100 mile long Lookout Mountain, but also by the dramatic interplay of clouds and sunlight across the mountain and its valleys. Little wonder former residents applied place names like Cloudland, Craigsmere, Rocktown and Lookout.

This is a land until recently relatively unknown to tourists, casual visitors and even outdoor recreational enthusiasts who have long been attracted to the mountains in the eastern part of the state. It has remained the province of local inhabitants, summer residents around Mentone, adventurous cavers and hang gliders seeking the best take-off point on the East Coast. Yet for those who discover it, this

Figure 2   CUMBERLAND PLATEAU & CHICKAMAUGA VALLEY (NORTH)

Continued on next page

©1990 THE GEORGIA CONSERVANCY, INC.

Figure 3   CUMBERLAND PLATEAU & CHICKAMAUGA VALLEY (SOUTH)

Cumberland Plateau region casts its own spell, luring one back again and again.

The Chickamauga Valley is not just one valley but a series of northeast-southwest trending valleys with limestone floors and ridges some 200 to 300 feet high, capped with more weather- resistant rock. Down through these valleys between Chattanooga and Atlanta, Union Army forces under General William Sherman pursued Confederate troops during the fighting which led to the Battle of Atlanta, near the end of the Civil War. Visitors to the military parks at Chickamauga, Missionary Ridge and Orchard Knob, as well as other areas such as the lovely and serene McLemore Cove will come away with a clearer understanding of how the natural geology of the region has helped shape recent human history.

Lookout Mountain Area

~LOOKOUT MOUNTAIN. Lookout Mountain is the southernmost extension of the Cumberland Plateau, which runs down the East Coast parallel to but inland from the Appalachian Mountains. Long and relatively flat on top, it extends for 100 miles in a diagonal that cuts across Alabama, Georgia and Tennessee. There are three miles of Lookout Mountain in Tennessee, 21 in Georgia and 76 in Alabama.

About 600 million years ago during the Cambrian period of the Paleozoic geological period, there was a vast tropical sea covering much of the area that is now Lookout Mountain. During the Carboniferous period, hundreds of millions of years later, tiny marine organisms, as well as scaly trees, plants and ferns died and decayed, helping create the sedimentary rock of the region, such as sandstone, limestone, shale and coal. Fossils showing evidence of these plants and animals are visible in the region. At the end of the Paleozoic era, mountain folding produced what we know today as Lookout Mountain.

The mountain is in one of the world's richest cave regions. When overlapping of the crusts occurred at the time the mountains were formed, faults were created. As water from streams or rain seeped into these faults, softer rock such as limestone was gradually dissolved, leaving only ledges of rock resistant to erosion. As a result, many miles of winding passages and underground streams run through the mountain.

CAVES OF LOOKOUT MOUNTAIN. In the northwest corner of Georgia, the northeast corner of Alabama and the southern part of Tennessee cavers have discovered a region linked by the Cumberland

Plateau and characterized by a vast network of caves cut through limestone rock. To cavers the region is not Tennessee, Alabama and Georgia, but "TAG" and they come from all over the world to explore its labyrinthine underground passages. Tennessee alone has more than 5,500 caves -- more than any other state. Ellison's Cave on Georgia's Pigeon Mountain is the deepest cave east of the Mississippi River.

A few caves in the region are commercial, open to the public for a fee. These include famous caves such as Ruby Falls in Lookout Mountain and lesser-known sites such as Sequoyah Caverns near Valley Head, Alabama.

Business volume varies greatly at different caves. Raccoon Mountain estimates some 10,000 visitors a year, while perhaps 350,000 see Ruby Falls.

LOOKOUT MOUNTAIN PARKWAY. [Fig. 2(1)] The designation is sometimes confusing because the "parkway" includes several roads, not just one. Nevertheless, this multi-highway driving route provides visitors to the region with an overview of the dramatic piece of geography between Gadsden, Alabama and Chattanooga, Tennessee that is Lookout Mountain. The route begins in Gadsden as AL 176 and runs in a northeasterly direction to Chattanooga. The mountain can be traversed not only in a north-south direction, but east-west as well. Visitors who explore county roads across the width of the mountain will have a better understanding of how this long flat Cumberland Plateau mountain differs from the peaks and ridges of the Blue Ridge Mountains.

SCENIC OVERLOOK. [Fig. 2(2)] On GA 157, look for a metal highway rail about 11.9 miles north of GA 48 (or 10 miles south of the intersection of GA 136 and GA 157 S.) which views McLemore Cove [Fig. 2(18)], a breached eroded anticlinal valley between Pigeon and Lookout Mountains.

ZAHND TRACT. [Fig. 2(3)] This is an area of large unusual rock formations characteristic of this region. Also present is a mixture of mesic, xeric and coastal plain plants. Most visible from the road is the mountain laurel, which is especially abundant and blooms in May. The plot is owned by the state of Georgia. The rocks are about 200 feet off the road, east of 157.

DIRECTIONS: *From the intersection of GA 48 go 12.9 miles on GA 157, or from GA 136 go 9.7 miles south on 157.*

JOHNSON CROOK. [Fig. 2(21)] Johnson Crook is a deep indentation or cove on the west side of Lookout Mountain, located entirely in Dade County, Ga. The valley of the crook is about 1,100 feet above

Mountain laurel
Kalmia latifolia

The leaves of this heath are reported to be poisonous. It is next to bloom after the flame azalea but precedes both Carolina and rosebay rhododendron. It has the most spectacular displays along streams where the plants can get full sunlight. Known to mountain people as "ivy" it forms "slicks" on dry, rocky south-facing slopes.

sea level, and the brow around it ranges from 1,900 to 2,100 feet. The village of Rising Fawn and impressive Fox Mountain are immediately to the west of the crook.

In September, 1863, shortly before the Battle of Chickamauga, an epic event occurred when 40,000 Union Troops marched from Rising Fawn east into the crook and up, over and down Lookout Mountain, building a road as they advanced and carrying with them all of the equipment of war.

McCARTY BLUFF. [Fig. 2(8)] (Lookout Mountain Flight Park and Training Center). Sixty miles of ridgeline and the unique thermal-producing qualities of the valley floor make this the premier hang gliding site on the East Coast. Pilots from all over the world sail high above the Lookout Mountain Ridge and fly for hours up and down the valley. There is usually activity every day, and spectators get a close-up, breathtaking view of winged participants jumping off the sheer cliffside. The East Coast hang gliding distance record was set here, a flight of 130 miles ending in Social Circle, Georgia. National and regional competitions are held here on a regular basis.

DIRECTIONS: *On GA 189, 7 miles north of 136.*
ADDITIONAL INFORMATION: *For information on flight training and equipment contact Lookout Mountain Flight Park and Training Center. (404) 398-3541.*

COVENANT COLLEGE. [Fig. 2(10)] Called the "Castle in the Clouds," a name first applied to the luxury hotel and gambling casino that first occupied this site in the late 1920's, Covenant is a four-year Presbyterian-affiliated college. A visit to the campus affords the visitor with the only unobstructed 360-degree panorama of the country beyond the mountain.

BROW PARK. [Fig. 3(22)] Here visitors can get a representative sample of what the views are like along the entire length of Lookout Mountain. Picnic tables, good sunset views.

DIRECTIONS: *0.2 mile north of Mentone, AL on County Road 89.*

~REFLECTION RIDING AND CHATTANOOGA NATURE CENTER. [Fig. 2(11)] Reflection Riding is a 300-acre nature preserve along Lookout Creek at the base of Lookout Mountain. It adjoins 2,000-acre Point Park and Lookout Mountain Battlefield National Military Park. The area is maintained in the style of an English natural landscape and is crisscrossed by winding paths and graveled roads. It gains its name from Reflection Pond, a landmark on the property, and the English word *riding*, meaning an inviting pleasure path. The Great Indian War Path and the St. Augustine and Cisca Trail

Beech
Fagus grandifolia

Beech prefers rich, moist soils and is most often found in ravines and along streams. Three altitudinal varieties have been described. Beech often grows with yellow birch at high elevations and may form stands as on the head of Buck Creek at White Oak Stamp. Its nuts feed a variety of wildlife. It was said to be one of the major foods of the now extinct passenger pigeon.

crossed Reflection Riding. Hernando de Soto's troop followed the Great Indian War Path over this area looking for gold. A grist mill operated by two Cherokees was on this site. Only the millstones remain today. In 1863 Union forces under General Hooker crossed Lookout Creek to engage the Confederate Army in the Battle of Lookout Mountain. Markers describing the battle are placed at many points along the drive.

Deep gorges, rock fields and moss-covered boulders provide interesting topography as well as shelter for many species of birds and other wildlife. The edges of Lookout Creek furnish habitat for bog plants, frogs and other small water creatures. Wildflowers and grasses cover the open meadows. Native rhododendron and azaleas have been planted on the mountain slope. The forest is predominantly oak with scattered groves of pine.

The 12 miles of trails are well marked and relatively easy walking. All of the trails are interconnected, so a hike can be as long or short as desired and flexible in destination. From the park border trail and the driving loop there are connections to the National Park Service trails. Maps are available at the nature center. The wetland walkway, accessible to handicapped visitors with wheelchairs, leads from the road in front of the nature center through the animal habitats to a lovely overlook beside the creek.

Along the three miles of driving loop, most of the trees and shrubs are identified, as are points of historical interest. During the blooming seasons of spring, summer and fall a variety of wildflowers can be seen. Plant identification guides corresponding to the numbered plant labels are available at the nature center. There are lots of stopping places along the way. Surrounded by ferns, the secluded gazebo overlooking Siren Pool has benches and shade where visitors can sit quietly and relax. The screened pavilion at the fragrance garden has benches and outside picnic tables.

Located at the gateway to Reflection Riding, the nature center features passive solar designed buildings containing a wildlife diorama, exhibits, a library, resource collections and a gift shop. An auditorium and solar greenhouse are next to the wildlife rehabilitation laboratory, where visitors can visit injured and orphaned wild animals, including hawks and owls. On weekends, programs including workshops, films, classes and interpretive walks are offered. Special programs are available upon request. Hand-fed Canada geese, mallards and wood ducks are year-round residents of Reflection Pond. Visitors are allowed to feed them.

DATES/HOURS: *Mon-Sat 9-5, Sun 1-5; closed holidays.*
FEES: *Adults $1.50; children $1.*
SPECIAL EVENTS: *Weekend programs, summer day camp, annual wildflower walk (mid Apr).*
DIRECTIONS: *From I-24 take exit I-75 (Brown's Ferry Road) south to US 41; go east to Garden Road; turn right (south) to Reflection*

*Riding and Nature Center. Garden Road is also reached from Scenic
Highway 148.*
ADDITIONAL INFORMATION: *Reflection Riding and Chattanoooga Nature
Center, Rt. 4, Garden Road, Chattanooga, TN 37409. (615) 821-
1160.*

~LOOKOUT CREEK. [Fig. 2(6)] Lookout Creek runs through Lookout
Valley, along the base of Lookout Mountain. It begins just across
the state line near the little town of Valley Head, Alabama. It then
flows northeastward, slicing across the extreme northwestern corner
of Georgia, then into Tennessee, where it empties into the mighty
Tennessee River at the base of Lookout Mountain in Chattanooga. It
weaves its way through Georgia for 30 miles, in and out of
wilderness areas and pasture land, offering the canoeist briskly
flowing flat waters and a moderate number of Class I shoals.
Scenery varies dramatically during the nine-mile run between the put-
in and take-out points described here. At one moment canoeists pass
through heavy forests, the next through open pastureland that offers
impressive views of Lookout Mountain, a constant companion to the
east. Although the headwaters of Lookout Creek are scarcely a mile
from the headwaters of Little River, these two neighboring rivers
flow in opposite directions. The former flows north, placidly
winding through Lookout Valley. The latter flows south, roaring
violently down the spine of the mountain. The explanation is that
although born in the same neighborhood, the streams belong to
different watersheds. Lookout Creek belongs to the Tennessee
Valley watershed; the Little River, to the Coosa Valley watershed.
This fact also explains why Lookout Creek can maintain its water
level, since it is filled by water running off the western slopes of
the entire Lookout Mountain Plateau, while its rocky-bottomed
neighbor up on the mountain, fed by a smaller watershed, can
quickly run dry.

DIRECTIONS: *The take-out bridge is on GA 136, 0.7 mile east of where
136 meets US 11 in Trenton [Fig. 2(6)]. The best take-out spot,
however, is not at the bridge but down a dirt road that runs south
along the west side of the creek for 0.2 mile to a good access point
above an old mill dam. To reach the put-in, return to Trenton on GA
136, turn left (south) on US 11 and drive 7.5 miles to Rising Fawn
[Fig. 2(6)]. Turn left (east) on Furnace Road and drive 0.3 mile to
the put-in bridge.*

Cloudland Canyon

~CLOUDLAND CANYON STATE PARK. [Fig. 2(7)] Located on the
western edge of Lookout Mountain, Cloudland Canyon is one of the

largest and most scenic state parks in Georgia. The park provides visitors with beautiful vistas of the rugged geology of this area and an excellent outdoor setting for the camper or hiker wanting to experience the beauty of the natural world. Cloudland was established in 1939 when the state of Georgia began the acquisition of land from several private landowners. Today it encompasses some 2,200 acres of beautiful mountain land. Until 1939, when construction of a Georgia highway through this area was finally completed, the only access was through Alabama or Tennessee. The park is perhaps one of the best places to view and understand the geology of northwest Georgia. An excellent guidebook, the *Geologic Guide to Cloudland Canyon State Park* by Martha Griffin and Robert Atkins, is available at the park office. It discusses the fascinating geology of this area at ten stations around the rim trails and along the trails to waterfalls on Daniel's Creek.

The park straddles a deep gorge cut into the west side of Lookout Mountain by Sitton Gulch Creek. The elevation here drops from 1,800 to 800 feet above sea level at the bottom of the gorge. The rimrock and steeper cliffs are resistant sandstone formed over 200 million years ago from beach and dune sands of an ancient shoreline. Shale layers below the sandstone are marked by a growth of pines. At the canyon bottom is a slope of rock fragments called "talus" and now heavily forested. The valley floor and gentle slopes seen in the distance are formed of fossil-bearing limestone.

FACILITIES: *75 tent and trailer sites, 16 rental cottages, 40-bed group camp, winterized group shelter, tennis courts, swimming pool, 30 walk-in campsites.*
DATES/HOURS: *Daily 7am-10pm year round; office open 8am-5pm.*
SPECIAL EVENTS: *Crafts in the Clouds, third weekend in May; Wildflower Program, May; Backpacking Trip, Oct.*
DIRECTIONS: *Located on GA 136, 8 miles east of Trenton and I-59, 18 miles northwest of LaFayette.*
ADDITIONAL INFORMATION: *Cloudland Canyon State Park, GA Department of Natural Resources, Rt. 2, Box 150, Rising Fawn, GA 30738. (404) 657-4050.*

~HIKING TRAILS OF CLOUDLAND CANYON STATE PARK.
The canyon's rugged beauty is a joy year round, each season offering special sights and sounds for visitors. A hike down Cloudland's trails to the canyon floor is a walk through millions of geologic years. Trails are well marked and easy to follow. The park provides good interpretive information about the history and geology of the area. Maps and directions to the trailheads are available in the park office.

WATERFALL TRAIL. 0.3 mile. Walk to two waterfalls on Daniel Creek.

Red tail hawk
Buteo jamaicensis

WEST RIM LOOP TRAIL. 4.9 miles. Part of the trail follows the canyon rim close to its edge. An overlook provides views into the three park gorges.

CLOUDLAND BACK COUNTRY TRAIL. 5.4-mile loop. Backpacking and camping are permitted on this trail. Stop by the park office to obtain a permit and pay the $3-per-person fee.

~FOSSIL SITE. [Fig. 2(9)] Pennsylvanian plant fossils. Fossils to be found include tree-fern-like plants called Sigillaria, small ferns such as Pecopteris, Alethopteris, Neuropteris, Archeopteris and others.

DIRECTIONS: *From the intersection of Ga 136 and GA 157 west of LaFayette, go north on 157, 5.7 miles. Turn left on Durham Road for 0.6 mile. There are large spoil banks on the right made up of minerals taken from coal mines nearby.*

~SEQUOYAH CAVERNS. [Fig. 2(5)] Also called Looking Glass Caverns because of the mirror-like reflection of cave formations in cave pools. A commercial tour lasts about 30 minutes. The path behind the log cabin labeled Sequoyah's Cabin leads to the entrance to a wild cave. It is interesting to compare this with the entrances to commercial caves. The Dogwood City Grotto, Atlanta chapter of the National Speleological Society, uses the pretty campground here for its annual fall gathering in October, when approximately 800 cavers gather for a weekend of cave exploring, camping and partying.

FACILITIES: *Campground, fishing pond, hayrides. Animals on the grounds include buffalo, Rocky Mountain sheep, goats, llama, black antelope and white fallow, spotted fallow and wild deer.*
DATES/HOURS: *Mar-Dec, open daily 8:30-5:30 (6 during summer months); Jan and Feb, Sat and Sun only 8:30-5.*
FEES: *Adults $5, children $3, under 6 free.*
DIRECTIONS: *Take the Hammondville/Valley Head exit or the Sulphur Springs/Ider exit off I-59 and follow signs.*
ADDITIONAL INFORMATION: *Sequoyah Caverns, Rt. 1, Valley Head, AL 30359. (205) 635-6423.*

~RUBY FALLS. [Fig. 2(13)] This is the most heavily promoted and commercially successful cave in the Southeast. Visitors on a recent tour were from Alaska, California, South Dakota and Japan. Visitors ride an elevator 260 feet down into the cavern. They then walk 0.4 mile one way, past a variety of rock formations to Ruby Falls, with its 145-foot cascade lighted from below with multicolored spots and accompanied by the theme from the movie *2001*. Tour guides are cheerful and enthusiastic college students.

FACILITIES: *Gift shop and lookout platform with good views of Chattanooga.*
DATES/HOURS: *8-9 daily.*
FEES: *Adults $6.*
DIRECTIONS: *Main entrance is on TN 148, 0.5 mile off US 41, 11, 64 and 72. From I-24 follow signs to Lookout Mountain.*
ADDITIONAL INFORMATION: *Ruby Falls, Scenic Highway, Chattanooga, TN 37409. (615) 821-2544.*

~EXPOSED COAL SEAM. [Fig. 2(19)] From Menlo take GA 48 west for two miles and stop just before reaching the brow of the mountain. Under massive sandstone on the left (south side of the highway) and over some shale is a thinly beaded seam of coal. One must climb the bank to see it. During the millions of years of the Carboniferous era, huge tree ferns and giant horsetails which were one to two feet in diameter and 60 or more feet high lived in the great swamps and river deltas that circled the northern hemisphere. As these plants died and fell to the earth the swamp water prevented them from losing their carbon by oxidation. After eons of peat formation these carbonized remains were compressed into layers of coal which have powered mankind ever since. To split a piece of coal and find the imprint of the leaves of these ancient forests must be one of the most significant experiences in natural history. Birmingham, AL, became a great metallurgical center because of the combination of coal and iron somewhat similar to the deposits around Lookout Mountain.

~RACCOON MOUNTAIN. [Fig. 2(14)] The absence of props such as dramatic music and sophisticated lighting allows the visitor to experience more directly the actual natural environment of the cave. Visitors may receive a personal tour by a knowledgeable caver. Wild tours -- explorations of parts of the cave not normally seen by those taking commercial tours -- leave every Saturday at 10 and Sunday at 1 and last about four hours. Hardhats, lights, rope and other necessary caving equipment are furnished.

DIRECTIONS: *From I-24 at Tiftonia/Lookout Mountain Exit, go north on US 41 and follow signs. From Lookout Mountain, follow 41 north.*
ADDITIONAL INFORMATION: *Raccoon Mountain, Rt. 4, Cummings Hwy., Chattanooga, TN 37409. (615) 821-9403.*

~NOCCALULA FALLS PARK AND CAMPGROUND. A rushing waterfall on Black Creek is the centerpiece of Noccalula Falls Park and Campground, located at the southwestern end of the Lookout Mountain Parkway. A re-created pioneer community depicts life of early settlers in this area of the Appalachian foothills. Some of the buildings were moved from their original sites to be preserved here. Among these are a house built in 1877 and a large cotton warehouse built in 1888. From March until September, a train circles the edge of the park, which includes a botanical garden. A stairway leads to the gorge below the falls and the Gorge Trail. Interesting rock formations are found in the center of the park.

FACILITIES: *Restrooms, concessions, swimming, camping, picnicking, tennis, restaurant, playground, dump station, store, laundry facilities.*
DATES/HOURS: *Park -- 8 until sundown year round; campground -- summer 7-7, fall 8-5, winter 8-4.*
FEES: *Adults $1.50; children 6-11, $.50; under 6 free. Camping fees: with water and electrical hookup $10 for 2 people, $1 for each additional person; tent with no hookups $4 per person.*
SPECIAL EVENTS: *Art On The Rocks, first Sun in May; Fall Fest, first Sun in Oct.*
DIRECTIONS: *East of I-59 on AL 211, Noccalula Road, at Gadsden, AL.*
ADDITIONAL INFORMATION: *Noccalula Falls Park and Campground, City of Gadsden, P.O. Box 267, Gadsden, AL 35999. (205) 543-7412 (campground), (205) 549-4663 (park).*

Pigeon Mountain Area

~PIGEON MOUNTAIN. [Fig. 2(4)] Pigeon Mountain and Lookout Mountain form a "V" like the thumb and index finger of a person's left hand held palm down, with Lookout being the index finger and Pigeon being the thumb. Nestled in the "V" shape is lovely McLemore Cove [Fig. 2(18)]. The northern tip of Pigeon Mountain lies about three miles west of LaFayette and stretches southwest for 10 miles, where it joins with Lookout. The mountain was named for the Passenger Pigeon, now extinct, which in the 1800's roosted there by the thousands. In the twenties and thirties some 30 families lived on Pigeon Mountain working small farms and perhaps making moonshine liquor. Their names have stayed behind as part of the landscape as in Rape Gap, Ellison's Cave and Pettijohn's Cave. The thirties, however, saw a lowering of the water table on the mountain, causing all the wells to dry up and the families to abandon their homes. To date, the water table has yet to return to its former level.

This is an area with many natural features of exceptional value for wildlife, recreation, historical, archeological and educational purposes. For 10 years it has been studied by scientists, who are still finding new and exciting plants, animals and natural environments. Some 21 rare plants and several rare salamanders are found here. The area was leased by the Georgia Department of

Northern red salamander
Pseudotriton ruber

It is always startling to turn over a rock and see this red creature with black spots. Mountaineers call them "red dogs" and believe that trout prefer them to species of other colors. Red salamanders occur in quite dry situations on the floodplains of mountain streams.

Natural Resources in 1969 as a wildlife management area. Since that time the state has purchased more than 13,000 acres of the mountain. The land is being managed primarily for wildlife and to protect and enhance its many natural features.

ADDITIONAL INFORMATION: *The Georgia Department of Natural Resources, Route 1, Floyd Springs Road, Armuchee, GA 30105. (404) 638-3944 or 295-6041.*

CAVES OF PIGEON MOUNTAIN. Like Lookout Mountain, Pigeon Mountain is laced with caves that wind all through the limestone rock. There are many cave entrances on the mountain, and it is an important location for cavers from all over the Southeast. One of these, Ellison's Cave, contains two exceptionally deep pits -- Fantastic Pit at 510 feet and Incredible Dome Pit at 440 feet. About 13 miles of Ellison's Cave have been explored and mapped but all indications are that it is much more extensive. In fact, it is likely that Pigeon Mountain is a vast system of underground caverns and stream channels. Pettijohn's Cave, near the base of the mountain on the eastern side, was first described in 1837. Approximately five miles of passageways in this cave have been mapped, and new passages are still being discovered. This cave has seen much more use than Ellison's and has sustained more damage to its mineral formations.

It should be emphasized that the underground can be an extremely dangerous area to explore for individuals unfamiliar with the skills required in caving. Entrances to caves should be explored only in the company of well-equipped, experienced cavers.

ADDITIONAL INFORMATION: *Because of the danger of caving, directions are not provided. For information on the sport of caving, contact the National Speleogical Society, Cave Ave., Huntsville, AL 35810.*

THE POCKET TRAIL. [Fig. 2(41)] A loop trail about six miles long. This steep trail climbs Pigeon Mountain and follows the ridgeline for 2.3 miles. The view to the northwest looks down on McLemore Cove, a valley of farmland between Pigeon and Lookout Mountains, and across to Lookout Mountain itself. Here the hiker has an excellent opportunity to observe and carefully climb on the unusual rock formations typical of this portion of the Cumberland Plateau. The fractured sandstone and limestone rock has been weathered and eroded over thousands and thousands of years into spires and teetering boulders that are most dramatic, particularly when perched -- as many of them are -- on the very edge of the mountain.

Several rare or uncommon plant species have been recorded here, making it one of the most remarkable botanical areas in northwest Georgia. There are at least eleven significant species associated with the small patch of mesic hardwood forest below the wet weather falls that are found almost nowhere else in Georgia. These include celandine poppy, Ohio buckeye, bent trillium, nodding spurge, lanceleaf trillium, wild hyacinth, log fern, harbinger of spring, Virginia bluebells, hairy mock-orange and blue ash. When the plants are in bloom the forest below the waterfall near the start of the trail is truly remarkable, with some species occurring in quite thick beds. The rocky slopes above The Pocket contain an unusual open forest community dominated by red cedar and chinquapin oak. It also includes the smoketree, a rarity in Georgia. Hedge nettle, another new occurrence for the state, was first observed on slopes above the open meadow.

DIRECTIONS: *From LaFayette take GA 193 west about 8 miles to Davis Crossroads. Turn left on Hog Jowl Road and go about 2.7 miles. When the road forks, take the left fork and pass Hermon Baptist Church on the left. At the top of the hill, just past the church, a paved road turns left. Turn there and follow the road (it is paved only for about 0.5 mile) into The Pocket. The road winds 1.6 miles past several fields and up a narrow mountain track that may require four-wheel drive in severe weather. Notice the falls to the right as the open area is reached. A cable across the road at the end of a small field prevents further auto travel. Park in the field. The hiking trail begins near a wooden sign beside Pocket Branch. Look for a small sign designating the trailhead and for blue blazes that mark the trail.*

ROCKTOWN HIKE. [Fig. 2(42)] About 1.0 mile one way. The exploration of the massive boulders within the 150 acres of Rocktown can easily consume the better part of a day. The biggest mistake visitors can make is not to allow enough time to inspect this unusual site. Some of the boulders are as large as three-story office buildings; a narrow pedestal supporting a caprock resembles a 25-foot tall champagne glass; deep inside a narrow dark crevice it is cool enough for hikers to see their breaths even though outside temperature may be close to 80 degrees.

The reddish rocks that hikers will see along the trail or imbedded in the sandstone formations of Rocktown are iron ore deposits. At one time there were 10 iron mines on the mountain. These deposits add a special visual interest to the Rocktown environment, because the softer sandstone erodes around them. Rocktown is easy to reach and would be a suitable hike for those of almost any age or physical condition. The trail is marked with white blazes.

DIRECTIONS: *From US 27 in LaFayette go west on GA 193 2.8 miles to Chamberlain Road; turn left and go 3.4 miles; turn right onto gravel marked by a wooden sign for Crockford-Pigeon Mountain Wildlife Management Area. Pass the Department of Natural Resources' Check Station and continue straight on the gravel road.*

Slimy salamander
Plethodon glutinosus

This is the most common terrestrial salamander, occurring under nearly every log in the forest. It is replaced by a different species at higher elevations. It is distasteful to predators and has a copious, sticky discharge that is difficult to remove from hands and fingers.

Where the road forks, 4.2 miles from the check station, continue on the right fork. Past some cleared fields on the left, there is a road to the left 1.3 miles after the fork. Turn left there and go 0.7 mile to a clearing near the trailhead.

WATERFALL BRANCH. A small stream containing a scenic waterfall. Several rare plants have been recorded on the east- and northeast-facing slopes in the vicinity of this stream, including the hairy mock-orange, the hedge nettle, the Alabama snow-wreath, the wild hyacinth, the nodding spurge and the state-protected twinleaf.

BLUE HOLE. A large spring located at the base of the eastern slope of Pigeon Mountain. The unusual bluish color of its waters, along with the fact that it represents a hydrological discharge of the extensive Ellison's Cave system, makes this a significant feature.

DICKSON GULF AND MCWHORTER GULF. These "gulfs" contain the important and rare Pigeon Mountain salamander, a species known from only four sites, all located along the eastern slope of Pigeon Mountain. The green salamander has also been collected from this area.

SAGPONDS. Water-filled depressions formed when underlying limestone strata are dissolved by groundwater and "slumping" occurs. Many of these sagponds serve as important groundwater recharge areas, slowly adding water to underground reserves. Several natural sagponds are found on top of Pigeon Mountain. Some of these have been valuable to scientists who drilled them through deep layers of peat and found ancient pollen samples which enabled documentation of the vegetation that covered the area during the Ice Age.

~MCLEMORE COVE. [Fig. 2(18)] A post-card-pretty valley nestled in the "V" formed by Lookout Mountain and Pigeon Mountain. The steep limestone and sandstone walls of the mountains form a dramatic backdrop for a scenic drive through the cove. The area is almost exclusively agricultural, with small dairy farms taking up most of the land. At the southwest end of the cove is a portion of the picturesque 11,500-acre Mountain Cove Farm. Red cedars which thrive on the limestone soil here are profuse throughout the cove, particularly along West Cove Road, as indicated by the names of the natural features and landmarks: Cedar Grove Creek, Cedar Grove community and Cedar Grove Church and Cemetery. Perhaps nowhere else in Georgia are so many cedars concentrated in such a small area.

The cove, which was named for Robert and John McLemore, sons of a white trader and a Cherokee mother, is just south of Chickamauga Battlefield. One of the Civil War battles took place at

Davis Crossroads.

Near Cedar Grove Methodist Church a large number of Union soldiers spent the night of September 17, 1863. Another antebellum structure is the 130-year-old plantation-plain style farmhouse where the Hise family has lived for generations. It is located a half mile south of Mt. Hermon Church on Hog Jowl Road. Most of the other old houses and buildings in the cove are not antebellum but date from the 1890's, when the railroad was built through the northern part of the cove.

DIRECTIONS: *Take GA 193 west from LaFayette 8 miles to Davis Crossroads. Note that the best view of McLemore Cove is from GA 157 atop Lookout Mountain.*

Military Parks

~CHICKAMAUGA AND CHATTANOOGA NATIONAL PARK. These sites became the first of four military parks established by Congress between 1890 and 1899, the others being Shiloh, Gettysburg and Vicksburg.

CHICKAMAUGA. [Fig. 2(15)] The Civil War battle of Chickamauga, in the northwest corner of Georgia, was the first of a series of decisive battles that culminated in the fall of Atlanta and brought the Civil War to a close. A Union force of about 58,000 men and a Confederate force of about 66,000 men clashed on the battlefield at Chickamauga on September 19 and 20, 1863. The result, after 34,000 casualties (3,969 dead), was that the Union Army retreated north to Chattanooga, then a town of about 2,500 people, and the Southern forces occupied Missionary Ridge and Lookout Mountain, which bordered the town. Troops from 29 of the 33 states east of the Rockies engaged in the campaign; four states had troops on both sides.

The Chickamauga Battlefield Visitor Center has an excellent museum containing artifacts related to the Civil War and the Fuller Gun Collection, which consists of 355 weapons dating from the Revolutionary War period through World War II. A 20-minute slide show is presented every half hour from 8 to 5 during the summer and 8 to 4 in the winter. Books on Civil War history and rental VCR tapes are available.

The major points of interest on the Chickamauga Battlefield, which when the battle was fought was dense woods and thick underbrush, can be reached by following a seven-mile driving tour. Monuments and markers along the road indicate the locations of units and batteries engaged in the battle.

The naturalist will also enjoy the Chattanooga National Park. It contains an outstanding array of protected natural areas with unique cedar glades, large trees, limesinks, springs, branches and trails.

FACILITIES: *Museum, orientation program, bookshop, guided tours, maps, brochures, driving tour.*
DATES/HOURS: *9 to 5 daily, year round.*
DIRECTIONS: *Exit I-75 at GA 2 and go west about 6 miles to US 27; go south to the park 1.0 mile from the town of Fort Oglethorpe.*

POINT PARK. [Fig. 2(12)] After the Battle of Chickamauga the Union Army retreated to Chattanooga, and the Confederate Army re-formed siege lines around the city with the intention of starving and freezing the Union troops into submission. Point Park, strategically positioned on top of Lookout Mountain, was the location of one of those siege lines. The dominance of the location over the city below cannot be fully grasped until one stands on the edge of Point Park and looks down on Chattanooga. A visit to this park is an opportunity, possible nowhere else in America, to visualize the grand strategy of a major Civil War battle. During the Battle of Lookout Mountain, termed the "Battle Above the Clouds" because during the fighting a band of mist and fog hung around the middle of the mountain, the Union Army drove the Confederates from their position and effectively gained control of the city.

Point Park is on the northeastern tip of Lookout Mountain. The welcome center contains a fine 13'x 30' mural painted by James Walker, an eyewitness to the battle. A tape recording provides a narrative that describes the scene and effectively draws the visitor into the action. The small Ochs Museum in the park displays clothing, equipment and photography pertinent to the battle.

DIRECTIONS: *From I-24 in Chattanooga take the Lookout Mountain exit and follow the signs for Lookout Mountain Parkway (which is Broad Street and also Hwys 11, 41, 64 and 72). Follow the signs for Ruby Falls (Point Park is past that) and, when past the Falls, pick up the signs for the Cravens House and Point Park. The route goes up the mountain on TN 148 (Scenic Highway).*

ORCHARD KNOB. [Fig. 2(16)] This hill in front of Missionary Ridge was initially the forward position of the Confederate defense line. It was taken by Union forces, and from here General Ulysses Grant commanded the assault on Missionary Ridge. On November 25, 1863, a prearranged signal of six cannon shot from this hill signaled the beginning of the battle for the ridge. Visitors will find a half dozen state monuments and a number of cannon, but the real reason to visit Orchard Knob is the geographical perspective it gives to the fighting between Lookout Mountain and Missionary Ridge.

DIRECTIONS: *Follow Broad Street in Chattanooga to Fourth St. Turn* *right and pass the Erlanger Medical Center. Turn right onto Orchard Knob Ave. Note that just before Orchard Knob Ave is Holtzclaw; turn right there to see the National Cemetery.*

MISSIONARY RIDGE. [Fig. 2(16)] Missionary Ridge was occupied by the Confederate forces after the Battle of Chickamauga and was part of the siege line around Chattanooga. During the battle for the city, Union troops attacked and captured the ridge. Along the ridge are remarkable views of Orchard Knob, Chattanooga and Lookout Mountain. The entire length of the ridge was occupied by Confederate forces and formed part of the siege line. Markers, plaques and gun positions give details of troop positions and describe the action in which various units participated. The historical markers are dispersed among elegant houses.

DIRECTIONS: *From Orchard Knob continue on Third St. Turn right on Glenwood and left on Oak, which merges with Shallowford and then intersects with Crest Road to run along Missionary Ridge.*
ADDITIONAL INFORMATION: *Chickamauga and Chattanooga National Military Park, Point Park and Lookout Mountain, National Park Service, P.O. Box 2128, Fort Oglethorpe, GA 30742.*

Black locust
Robinia pseudo-acacia

While not confined to the mountains, the black locust commonly seeds into mountain coves following heavy logging or other disturbance. Its wood is much in demand for fence posts, since it contains a chemical which prevents fungal growth.

Little River (see Fig. 4)

~LITTLE RIVER CANYON. [Fig. 3(26)] Little River Canyon on long, flat Lookout Mountain is the deepest gorge in the eastern United States. With an average depth of 400 feet, it is 600 feet at its deepest point and three-quarters of a mile across. Little River flows right down the middle of the canyon and, therefore, down the spine of Lookout Mountain, making it the only river in North America to flow its entire length along a mountaintop.

Geologists have devised two theories to explain the canyon's formation, neither of which has been proved or disproved. One is that the river may have once flowed underground until its roof overhead caved in and exposed it. Or perhaps an upheaval within the earth opened up a crevice which was enlarged over time by the erosive action of the river formed within it.

~DESOTO FALLS. [Fig. 3(23)] In addition to a beautiful 100-foot waterfall, there is a dam creating a lovely mountain lake which provides swimming, fishing and boating.

~DESOTO STATE PARK. [Fig. 3(24)] This fine Alabama state park has approximately 20 miles of easy-to-follow, well marked hiking trails. Rustic foot bridges span many of the streams; unusual rock formations and rare forms of plant life are found along these trails.

FACILITIES: *This fine state park has a variety of lodging, including rustic log cabins, mountain chalets, a lodge, and a 25-unit motel, as well as campgrounds. The information center has a coin-operated laundry, restrooms, country store and a local craft and gift shop. The store is stocked with all items necessary for camping, picnicking and housekeeping in the cottages. Additional facilities include a picnic area with rustic stone shelter, picnic tables and grills, volleyball court and ball field (equipment may be checked out at the country store), Olympic-size pool and two unlighted tennis courts.*
DIRECTIONS: *On Alabama county road 89. Follow signs from Mentone, AL.*
ADDITIONAL INFORMATION: *For general information on DeSoto State Park camping, hiking and picnicking contact DeSoto State Park, Rt. 1, Box 210, Fort Payne, AL 35967. (205) 845-0051. For information on the lodge, reservations for cottages or rooms contact DeSoto State Park, Rt. 1, Box 205, Fort Payne, AL 35967. (205) 845-5380.*

~DESOTO SCOUT TRAIL. [Fig. 3(25)] This is a 12-mile trail that begins at Comer Scout Camp and follows the West Fork of Little River to a spot north of AL 35. Inquire at the DeSoto State Park

Hellbender
Cryptobranchus alleganiensis

This grotesque creature is our largest salamander, over twenty inches long. It lives under rocks in well-oxygenated mountain streams but only in Tennessee River tributaries on the north side of our Blue Ridge.

Guide To The North Georgia Mountains

Figure 4   LITTLE RIVER

information center for detailed directions to the trailhead. (205) 845-0051. The trail is closed during November, December and January.

~GRACE HIGH FALLS. [Fig. 3(27)] The highest waterfall in Alabama, it is located on the south side of Bear Creek Canyon but can be seen only from the north side of the canyon.

~LITTLE RIVER CANYON HIKING TRAIL. [Fig. 3(28)] This six-mile hiking trail follows the north bank of Little River. (Note: A flood in 1985 brought 15 inches of rain in three hours to the canyon and resulted in road washouts, rock slides and tree falls. When this trail was last hiked by our reviewer, those obstructions had still not been cleared, making the trail difficult to follow, particularly on the north end.)

DIRECTIONS: *To begin the trail at its northern end, follow the Little River Canyon Rim Road (AL 275) to its intersection with 176. There on the rim road see an abandoned chairlift that at various times has transported tourists to and from the canyon floor. The trail down to the river is just a few yards north of the chairlift. It is extremely steep. The trail leads south along the river. The easiest access is from the southern end of the trail at Canyon Mouth Park, a county park operated by Cherokee County. The trail, at this point designated the JFK Trail and marked with yellow blazes, begins at a dirt-and-gravel parking area on the back side of the park.*
ADDITIONAL INFORMATION: *The park manager at Cherokee County Park will discuss setting up a shuttle to the northern trailhead -- a good idea since cars have been vandalized along Rim Road. Contact Little River Canyon Mouth Park, Rt. 2, Box 150, Cedar Bluff, AL 35959. (205) 779-6814.*

~RIM DRIVE. A 22-mile drive along the western rim of Little River Canyon. The road passes a dozen lookout points and is a rewarding way to experience one of the most outstanding natural landscapes in the Southeast.

~LITTLE RIVER CANOE TRIP. [Fig. 3(29)] Little River is classified as an Alabama Wild and Scenic River. It would have qualified as a National Wild and Scenic River had it not been for the now abandoned chairlift near the intersection of 176 and Rim Road. It is the only river in America that flows its entire length on top of a mountain. Etched deep in the spine of the long Alabama portion of Lookout Mountain, it flows through the deepest canyon east of the Rockies.

Born in the uplands around Mentone, Little River grows until it reaches the dramatic 100-foot DeSoto Falls at DeSoto State Park. It is a pretty Class II run until it is joined by its east fork just above

Vasey's trillium
Trillium vaseyi

In rich, moist areas this trillium has huge leaves and stands nearly two feet tall. You need to lift the wide leaves to see the remarkable maroon-colored flower nodding below.

THE GEORGIA CONSERVANCY

the AL 35 Bridge. Just below the bridge it takes a lethal, 60-foot plunge downward and the Little River Canyon is born dramatically.

When the water level is right, the river is a fast and heavy whitewater run of repeated Class II, III and IV rapids. Only experienced canoeists should attempt it. Even then, it should be run only after careful preparation and on-the-spot information checks with the DeSoto State Park information office. There are no water gauges in Little River, and levels can change from unrunably bumpy in low water to suicidally heavy in high water. This river requires a support team of at least three canoes equipped with heavy throw ropes, life vests and helmets. The canyon section of the river runs 16 miles from the AL 35 Bridge to Canyon Mouth Park, but only half of this is suitable for canoeing.

The run from Eberhart's Point to Canyon Mouth Park is approximately eight miles, but the distance is deceptive. Canoeists will need all the daylight hours available for unpredictable portages and unavoidable delays. Once in the canyon one has no way out but downriver. In moderate water some of the rapids must be portaged. Do not try to run the section of the river from AL 35 to Eberhardt's Point. According to park officials, most who try this end up having to rope themselves and their damaged canoes up the 500-foot cliffs to get out. Consider coordinating a canoe trip with an accompanying hiking party. This will provide additional support for the put-in portage and other necessary portages around unrunable rapids. (See hiking trail, above.)

DIRECTIONS: *To put in and take out, from Rome go west on GA 20 into Alabama. About 10 miles into Alabama, turn north on AL 35 continuing to the Little River Canyon Bridge. At the northwest corner of the bridge begins the Canyon Rim Parkway. Follow this for approximately 15 scenic miles to Eberhart's Point, the site of a now defunct chairlift. Several trails lead down the canyon wall to the put-in. Each is tortuous and long, a portage of almost 600 feet virtually straight down. Only the most determined of paddlers will attempt it. Vehicles can be shuttled to the take-out at Canyon Mouth Park or, alternately, at AL 273 if the park is closed.*

~EAST FORK OF LITTLE RIVER CANOE TRIP. [Fig. 3(30)] The east fork of Little River provides the average canoeist with a safe yet exciting way to experience this canyon area without having to face the dangers and difficulties of Little River Canyon further downstream. Located north of the actual canyon area, the east fork is a canoeable Class I - III tributary for paddlers of beginner and intermediate skills. It begins in the southwest corner of Georgia's Walker County and flows into Alabama for a distance of 16 miles before it joins with the west fork to form Little River. The information here covers the last 6.0 miles of the east fork (from Lake Lahusage to the confluence with the west fork) and the first 5.0

miles of the Little River (down to the AL 35 bridge). It is just beyond this bridge that the Little River takes its dramatic plunge into the canyon. The total canoeing distance from this run is 11.2 miles, a distance that can be covered in one full day of paddling.

DIRECTIONS: *For the shortest and fastest shuttle, leave the take-out bridge on AL 35 and go south on this road for 3 miles until it meets County Road 15 at Blanche, AL. Turn left (NW) on County Road 15 and go 11 miles (crossing back into Georgia) to Menlo. There, turn left onto GA 48 and go 4 miles to the Alabama state line. Two hundred yards past the state line sign is a paved road to the left, the Old Dam Road. Turn left here and go 1.4 miles to the dead end at the put in [Fig. 3(20)].*

For a more scenic shuttle, only 4.8 miles longer than the one above, go north from the take-out bridge on AL 35 for 5.4 miles then turn right on AL 89 (the DeSoto State Park Road) and follow this road through the state park, past DeSoto Falls for 11.4 miles to Mentone. In Mentone, turn right on AL 117 and go 6 miles, arriving at the Old Dam Road leading off to the right, about 200 yards before the Georgia state line. Follow the Old Dam Road 1.4 miles to the put-in.

MAP REFERENCES: *USGS 1:100,000 series: Chattanooga - Chickamauga - Rome.*

Armuchee Ridges

Unlike the Cumberland Plateau's broad flat-topped mountains complete with streams, the Armuchee Ridges are true ridges, relatively narrow and linear. Roadside ditches along Taylor Ridge are filled with multimillion-year-old fossils from former sea floors. There are also "pockets" or coves, outcrops of iron ore, and attractive waterfalls to provide visitors with pleasant travel destinations.

Instead of both sides of these ridges being similar, as in the Cumberland Plateau, here opposite sides are different. For example, on Taylor Ridge the western summit face is sandstone, while the east face cliffs are hard chert, a non-crystalline quartz. Rocky Face is similar, except that siltstones underlie its western flanks instead of limestone. These differences in rockface lead to changes in both topography and plant communities.

~TAYLOR RIDGE. [Fig. 5(1)] extends as one geological unit from the village of Holland on GA 100 in Chattooga County northwestward beyond the Tennessee line. Remnant of an ancient, larger ridge which once reached all the way to Lookout Mountain, it eroded over a period of some 200 million years. In the valley between Taylor Ridge and Lookout Mountain are located the towns of Summerville, LaFayette and Ringgold. The ridge is broken by a gap at Ringgold, the Ringgold Cut, where its name is changed to Whiteoak Mountain, although it is the same structure geologically. GA 100 passes the southwest tip of the Ridge. It is crossed by US 27 between Gore and Summerville, by GA 136 between Villanow and LaFayette, by I-75 at Ringgold and by several U.S. Forest Service roads. Because of federal ownership both John's and Horn Mountains are in a wildlife management area. Gate closure is seasonal; some gates are open only for hunting.

Geological time periods which can be observed in road cuts are Silurian (the age of fishes) and Mississippian (the carboniferous "coal age" and the age of amphibians).

~TAYLOR RIDGE TRAIL. [Fig. 5(2)] 2.4 miles. The trail, for foot traffic only, runs along the Ridge to FS Road 635-A.

DIRECTIONS: *Take GA 136 east from LaFayette for about 7 miles to the top of Taylor Ridge. Turn right (south) onto FS 217 (at gate). The trail begins at this point in the left fork of the road.*

~CHICKAMAUGA CREEK TRAIL. [Fig. 5(3)] 6.2 miles. A loop trail which begins and ends at the end of Ponder Creek Road. Foot travel only.

Timber rattlesnake
Crotalus horridus

You can hike for years in the mountains without seeing a rattlesnake. They are patchy in distribution and live in isolated areas near rock cliffs where they "den" in the winter. This snake is not aggressive and seldom even rattles, preferring that you pass it by unnoticed. Just watch where you put your feet and hands in thick brushy places.

Figure 5 ARMUCHEE RIDGES

DIRECTIONS: *Take GA 136 east from LaFayette for 9 miles. Turn left onto Ponder Creek Road and go about 0.6 mile. Take the right fork onto FS 219 to the end of the road. The trail can also be reached along FS 250, located at the intersection of GA 136 and Taylor Ridge.*

~**HOUSTON VALLEY ORV AREA.** [Fig. 5(4)] This 2,600-acre off-road vehicle area has a network of trails for motorbikes and all-terrain vehicles. Timbering is conducted in this area, so visitors are asked to stay on the trails.

DIRECTIONS: *From I-75 take the LaFayette exit 133 west onto GA 136 connector and go 7 miles. Turn right at GA 136 and go 11 miles. Turn right onto GA 151 and go 6 miles to Nickajack Road, located beside Wood Station Volunteer Fire Department. Follow Nickajack Road for 2 miles, crossing Taylor Ridge. At the base of Taylor Ridge, turn right onto Capehart Road and go 1 mile until the pavement ends. A parking area for Houston Valley is on the left at the beginning of a USFS gravel road.*

~**HIDDEN CREEK RECREATION AREA.** [Fig. 5(5)] The recreation area is located on a creek which appears and runs clear and cool for a day or so, then disappears. The area is a prime example of an oak-hickory forest, with a few beech trees in low-lying areas. There is a wide variety of flowering shrubs and plants. Dogwood, sourwood, hickory, maple, yellow poplar and red oak abound. The varied forest conditions offer excellent opportunities for the birder. There are no hiking trails but many dirt roads to walk.

FACILITIES: *16 campsites with tent pads, picnic tables and fire rings are seldom full, even on weekends; water pump near the entrance; sanitary facilities.*
DATES/HOURS: *Memorial Day - Oct 31.*
DIRECTIONS: *Exit I-75 onto GA 156 at Calhoun; go southwest for 7.5 miles; turn right (northwest) on FS 231 and go 2 miles; turn right (north) on FS 228 and go 4 miles.*
ADDITIONAL INFORMATION: *Hidden Creek Recreation Area, U.S. Forest Service, Armuchee Ranger District, 706 Foster Blvd., LaFayette, GA 30726. (404) 638-1085.*

~**THE POCKET RECREATION AREA.** [Fig. 5(6)] Not to be confused with the pocket on Pigeon Mountain, it got its name because it lies in a low pocket created by the steep ridges of Horn Mountain, which surrounds it on three sides. From 1938 through 1942 it was the site of a Civilian Conservation Corps camp. The foundations of the old structure are still visible. A large, clear, ice-cold spring bubbles up in the middle of the picnic area and flows through the recreation area as a refreshing creek for wading. Watercress grows abundantly in this spring.

FACILITIES: *Camping, picnicking, hiking, restrooms (handicapped facilities), drinking water.*
DATES/HOURS: *6-1, Apr-mid Nov.*
SPECIAL EVENTS: *Campfire program on weekends.*
FEES: *Campsites $5.*
DIRECTIONS: *Exit I-75 onto GA 136; go approximately 14 miles west toward Villanow; 0.5 mile east of Villanow, turn left (south) on Pocket Road, county road 230, and go approximately 7 miles past Keown Falls.*

~THE POCKET TRAIL. [Fig. 5(7)] A well maintained and clearly marked hiking trail makes an east 2.5-mile loop from the picnic area along low-lying streambeds and back to the campgrounds. When spring arrives, azaleas, dogwood, sourwood and mountain laurel enliven the area with color. In the fall it is brilliant with the leaves of hickory, maple, oak, beech and yellow poplar. The soil's subsurface in this area, made up of white limestone, erodes more easily than the harder rocks which make up the higher elevations in northwestern Georgia. This erosion has resulted in the area's unusual topography.

DIRECTIONS: *See The Pocket, above.*

~KEOWN FALLS SCENIC AREA AND HIKE. [Fig. 5(8)] This scenic area was set aside because of the unique rock bluffs and high elevation swampy areas formed from springs. Keown Falls, named for land surveyor Gordon Keown, are twin falls located along two spring-fed streams within the 218-acre scenic area. The larger tumbles 60 feet and the smaller about 40 feet. During summer the streams may become dry. A sign posted at the trailhead informs visitors whether the falls are flowing. The area is scenic even when the falls are dry. The 1.8-mile Keown Falls Loop Trail begins and ends at the picnic area parking lot. It is unmarked but easily followed. The northern part of the loop provides views of moisture-loving cove hardwood tree species, and the southern portion gives views of tree species indicative of dry ridges. This trail may be used to access the 3.5-mile John's Mountain Loop Trail, which is marked with white blazes. An overlook at the top of John's Mountain offers a scenic vista of Taylor Ridge, Lookout Mountain and the surrounding valley.

Keown Falls Recreation Area, located adjacent to the scenic area, offers an abundant variety of colorful wildflowers and shrubs. Mountain laurel blooms throughout the late spring and early summer months; both the pink and white varieties bloom in June. Azaleas and dogwood add to the springtime color. The mixture of hickory,

Red squirrel
Tamiasciurus hudsonicus

About half as large as a gray squirrel, red squirrels have white and black stripes down their sides. This frisky squirrel prefers evergreens, especially spruce-fir, but has been found as far south as Jack's Gap on the Georgia Blue Ridge (Brasstown Bald sector). Red squirrels have been seen in the city limits of Clayton where they feed on the cones of the Virginia pine.

sourwood, oak, beech and yellow poplar presents a brilliant spectrum for autumn leaf watchers. The picnic area located in a forest at the foot of John's Mountain has a flowing creek where children can wade and tired hikers can cool their feet.

FACILITIES: *Parking, picnic area with tables and pedestal grills, restrooms, hand pump for water, hiking trail. Maps and brochures available at the U.S. Forest Service office (see below).*
DATES/HOURS: *Dawn to dusk every day, Apr-Oct 31 (opening date subject to change).*
DIRECTIONS: *Take GA 136 east from LaFayette for 13.5 miles; turn right (south) at Villanow onto Pocket Road; go approximately 5 miles to the Keown Falls entrance road, FS 202.*
ADDITIONAL INFORMATION: *Keown Falls Recreation Area, U.S. Forest Service, P.O. Box 465, Lafayette, GA 30728. (404) 638-1085.*

~JOHN'S MOUNTAIN TRAIL. [Fig. 5(9)] 3.5 miles. This loop trail begins and ends at the John's Mountain Overlook located at the end of FS 208. The trail connects with the Keown Falls Trail above the falls.

DIRECTIONS: *Take GA 136 east from LaFayette for 13.5 miles. Turn right (south) past Vilanow onto a county road (Pocket Road) and go about 4 miles. Turn right onto FS 208 to the observation deck.*

~ARMUCHEE CREEK CANOE TRIP. [Fig. 5(10)] This is a canoe float through peaceful rural surroundings with excellent fishing for redeye and largemouth bass, red breast bream and catfish. The trip lasts from four to five hours for those who do not fish, and a day or more for those who do. Twenty minutes is required to float from the put-in to the bridge at Ebenezer Church; three hours, from the church to US 27 bridge north of Armuchee (an alternate take-out); and an additional hour, from there to the take-out in Armuchee. Livestock may be present where the creek winds through a cattle pasture and a pig farm; these are quickly passed, however.

DIRECTIONS: *From Rome take US 27 north to Armuchee; then take the Haywood Valley Road north to Ebenezer Baptist Church; cross the bridge just beyond the church and turn right. Follow this unnamed road to the next bridge, which is the location of the put-in. The take-out is in the Armuchee Community. Following 27 north from Rome, turn left on the first road after crossing the creek. The Armuchee post office is on the right after the turn. Go 0.25 mile to the creek.*

~FOSSIL SITES. This region of Georgia contains numerous fossil deposits. Many are exposed in road cuts which are accessible to the public.

Two-lined salamander
Eurycea bislineata

MISSISSIPIAN SITE. [Fig. 5(11)] From Rome take US 27 north 18.8 miles to the Gore intersection. Go 0.3 mile from Gore, turn right (north) onto a Forest Service road and park almost immediately by a gate. Walk up an old woods road to the left. There are many crinoid stems, some brachiopods, some bryozoa and rare small geodes. At this site the best picking is after a hard rainfall which tends to expose the fossils.

SILURIAN FOSSIL SITE. [Fig. 5(12)] From the Gore intersection, above, go an additional 1.5 miles; turn left at the top of Taylor Ridge on a Forest Service Road; go 0.2 mile. In the road bank on the right find chunks of iron ore containing Silurian cephalopods such as Homotoma. Usually one must break open the ore to find the fossils. They are very small -- 5 to 15 mm long and 2 to 3 mm in diameter.

~JAMES H. "SLOPPY" FLOYD STATE PARK. [Fig. 5(13)] The park covers 269 acres at the base of Taylor Ridge. It was named for a Georgia state representative who served in the legislature from 1953 until his death in 1974.

Two fishing lakes have wooden porch swings along their shorelines where visitors can sit and relax. Trails circle each lake. Rental boats are available and private boats are welcome. Only rowing, paddling or trolling motors are permitted. The lakes are stocked with channel catfish, bream and bass and are open for fishing all year round. The park has a program of wildflower planting and an ongoing program for restoring the bluebird population.

FACILITIES: *25 shaded tent and trailer campsites with water and electrical hookups, within walking distance of the lake; a primitive camping area with only water and pit toilets, available for organized groups; two picnic shelters; fishing; boat ramps and docks; boat rental; hiking; playground; trailer dump station.*
DATES/HOURS: *7am-10pm year round; office open 8am-5pm.*
DIRECTIONS: *2.0 miles south of Summerville on US 27, turn south onto well-marked road to the park.*
ADDITIONAL INFORMATION: *James H. "Sloppy" Floyd State Park, Georgia Department of Natural Resources, Rt. 1, Box 291, Summerville, GA 30747. (404) 857-5211.*

MAP REFERENCES: *USGS 1:100,000 series: Chattanooga - Chickamauga - Rome - Cleveland - Dalton - Cartersville.*

Great Valley

The Great Valley, situated between the Armuchee Ridges and the Cohutta Mountains, has long presented to all types of life an easy route from the coastal lowlands of Alabama to the north Georgia mountains and further north into North Carolina and Virginia. This was true even in prehistoric times when such animals as barking tree frogs and cottonmouthed moccasins moved northward along the sluggish streams, swamps and oxbow lakes of the Coosa River. These watery roads were probably main trading routes between Creek and Cherokee nations. The names of great rivers like Conasauga, Oostanaula, Coosawattee and Etowah attest to their Indian heritage. Etowah Mounds, Georgia's best known Indian village, is near the junction of the Etowah and Pumpkinvine Creek. The wide bottomlands of the valley, their timbers already killed in many areas by beaver, presented fertile settings for the corn-bean-squash agriculture of the Mississippian period of Indian culture (1000 A.D. - 1500 A.D.) Here in this region Indians trapped great spawning runs of fish such as the small mouthed buffalo and the fresh water drum. Tons of these fish were captured, smoked and dried. The unpolluted rivers were also full of large freshwater clams. Chestnuts, black walnuts and acorns of the lush valley forest, together with abundant game, supplemented the Indian diet.

The first white settlers must have eyed the Great Valley as a land of Eden when they arrived. As settlement of the territory continued, the Coosa River system opened up a large market for the goods grown here.

~THE CHIEFTAIN'S MUSEUM. [Fig. 6(1)] Located on the banks of the Oostanaula River, this was the nineteenth-century home of Major Ridge, a prominent Cherokee Indian who, along with his family, operated a ferry boat, owned a store and lived as slave-owner planters. The museum in the white clapboard plantation house contains exhibits describing Ridge's life and the history of Rome and northwest Georgia. Visitors can walk on a paved trail along the river. There is also an archeological dig at the site.

DATES/HOURS: *11-4 Tue-Sat, 2-5 Sun; closed Mon.*
FEES: *Adults $1, children free, groups $.75 per person.*
DIRECTIONS: *Located in Rome on Riverside parkway between GA 53 spur and US 27.*
ADDITIONAL INFORMATION: *The Chieftain's Museum, 501 Riverside Parkway, P.O. Box 373, Rome, GA 30162. (404) 291-9494.*

Figure 6   GREAT VALLEY

Northern red oak
Quercus rubra

This is a prize timber tree but seldom reaches a density of over 10 percent of the forest. It is a principal tree on most of the high ridges of the southern Appalachians between 3000 and 5000 feet. Along the Appalachian Trail, red oaks are often dwarfed and bonzaid by altitude and wind, and 200-year-old trees may be only 12 inches in diameter.

~MARSHALL FOREST NATURE PRESERVE. [Fig. 6(2)] Marshall Forest, an old-growth forest with remnants of virgin forest, was designated Georgia's first National Natural Landmark in 1966. The 104-acre forest was donated to The Nature Conservancy in 1976 by the Marshall family, who had owned and protected it for nearly a century. About 300 plant species, including 46 tree species, grow here. The trees are a mixture of northern and southern species. Northern red oak and chestnut oak are near the southern limits of their ranges, while longleaf pine is near its northern limit. The forest is home to several rare or unusual species. Access to the area is by special permission or guided tour only. Tours are provided by the Marshall Forest Stewardship Committee and may be arranged by calling the office. Students from several colleges and universities in the state have used the forest as a research site.

There are five trails, but most tours are conducted on the braille trail, which was designed for the visually impaired. Unfortunately, all of the trails are unkept. Lists of plants, birds and trees are available.

FACILITIES: *Tours, braille trail, other trails. Note: Access to the forest is by reservation only.*
DIRECTIONS: *In Rome go west on Shorter Ave. (GA 20); turn south (left) on Horseleg Creek Road. Forest begins approximately 0.5 mile from Rome city limits.*
ADDITIONAL INFORMATION: *Marshall Forest Nature Preserve, The Nature Conservancy, Chamber of Commerce, Rome, GA 30161. (404) 291-0766.*

~LOCK AND DAM PARK. [Fig. 6(3)] Mayo's Bar Lock and Dam were built on the Coosa River at Horseleg Shoals to facilitate the movement of steamboats and barges upstream from Alabama, to Rome. As many as 50 steamboats operated on the Coosa River between Rome and Greensport, Alabama during the mid- to late-1800's. These had difficulties navigating through shoals located throughout the river. The worst of these was Horseleg Shoals, and local citizens built temporary dams to create a deeper pool of water. Congress ordered a survey of the Coosa River in 1870, but it was not until 1913 that the lock and dam near Rome was completed. By the time of its completion, only three commercial boats remained on the river, and one of these was the Corps of Engineers' dredge. The steamboats turned to transporting passengers for picnics, parties and hunting and fishing trips. River traffic dwindled until the lock was finally closed in 1941.

FACILITIES: *25 campsites equipped for recreational vehicles, fishing, hunting, picnicking, boat launch ramp, boat dock, fuel and supplies, restrooms, canoe rental, trail, handicapped facilities, brochures, maps, restaurant, dump station.*

DATES/HOURS: *8-6 Mon-Fri, 7-7 Sat-Sun; closed Christmas and New Year's Day.*
FEES: *Individual camping $8-$10, groups $1.50 per person ($15 minimum).*
DIRECTIONS: *On the Coosa River 7.5 miles south of Rome. Take US 27 to Walker Mountain Road; turn west; go 3.4 miles to park.*
ADDITIONAL INFORMATION: *Lock and Dam Park, Rome-Floyd County Parks and Recreation Authority, 181 Lock and Dam Road, Rome, GA 30161. (404) 234-5001.*

~CAVE SPRING. [Fig. 6(4)] Cave Spring, settled in 1829, is a picturesque village in beautiful Vann's Valley. Definitely off the beaten track (about eight miles east of the Alabama border, fifteen miles south of Rome), the small community has been able to preserve its charm and integrity from modern development. Over 90 structures in Cave Spring are listed on the National Register of Historic Places.

Cave Spring's original claim to fame is its mineral spring flowing from a cave. The cave is in Rolater Park, which covers 29 acres of natural landscape inside the village. Little Cedar Creek flows through the park and village. The park has covered pavilions and picnic tables under beautiful trees. The large limestone cave is a popular attraction. It is open to the public during the summer and boasts a cool temperature of 56 degrees. The mineral spring has a capacity of about four million gallons a day of the "purest water in Georgia, " which is now being bottled and sold in stores. There is a 1.5-acre swimming pool, the second largest in Georgia, which is fed by spring waters. The Hearn Academy Inn is also on park grounds. Begun in 1839 as a dormitory for the Hearn Manual Labor School, it has been restored by the Cave Spring Historical Society, which offers tours of the building during Country Festival Week. Bed and breakfast are available here, as well as catered parties and weddings by reservation.

Also in Cave Spring is the Georgia School for the Deaf. Its first five students were admitted in 1846. The school is still in its original location.

FACILITIES: *Historic village with many old buildings; 29-acre Rolater Park with limestone cave, mineral spring, swimming pool and picnic tables. Hearn Academy Inn features bed and breakfast (404) 777-8439; antique shops in village, including Country Roads Antique Mall, 14,000 square feet; two village restaurants feature home cooking.*
SPECIAL EVENTS: *Annual Country Festival and Road Race, second weekend in June, incudes tours of Hearn Academy and arts festival.*
DATES/HOURS: *Rolater Park 7am-9pm year round, staff on duty Memorial Day to Labor Day. Swimming pool 10-5; cave 11-4 and by request.*
FEES: *Pool $1.50, cave $1.*

DIRECTIONS: *On US 411 about 15 miles south of Rome.*
ADDITIONAL INFORMATION: *Hearn Academy and Rolater Park (404) 777-8439.*

~BERRY COLLEGE (DRIVING TOUR). [Fig. 6(5)] Berry College was founded around the turn of the century by the remarkable Martha Berry. She lured industrialists such as Henry Ford and politicians such as Teddy Roosevelt here and convinced them to support her efforts to educate rural mountain children getting their first chance at formal schooling. It has one of the largest campuses in the world (28,000 acres). In the early years studies were conducted in log cabins which still stand, well preserved, but now Berry students use 40 more-modern buildings. Most of the property owned by the College is farmland which is worked by students in accordance with the founder's idea that every student should work part time on campus to help defray tuition costs. The campus is testimony to one woman's determination to bring education to children of the mountains. A tour of its grounds and buildings provides the visitor with insight into the isolated, hard, determined and proud nature of life in these hills during the first half of the century. The guard at the main entrance has maps for a self-guided tour. Highlights of this include the Gothic architecture of the Ford Quadrangle; the old mill wheel, one of the largest overshot waterwheels in the world; and picturesque agricultural buildings.

DIRECTIONS: *From Rome, follow US 27 north to the Berry College campus on the left.*
ADDITIONAL INFORMATION: *(404) 232-5374.*

~ETOWAH MOUNDS. [Fig. 6(6)] The Etowah Mounds and Village of the Mississippian Indians were occupied between 700 and 1650 and flourished from about 1000 until 1500. Several thousand Indians may have lived in this fortified town at its peak. It was the center of political and religious life in the valley and home to the chiefs who directed the growth, storage and distribution of food.

Three flat-topped ceremonial mounds that served as platforms for temples or residences for chiefs and priests are located on the floodplain at the juncture of the Etowah River and Pumpkinvine Creek. The village was surrounded by a stockade and deep ditch on all but the river side. It was linked to other Mississippian towns by the Etowah River. Visitors may take a self-guided tour of the Mounds. The entire walk is a little over 0.5 mile.

An excellent museum explains the archeological interpretations of the lives of people of the community. Many artifacts, including ceremonial objects, pottery tools and many shell beads, are on display. This is the only archeological site in northwest Georgia open to the public.

Big brown bat
Eptesicus fuscus

FACILITIES: *Archeological site, museum with audio visual show, maps and brochures, nature walks, bus parking, benches by the river.*
DATES/HOURS: *9-5 Tue-Sat, 2-5:30 Sun; closed Mon (except some legal holidays), Thanksgiving and Christmas Day.*
SPECIAL EVENTS: *Indian skills day (spring); artifacts identification days (Apr and Nov); astronomy programs.*
FEES: *Adults $1.50; children 6-12 $.75; group rates available.*
DIRECTIONS: *From I-75 take exit 124 onto GA 61, go through Cartersville to Indian Mound Road; follow signs to the mounds, 6 miles.*
ADDITIONAL INFORMATION: *Etowah Mounds Historic Site, Georgia Department of Natural Resources, 813 Indian Mounds Road, S.W., Cartersville, GA 30120. (404) 387-3747.*

~**WILLIAM WEINMAN MINERAL MUSEUM.** [Fig. 6(7)] This museum, the largest mineral museum in the Southeast, was established in 1983 by the Cartersville Tourism Council with a donation from the family of William J. Weinman, a pioneer in barite mining in Bartow County. It is dedicated to the collection and exhibition of minerals, rocks, gemstones and fossils from Georgia and around the world. It provides lapidary and identification services. Part of the facility is set aside for lapidary research and classroom activities. A new wing and a library were added in 1987, and a new paleontology wing is being planned.

The Georgian Exhibit Hall features a simulated limestone cave with a waterfall that dramatizes the dynamics of cave formation. It also houses a local mining display, local fossil finds and other specimens from Georgia. Many of the exhibits throughout the museum may be touched.

Lectures by a museum consultant on a variety of topics including rock and mineral identification, birthstones, fossils and fossilization and the solar system may be scheduled by appointment.

FACILITIES: *Touch-and-feel exhibits, guided tours on request, film, special lectures by appointment, library, handicapped access, gift and book shop.*
DATES/HOURS: *10-4:30 Tue-Sat, 2-4:30 Sun; closed Mon and holidays.*
FEES: *Adults and children 12 and over $2; seniors $1.50; children 6-12 $1; group rates for 15 or more; 50% discount for children under 12; 2 free adults with grade school group. Reservations required for groups.*
SPECIAL EVENTS: *Annual rock swap, second Sat in Jun.*
DIRECTIONS: *On the southwest side of the intersection of US 411 and I-75, Exit 26.*
ADDITIONAL INFORMATION: *William Weinman Mineral Museum, Cartersville Tourism Council, P.O. Box 1255, Cartersville, GA 30120. (404) 386-0576.*

~NEW ECHOTA. [Fig. 6(8)] By 1825 the Cherokee Nation had discarded the tribunal council of chiefs as a ruling body and patterned their government on the republican form of the United States. In November, 1825, the legislature of the Cherokee Nation, which covered the area from eastern North Carolina westward through northern Georgia into northeastern Alabama and eastern Tennessee, established its capital at New Echota. Among the many buildings constructed there were a number of commercial buildings, a legislative hall, a supreme court building and a mission station.

Prior to 1827 Sequoyah created the first written form of the Cherokee language. In response to this, the American Board of Commissions for Foreign Mission, which was based in Boston, underwrote most of the cost of establishing a print shop in New Echota. A member of the Board, Samuel A. Worcester, settled in the community in 1827.

Thirteen years after the establishment of New Echota, the United States Congress ordered the removal of the Cherokees to the West. This forced march in the winter of 1838-39 caused the death of 4,000 people and became known as the Trail of Tears. After this, the town quickly fell into disrepair, and by the 20th century the site was lost.

In the early 1950's a group of Calhoun citizens purchased 200 acres of the original site and deeded it to the state of Georgia. Five buildings have been reconstructed, and guided tours are available.

FACILITIES: *Guided tours, museum with slide show, nature trail, picnic area, bus parking.*
DATES/HOURS: *Open year round, 9-5 Tue-Sat, 2-5:30 Sun; closed Mon, Thanksgiving and Christmas.*
FEES: *Adults $1.50, children 6-12 $.75, group rates available.*
SPECIAL EVENTS: *Cherokee Festival, Oct; New England Christmas, Dec.*
DIRECTIONS: *From I-75 take exit 131 (north of Calhoun) onto GA 225, go east 1 mile.*
ADDITIONAL INFORMATION: *New Echota State Historic Site, Georgia Department of Natural Resources, 1211 Chatsworth Highway N.E., Calhoun, GA 30701. (404) 629-8151.*

~VANN HOUSE. [Fig. 6(9)] The house built by the Cherokee chief, James Vann, in 1804 and called "Showplace of the Cherokee Nation" is preserved as the Vann House Historic Site. James Vann, son of a Scottish trader and a Cherokee woman, helped establish the Moravian mission at Spring Place in 1801. In sponsoring the mission school, he contributed to the education of the Cherokee young, including several of the nation's future leaders. He was reputed to be generous when sober and pugnacious when drinking -- which was often. He was shot at Buffington's Tavern on February 21, 1809, at age 41. He had expected to leave his vast holdings to his young

THE GEORGIA CONSERVANCY

son, Joseph, but the Council of Chiefs intervened to divide the property between his widow and all of his children.

Joseph Vann managed nevertheless to acquire the house and much of his father's other property. An even better businessman than his father, he became known as "Rich Joe Vann" by the Indians and whites alike. During the 1830's push for Indian removal in Georgia, Vann made the mistake of hiring a white man as overseer of his plantation. Thus he unwittingly violated a new Georgia law declaring illegal a white man's working for an Indian. Because of this, his house and land were claimed by the state. During a dispute over ownership between a white boarder in the house and the Georgia Guard, the stairway was set on fire. The charred flooring is still visible.

When turned out of their home in Georgia, the Joseph Vann family moved first to a farm he owned in Tennessee and then traveled by steamboat to Webbers Falls, Oklahoma, where he built a duplicate of the Georgia Vann House. That house was also destroyed by Union forces during the Civil War. In the 1840's the Federal Government, after much litigation, paid Joseph Vann $19,605 for his property in Georgia: a fine brick house, 800 acres of cultivated land, 42 cabins, six barns, five smokehouses, a grist mill, a sawmill, a blacksmith shop, eight corn cribs, a shop and foundry, a trading post, a peach kiln, a still, 1,133 peach trees, 147 apple trees and more.

Joseph Vann operated a steamboat line after he moved to Oklahoma. He met his death in October, 1844, when an overheated boiler on his steamboat exploded during a race with another vessel on the Ohio River.

After deteriorating for 150 years, the house and three acres were purchased by the community and presented to the Georgia Historical Commission in 1952. The house was restored and dedicated in July, 1958. Many priceless relics of the family were returned to the house as exhibits.

FACILITIES: *Restrooms and picnic area; brochures and tours available.*
DATES/HOURS: *House open Tue-Sat 9-5, Sun 2-5:30; closed Mon (except legal holidays), Thanksgiving and Christmas.*
FEES: *Admission $1.50 per adult, children 12 and under $.75, under 6 free. Groups $1.25 per person, children $.50 with advanced notice.*
DIRECTIONS: *Located on the outskirts of Chatsworth between Dalton and Chatsworth at the intersection of GA 225 and GA 52.*
ADDITIONAL INFORMATION: *Vann House Historical Site, Georgia Dept. of Natural Resources, Rt. 7, Box 7655, Chatsworth, GA 30705. (404) 659-2598.*

MAP REFERENCES: *USGS 1:100,000 series: Chattanooga - Rome - Chickamauga - Rome - Cleveland - Dalton - Cartersville.*

The Western Blue Ridge

The area known as the Western Blue Ridge includes the Cohutta Mountains and Wilderness, Big Frog Wilderness, Conasauga Lake, Carters Lake, Fort Mountain State Park, the Copper Basin and the Rich Mountains. Positioned between the Great Valley and the Eastern Blue Ridge Mountains, the Western Blue Ridge section of the Georgia mountains has a character and wildness all its own. Geologically, these mountains have more in common with the Great Smokies to the north than with their immediate sandstone and limestone neighbors to the west or the highly metamorphosed crystalline rock to the east. Because of its diversity this region offers some of the greatest possibilities for ecological ramblings found anywhere in the mountains.

Figure 7   COHUTTAS ACCESS MAP

New England cottontail
Sylvilagus transitionalis

This high mountain species is reddish in summer, and there is a dark patch between the ears. This rabbit ranges down the high ridges of the Appalachians and reaches its southern limits in Georgia.

The Cohutta Wilderness

The Cohutta Wilderness covers 37,000 acres (about 60 square miles) that spill over the Georgia/Tennessee border and lie within the 95,000-acre Cohutta Wildlife Management Area. It was designated as a wilderness in 1975. Hemp Top was added in 1986, making this the largest mountain wilderness area in the East outside the Smokies. Fortunately much of the surrounding non-wilderness has been placed in forest service category "M-15," which prevents the construction of any new permanent roads.

The Cohuttas share a unique distinction with the Rich Mountains in having round, flat-topped ridges and peaks covered with deep, black soils. In most of the Eastern Blue Ridge, on the other hand, the higher one goes, the rockier and thinner the soils. This characteristic of the Cohuttas profoundly affects the plant communities. Rich-soil ridges are often carpeted with lush ferns and knee-high herbs.

The wilderness lies in the southern Appalachian highlands and, like most of north Georgia's highlands, enjoys a botanically rich mixture of temperate climate plants. North meets South in Georgia's mountains, with northern species mixing with their southern kin. Many northern species are at their southern limits here. Within the southern highlands is contained the greatest mixture of temperate climate plants in the world, save eastern temperate Asia, located on the same latitude.

The wilderness is home to a variety of wildlife: deer are plentiful, black bears make their home here, as do wild boar and a variety of smaller creatures such as bobcats and squirrels.

T.P.'s Country Store (see Eton access below) and Greg's General Store (see Cisco access below) display the trophies of local hunters and are good places to get a close-up look at some of the kinds of creatures that inhabit the wilderness. At Greg's General Store, for example, are a stuffed 200-pound black bear, the head of an eight-point buck and that of a wild boar that weighed more than 500 pounds when killed. Store regulars are quick to relate that a bear twice the size of the stuffed one was killed just a quarter-mile away.

The wilderness is also located on the Appalachian flyway for birds, especially warblers, tanagers, thrushes and vireos. Because the climate more resembles that of New Jersey than of Georgia, birds nest here that do not nest in the valleys below. Rose-breasted grosbeak, scarlet tanager, dark-eyed junco, chestnut-sided warbler, black-throated blue warbler and black-throated green warbler are but a few examples. These are all birds that nest in the North or in mountainous regions of the South such as this.

Few of the visitors who enjoy the Cohutta Wilderness realize its history of logging; seventy percent of the area was logged between 1915 and 1930. Three or four logging camps, each with 80 to 100 men, were operated simultaneously in the area. Railroads were built

Figure 8   COHUTTA WILDERNESS (LAKE CONAUSAGA)

by hand and ran up the Jacks and Conasauga Rivers. Trestles built over the river often were washed away by floods. Bunk cars were winched three and a half miles up hillsides. Logs were skidded out with horses, and cable logging was done in the inaccessible areas. Logging was completed in the Conasauga River drainage in 1928 and started along the Jacks River in 1929. The Depression halted logging for about three years. During that time the loggers worked in the Civilian Conservation Corps building some of the facilities still used in the area. After the Depression, Beech Creek, Rough Creek, Rock Wall, Poplar Creek and Penitentiary Creek areas were logged. The railroads were dismantled and the rails removed in 1937. Remnants of ties and trestles can be found today. Also one can occasionally find dynamite drills in rocks, spikes, cables, steel support rods, horseshoes and old building foundations.

While in operation, the Conasauga River Lumber Company sawmill sawed 80,000 board feet a day. It was from this company that the U.S. Forest Service acquired a large portion of the area in 1934 and 1935. Farms have converted back to forests, roads have been turned into hiking trails and the area is returning to the way it was when only native Americans lived here.

~ACCESS TO THE COHUTTA WILDERNESS. The following guide provides an overview of the Cohutta Wilderness, a way to come to terms with the whole experience before beginning a detailed exploration of any one trail. The map provides information on access roads to the wilderness from five towns and villages on its border. Also shown are Forest Service roads bordering the area and designated trails which cross it. Trailheads are generally well marked and parking areas are provided. All of the roads that border the wilderness are one-lane dirt, sometimes with a coating of loose gravel. They are wide enough for two cars to pass cautiously. Curves are sharp and hard to see around.

Often rock breaks through the road surface, creating a washboard ride. Although a four-wheel-drive vehicle would be the ideal transportation on these surfaces, most cars in good condition will have little trouble. Some roads are closed depending on weather conditions, so it is recommended that one call the Cohutta Ranger District of the U.S. Forest Service (404 695-6736) in advance of a trip to check road conditions.

ELLIJAY ACCESS. [Fig. 7(1)] From the Ellijay Square go west on GA 52, 9.5 miles to FS 18. There is a sign for Lake Conasauga Recreation Area; turn right. After 1.3 miles the pavement ends. At the fork, take the left fork over a one-lane bridge. Continue on FS 18, which is marked just across the creek. At 3.5 miles is an intersection where FS 68 turns sharply to the right. Take 68 turning up a steep incline. At mile 4.5 is a nice level picnic or camping area, and at mile 5.7 is Holly Creek Checking Station. Soon, at mile

Bobcat
Felis rufus

Along with the red and grey fox, the bobcat is a principal predator at the top of the food chain which begins with colonization of a fallen leaf by bacteria and fungi on the forest floor. While the bobcat will attack deer sometimes, it cannot effectively control their numbers, a job once handled by cougars and wolves.

6.0, the road forks, with FS 90 going to the right; stay on 68. Find Barnes Creek Picnic Area for day use at mile 7.2; a wooden platform extends out over a small waterfall. At mile 9.5 is the intersection marked Potato Patch Mountain on the map.

ETON ACCESS. [Fig. 7(2)] From Chatsworth take US 411 north to Eton. Turn right at the only traffic light onto Fourth Avenue (State Hwy. 286 ends here). Set the odometer at 0.0 where Fourth Avenue begins at US 411. Mile 1.1, Grassy Mountain intersects from the left. Mile 1.5, the road forks at T.P.'s Country Store; bear left on the CCC Camp Road. Mile 3.8, Crandall Road intersects from left. At mile 4.2 Cool Springs Road intersects from right. At mile 5.1, the road, still CCC Camp Road, passes through a scenic valley with Fort, Beaver and Tatum Mountains in the background. The pavement ends at mile 6.1. Mile 7.0 is the start of a nice drive along a creek. At mile 7.2 the view looking upstream through the trees at Emery Creek is a fine sight. Mile 10.3 is the intersection of 18 and 68. (Note the CCC Camp Road and FS 18 at some point become the same road). From this point, refer to the Ellijay Access (above) beginning at mile 3.5. If there is time for exploring only one access point to the Cohutta Wilderness, this should be it. The valley drive and the drive along the creek make this one of the most visually rewarding ways to approach the wilderness.

CRANDALL ACCESS. [Fig. 7(3)] From Chatsworth take US 411 north. Pass through Eton approximately 2.5 miles. Watch for a green and white sign marked "Crandall" on right. Cross railroad tracks and turn right. Take first left at post office (note USFS sign for Lake Conasauga). Set the odometer at 0.0 here. The paved road ends at mile 0.5. Mile 6.7, Hickey Gap. Mile 8.9, intersection with FS 17.

CISCO ACCESS. [Fig. 7(4)] GA 2 intersects US 411 here at Greg's General Store in Cisco. Set the odometer at 0.0 here. Go east toward the Cohuttas as if continuing on GA 2. At mile 0.7 pass county road 169 on the right. Mile 1.0 marks the end of the pavement. Take the right fork at the "Y" intersection at mile 1.6. (County road 210 bears left.) At mile 3.2, FS 17 comes in from the right, FS 16 goes left. Follow 16 just across the state line into Tennessee to the start of Jacks River Trail (note FS road 51 branches to right just after crossing the river. Stay left on FS 16).

BLUE RIDGE ACCESS. [Fig. 7(5)] Set the odometer at 0.0 at the intersection of US 76 and GA 5 in Blue Ridge. Go north on GA 5. Take old SR 2, which turns to the left at mile 3.2. At mile 6.9 are Fightingtown Creek and McKinney Crossing. At mile 11.3 the pavement ends. At 13.3, after a long climb up the mountain, look for the sign, "Cohutta Wildlife Management Area, Watson Gap." Bear left on FS 64. Mile 17.6 marks Dyer Gap. Where 64-A forks to the left, stay on 64, the right fork. Mile 18.3, cross south fork of the Jacks River. Mile 18.4, 64-B intersects on left. At mile 20.2 the Mountain Town Creek Trail is on the left. At mile 22.9, Three Forks and East Cowpen Trail.

~HIKING TRAILS OF THE COHUTTA WILDERNESS. With 95 miles of trails, the Cohutta Wilderness is a hiker's dream come true. All the trails are easily followed and blazed, with the exception of Jacks River Trail downstream from the falls. After heavy rains, both the Jacks and Conasauga Rivers can become raging torrents, virtually impossible to cross safely. Those planning a hike to the Cohutta Wilderness should watch weather forecasts carefully. Bring a rope to cross the rivers more safely, and if water is raging don't even try. In bad weather a trip may get extended. Be prepared for this sort of thing with extra food. Make sure people know the route of the hike and expected time of return. Even in low water, plan on getting wet. For example, the Conasauga River Trail between Betty Gap and FS 17 has 38 river crossings. Hiking boots will quickly become soggy footweights. Many experienced hikers on the Conasauga and Jacks River Trails wear old tennis shoes and simply resign themselves to having wet feet. Bring dry shoes for camp.

Camping is permitted anywhere except in the trails and at trailheads. The trick is to find a spot flat enough. Fires are permitted using dead and down wood only. No permits are required. Please obey wilderness regulations posted on bulletin boards at trailheads.

Text mileages are from Tim Homan's book, *The Hiking Trails of North Georgia*. Homan's figures are regarded as accurate, since he walked and rewalked the trails using a measuring wheel. Wilderness maps are available from U.S. Forest Service District Office in Chatsworth or from patrolling Forest Service officers.

Wilderness maps are available from U.S. Forest Service District Office in Chatsworth or from patrolling Forest Service officers.

CONASAUGA RIVER TRAIL. [Fig. 8(6)] From Betty Gap to the parking area at Forest Service Road 17, 13.1 miles. A popular hiking trail. Bray Field can accommodate perhaps 100 campers.

CHESTNUT LEAD TRAIL. [Fig. 8(8)] From the parking area at FS 68 to its junction with the Conasauga River Trail, 1.8 miles. Provides a good look at skeletons of giant chestnut trees that thrived in this forest before the chestnut blight.

PANTHER CREEK TRAIL. [Fig. 8(9)] From the Conasauga River

American chestnut
Castanea dentata

While it ranged into the upper Piedmont, this tree reached remarkable densities and large size in rich mountain coves and on slopes and rounded ridges with deep black soil. Its untimely death in the 30's by an Asiatic fungus deprived many animals of a major fall fattening food that enabled them to survive the winter. Our forests are still adapting to this loss, and tulip poplar now grows on many of the sites once occupied by chestnut.

Trail to the East Cowpen Trail, 3.4 miles. Passes a high waterfall. A popular trail.

HICKORY CREEK TRAIL. [Fig. 8(10)] From the trailhead at FS 51 to trailhead at FS 630, 8.6 miles.

EAST COWPEN TRAIL. [Fig. 8(11)] From the parking area at Three Forks to the trailhead at FS 51, 7.0 miles. Follows the former route of old Georgia state highway 2, a rough dirt road showing 2signs of years of off-road vehicle abuse. Though not necessarily a good destination trail, it can provide relatively quick access to other trails.

JACK'S RIVER TRAIL. [Fig. 8(12)] From the parking area at Dolly Gap to the trailhead in Alaclusy Valley, 16.7 miles. The longest and wettest trail in the Cohutta Wilderness. Often crowded, 100 campers is not unusual at the falls. The least-used portion of the trail is from Alaclusy to Jack's River Falls. In the middle of Horseshoe Bend are several beautiful spots to camp.

SUGAR COVE TRAIL. [Fig. 8(13)] From Rough Ridge Trail to Jack's River Trail, 2.2 miles.

PENITENTIARY BRANCH TRAIL. [Fig. 8(14)] From the Hemp Top Trail to Jack's River Trail, 3.5 miles.

ROUGH RIDGE TRAIL. [Fig. 8(15)] From East Cowpen Trail to Jack's River Trail, 7.0 miles.

HICKORY RIDGE TRAIL. [Fig. 8(16)] From East Cowpen Trail to Jack's River Trail, 3.5 miles. Not heavily used.

BEECH BOTTOM TRAIL. [Fig. 8(17)] From FS 62 to its junction with the Jack's River Trail, 4.0 miles.

RICE CAMP TRAIL. [Fig. 8(18)] From FS 51 to the Jack's River Trail, 3.9 miles.

HORSESHOE BEND TRAIL. [Fig. 8(19)] From FS 51 to the Jack's River Trail, 3.0 miles. Not heavily used.

HEMP TOP TRAIL. [Fig. 8(20)] From the trailhead at Dolly Gap to Big Frog Mountain, 6.0 miles. Not heavily used.

~OFF-ROAD-VEHICLE TRAILS ON THE COHUTTA RANGER DISTRICT

WINDY GAP CYCLE TRAIL. [Fig. 8(22)] 5.0 miles. Designed for experienced trail bikers. Take US 411 north from Chatsworth for 4.0 miles. Turn right (east) at the traffic light in Eton and go about 5.0 miles. Turn left on FS 218 (Muskrat Road) and travel 3.0 miles to the trailhead.

MILMA CREEK ORV TRAIL. [Fig. 8(22)] 4.0 miles. Suitable for all-terrain vehicles. Connects Windy Gap Cycle Trail and Tibbs Trail. Access is by Windy Gap Cycle Trail. See directions above.

TIBBS ORV TRAIL. [Fig. 8(22)] 5.0 miles. Suitable for all-terrain vehicles. Note that this trail is closed by a gate at both ends. Access through Windy Gap Cycle Trail and Milma Creek ORV Trail. See directions above.

ROCKY FLATS ORV TRAIL. [Fig. 8(23)] 5.0 miles. Suitable for 4-wheel-drive vehicles. Trail is 3.0 miles east of Crandall off Mill Creek Road (FS 630) on the right.

TATUM LEAD ORV TRAIL. [Fig. 8(24)] 7.0 miles. Suitable for 4-wheel-drive vehicles, motorbikes and all-terrain vehicles. Trail deadends on private property. Take GA 52 east from Chatsworth nine miles. The trail is located 0.5 mile past the Cohutta Lodge on the right.

Lake Conasauga.

Nineteen-acre Lake Conasauga, located at 3,150 feet, near the summit of Grassy Mountain, is the highest lake in Georgia. The name Conasauga is derived from the Cherokee word *kahnasagah*, meaning "grass, sparkling water or strong horse," according to various sources. Grassy Mountain, at 3,682 feet, is one of the higher mountains in the area, and the grassy Ball Field is nearby.

Conasauga River and Lake Conasauga do indeed sparkle. The metaphor of a strong horse may come from the river overflowing its banks and flooding after heavy rain. Whatever the source, a river, lake and several ancient Indian settlements in the area share the name Conasauga.

Lake Conasauga, the picnic area and U.S. Forest Service roads 18 and 68 were constructed by the Civilian Conservation Corps during the administration of Franklin D. Roosevelt.

A fully developed Forest Service campground is available. The 35 campsites have both tent and car pads. Restrooms and cold running water are centrally located. Most of the sites are not on the lake, but are very close. This is a heavily used campground, and on busy summer weekends it is likely to be full. There is an overflow camping area. No water is available but there are portable toilets. The group camping area is a large grassy field without tables, grills or water.

The entire recreation area is accessible from the day-use area, which has a restroom, water, tables, grills, two covered shelters and a parking lot. The large, heavily used but rarely full picnic area offers quiet solitude a short walk from the car. Food and equipment must be carried to the picnic tables and shelters, as none is next to the parking area. At the lake there is a developed swimming area with a dock and pea gravel bottom. There is no beach for sunbathing, but a pleasant grassy ledge instead. Swimming is restricted to the marked swimming area. The water remains cool most of the summer, though by July 4, it is quite comfortable.

Off the picnic road is a boat ramp and parking lot access road. The lake is limited to electric motors, rowing and paddling. It is a great place to canoe or raft.

Because the lake is heavily fished, fishing is poor, although some very large bass live in the deeps. Rainbow trout are stocked, and bream and crappie are also present.

~LAKE CONASAUGA RECREATION AREA. [Fig. 8(25)] A Song Bird Management Area, where the trees and other vegetation are managed to provide the best bird habitat. Over 100 species of birds can be seen. These include hawks, owls, woodpeckers, kinglets, thrushes, vireos, warblers, cuckoo, phoebe, flycatcher, chickadee, titmouse, nuthatch, brown creeper, wrens, tanager, grosbeak, bunting and red crossbill. A checklist of the birds is available from the Cohutta Ranger District Office.

Like most of Georgia's highlands, the elevation, climate, vegetation and nesting birds of Lake Conasauga are similar to those in Pennsylvania. Georgia's mountains are the approximate southern limit for eastern hemlock and eastern white pine. This is an excellent area in which to see a wide range of trees, shrubs, herbs and flowers representative of the southern highlands, including the yellow birch and mountain camellias. A plant list is available from the Ranger District Office.

FACILITIES: *Parking, camping, picnicking, swimming, boating (electric motors only) canoeing, fishing, trails, drinking water, restrooms.*
DATES/HOURS: *Paid campsites open second Fri in Apr-last weekend in Oct. Overflow camping area open all year.*
FEES: *Campsite $5.*
DIRECTIONS: *From Chatsworth take US 411 north 4 miles; turn right (east) at traffic light at Eton; follow this country road making no turns until the pavement ends and it becomes FS 18; turn left (northeast) on FS 68 for 10 miles. From Ellijay take US 52 west from the square for about 7 miles to FS 18, marked with a sign for Lake Conasauga Recreation Area. Follow the paved road. Where the pavement ends, cross one-lane bridge. FS 18 marked here. Continue to the junction with FS 68; turn right and follow the signs to Lake Conasauga.*
ADDITIONAL INFORMATION: *U.S. Forest Service, Cohutta Ranger District, 401 Old Ellijay Road, Chatsworth, GA 30705. (404) 695-6736.*

~HIKING TRAILS AROUND LAKE CONASAUGA:

Lake Conasauga Trail. [Fig. 8(25)] 1.2 miles. An easy walk around the lake, passing through tunnels of rhododendron and crossing picturesque bridges. Interesting ferns, wildflowers, shrubs, trees, birds and scenic views of the lake are found along the trail.

GRASSY MOUNTAIN TOWER TRAIL. [Fig. 8(26)] 1.6 miles. From the dam on Lake Conasauga to the old fire tower atop Grassy Mountain, this trail makes an easy ascent along the ridge.

SONGBIRD TRAIL. [Fig. 8(27)] 1.3 miles. This trail begins at a small meadow just below the recreation area and then runs along a small brook through the Songbird Management Area, a series of clearcuts which provide a variety of vegetation valuable to many songbirds. Interpretive nature walks are offered on certain Saturday afternoons between Memorial Day and Labor Day.

White pine
Pinus strobus

In the eastern Blue Ridge this stately tree is confined to ravines and narrow floodplains where it comes in after heavy logging. Beautiful stands occur along the Chattooga above Burrell's Ford Bridge and up Reed Creek, a tributary above the Hwy 28 bridge. In the western Blue Ridge it occupies moist, lower slopes north and west of the Russell Scenic Highway, and in the lower Cooper Creek basin.

~THE CONASAUGA RIVER. [Fig. 8(28)] The Conasauga River is born deep in the Cohutta Wilderness. From its inception, it flows north through a series of almost inaccessible steep gorges before reaching the Alaclusy Valley. Here it appears to rest for a couple of miles before its confluence with the Jacks River and return to whitewater. This upper section offers beautiful rough country hiking. Considered uncanoeable by most, at very high water levels it provides a few hardy souls a wildwater experience hard to beat. The section beginning where the Conasauga leaves the valley at its confluence with the Jacks is much more suited to recreational paddling. Here the river turns westward to cut across several ridges before bending south to join the Coosawattee and eventually become part of the Coosa River system.

This is a crystal clear mountain stream which during the summer lacks sufficient water for easy navigation by canoe. Most of the rapids are intricate Class I or Class II mazes -- excellent water to help sharpen water reading skills. There is one Class III rapid thrown into the middle of the run to keep paddlers alert on this exceptionally scenic river.

The Conasauga is normally high enough to run during the winter and spring months. Even at these higher levels it will remain clear. Since this river rises rapidly in time of flood, avoid putting in if it is cloudy and turbid. There are no specific hazards for intermediate or advanced canoeists, although the one Class III rapid could cause problems for less experienced paddlers. Cold-weather paddling trips are for experienced groups only. Full wet-suit protection and complete safety and first-aid gear are essential.

DIRECTIONS: *Travel north on US 411 over the Georgia state line. The Conasauga River bridge, which is the take-out point, is just a couple of miles across the line in Tennessee. To return to the put-in, continue north on 411 to the first paved road on the right next to a service station; this is Sheeds Creek Road; turn right. The pavement soon ends, but the road bed is solid and will present no problems. Follow this same road for about 7 miles over several ridges until it drops down into a small valley. Several camping areas as well as the river will be visible on the right, followed by a large steel bridge. This is the Jacks River Bridge and marks the confluence of the Jacks and Consauaga Rivers. There are several good launch sites in this area.*

American toad
Bufo americanus

Chestnut oak
Quercus prinus

With the largest acorn of our mountain oaks, the chestnut oak is found mostly on rocky ridges with shallow soils. Many lower ridges are dominated by this tree while northern red oaks occupy the higher, wetter ridges.

Big Frog Wilderness

The Cohutta Wilderness extends into Tennessee as far as the Eastern Continental Divide. Protruding from it is the isolated hulk of Big Frog Mountain. Big Frog is not a huge mountain (4,224 feet), but like Grassy Mountain (3,692 feet) in the Cohuttas it appears more dominant because it stands alone. Lacking the protection of other mountains, it receives the full impact of cold fronts and other climatic events. In addition it receives high rainfall. Big Frog is a scenic mountain. The top is forested; northern hardwoods are present, as is a boulderfield on the north side.

~ROAD ACCESS AND HIKING ACCESS TO BIG FROG WILDERNESS:

COPPERHILL ACCESS. From Blue Ridge take GA 5 north to the Tennessee line. Pass through Copperhill and in about 2 miles take 251 west. Cross the Ocoee River and continue on 251 for 5.8 miles. Cross Tumbling Creek and intersect FS road 221 [(Fig. 9(2)]. Turn north on FS 221 Peavine-Sheeds Creek Road. Off this road one will pass 5 trailheads to Big Frog Mountain. Note that at each trailhead, the distance from the trailhead to Big Frog Summit is given. Set the odometer at 0.0. At 2.0 miles pass Tumbling Creek Campground [(Fig. 9(3)]; at 5.6 miles reach Licklog Ridge Trail [(Fig. 9(4)] (5.6 miles to summit); at 8.4 miles reach Big Frog trailhead [(Fig. 9(5)] (5.2 miles to summit); at 13.2 miles reach Big Creek trailhead [(Fig. 9(6)] (5.2 miles to summit); at 14.8 miles reach Wolf Ridge trailhead [(Fig. 9(7)] (7.6 miles to summit; at 17.2 miles pass the turnoff on Big Frog Road (gated) [(Fig. 9(8)]; at 18.8 miles reach a fork in Alaclusy Creek Valley. Turn south on FS 221. Just north is the Sylco Campground. Continue down FS 221 but go straight when FS 221 turns west at 22.8 miles. One will reach Ciscoon on US 411 in 8 to 10 miles.

CHATSWORTH ACCESS. The Big Frog trails can be reached from Chatsworth by reversing the above directions.

OCOEE RIVER ACCESS. From Copperhill north on TN 68 go 28 miles to US 64 intersection. Take 64 west and go 8 miles. Take the first left road [(Fig. 9(9)] after the highway begins running along the river. Just below this is the put-in for rafting the famous Ocoee River. After crossing the river one passes the USFS Thunder Rock Campground. Go 4.0 miles to intersect the Peavine-Sheeds Creek Road, FS 221 [(Fig. 9(10)], between Licklog Ridge (east) and Big Frog (west) trailheads. Note: It is well worth a few moments to drive down the Ocoee Gorge just to watch the rafts go by. This whitewater trip rivals the Chattooga in excitment, but not as a

Figure 9   BIG FROG MOUNTAIN WILDERNESS

wilderness experience, since US 64 closely follows the Ocoee.

CHESTNUT MOUNTAIN TRAIL. [(Fig. 9(11)] Approximately 10 miles east of US 411 on FS 221, Peavine-Sheeds Creek Road, turn east on FS 62 and go 6 miles to the trailhead. Hike 3.2 miles to Big Frog summit along Chestnut Mountain and Wolf Ridge.

MAP REFERENCES: *For Cohuttas and Rich Mt., USGS 1:100,000 series: Cleveland - Dalton - Cartersville, USGS 1:24,000 series: Cashes Valley - Blue Ridge - Wilscot - Ellijay - Ticknetley - Noontootla.*
County Highway Maps: Gilmer - Murray - Fannin - Gordon.
For Big Frog, USGS 1:24,000 series: Epworth - Ducktown - Hemp Top - Caney Creek.

The Western Blue Ridge

Carters Lake

Located 12 miles south of Chatsworth off US 411, 3,500-acre Carters Lake [Fig. 10(1)] was constructed by the U.S. Army Corps of Engineers in 1977. The lake provides many recreational opportunities including boating, swimming, camping, hiking and fishing. A large area near the dam on the south shore has been developed by a concessionaire as The Blue Ridge Mountain Marina Resort, the only developed area permitted on the lake. In a road cut below the dam one can see the Cartersville-Great Smoky Fault where Western Blue Ridge rocks rest against those of the Great Valley.

DATES/HOURS: *The resource manager's office and visitor center is open year round Mon-Fri 8-4:30; summer Sat and Sun 1-6.*
DIRECTIONS: *Access via GA 136 east from US 411. Follow signs.*
ADDITIONAL INFORMATION: *Contact the Resource Manager's office, Carters Lake, P.O. Box 86, Oakman, GA 30732. (404) 334-2248.*

~CAMPING AT CARTERS LAKE: (Obtain map at Resource Manager's office.)

HARRIS BRANCH PARK. Group camping only. Shelter, 6 tables, large grill, 10 tent pads, running water, 2 comfort stations. Public beach open daily Apr until mid-Sep. Reservations required. Gates open at 9 and close at 9. Closed Oct-Mar.

DOLL MOUNTAIN PARK. 65 campsites, 28 with electrical and water hookups; 2 comfort stations with shower facilities and a recreational dump station. Fee: $8 for those campsites with electrical hookups, $6 for those without. No reservations, campsites rented on a first-come, first-served basis. Gate open 8am-11pm. Closed Oct-Mar.

RIDGEWAY PARK. 22 campsites, pit toilets, boat ramp and dock. Accessible by dirt road only.

FEES: *$4. Remains open during off season, Oct-Mar, when sites are free.*

WOODRING BRANCH. 31 campsites, all with electrical and water hookups; comfort station and boat ramp. Another 12 campsites with pit toilets and a hand-operated water pump are available.

FEES: *$8 with water and electrical hookups; $4 Without.*
DATES/HOURS: *Gate open 8am-11pm. Closed Oct-Mar.*

Figure 10   CARTERS LAKE

~Hiking At Carters Lake: (Obtain map at resource manager's office.)

Hidden Pond Trail. About 0.5 mile. The trail was constructed to provide access sites for bird watchers. Two bridges are part of the trail; one 20-foot bridge spans the stream near the entrance to the management area and a 210-foot structure goes across a beaver pond. An observation platform upstream at the edge of a second beaver pond provides a view of an active beaver lodge and offers an excellent opportunity for viewing water fowl. Located near the entrance to the management area.

Tumbling Waters Nature Trail. Approximately one mile through a secluded valley carved by a mountain stream. The trail includes two viewing platforms located above a cliff from which hikers can view Trails Creek cascading into Carters Lake. Trailhead located in Ridgeway Park.

Big Acorn Nature Trail and Burnt Oak Nature Trail. About 0.5 mile. Easy trail along a wood chip path. Signs identify trees and shrubs. Trailhead at the Carters Lake Visitor Center.

Blue Ridge Mountain Marina Resort. Cabins and rooms, rental houseboats, convenience store, pontoon and fishing boat rental, guided fishing trips, snack bar and boat repair.

~Canoeing Trips

The Coosawattee River. [(Fig. 10(2)] The Cartecay and Ellijay Rivers meet in the town of Ellijay to form the Coosawattee, one of the largest rivers in north Georgia. Once out of town, the river turns west through the southern Cohuttas, carving downward more than 500 feet in 22 miles through a spectacular gorge and emerging through a narrow breach into what geologists call the Great Valley. The highest earthen dam east of the Mississippi now fills that breach, and Carters Lake has inundated more than half the river, including the biggest rapids and the highest cliffs. This gorge was second only to Tallulah Gorge in grandeur. In fact, canoeing insiders believe that James Dickey's novel-turned-movie, *Deliverance*, which was filmed on the Chattooga, was actually written more with the Coosawattee in mind. A fine run of intermediate difficulty remains on the upper section, past forested bluffs. Because of the open nature of this river, with wide views of the surrounding trees, it is most scenic in April, when the woods are leafing out, and in October, during the fall color display. Although the river gradient is almost 30 feet per mile in places, the rapids do not exceed Class III and are separated by easy, flat sections which allow paddlers to relax and enjoy the scenery.

DIRECTIONS: *To find the put-in, first locate the GA 5 bridge over the Coosawattee south of Ellijay. On the north side of the bridge, turn west on Legion Road and drive about a mile to where the road comes just to the river's edge [(Fig. 10(2)]. One can also put in a couple of miles upstream at the Gilmer County Park, just south of the intersection of GA 5 and GA 282 [(Fig. 10(3)]. To reach the take out, go back out Legion Road to GA 5, up to GA 282, and west about 8 miles, watching for a large sign to the Ridgeway access area. Follow the signs to the boat ramp [(Fig. 10(4)].*

TALKING ROCK CREEK. [(Fig. 10(5)] Talking Rock Creek is a beautiful, clear mountain stream deeply etched into the canyon-like foothills of the Cohutta and Blue Ridge Mountains, just northwest of Jasper. Generally running northwest, it empties into the reservoir below Carters Lake Dam. Canoeists experience wild and remote country, high cliffs and primitive mountain scenery, as well as Class I - III rapids.

DIRECTIONS: *The put-in and take-out are about 9.0 miles apart on GA 136. The put-in bridge is about 2.0 miles north of Blaine [(Fig. 10(5)], and the take-out bridge is where the creek runs into the reregulation reservoir below Carters Lake Dam [(Fig. 10(6)]. Total distance from bridge to bridge is about 15.0 miles. Steady paddling by experienced canoeists makes a 6.0- to 8.0-hour trip feasible. Expect possible headwinds during the last 3.0 miles, which could extend the length of the trip.*

MAP REFERENCES: *For Cohuttas, Rich Mt. and Big Frog, USGS 1:100,000 series: Cleveland - Dalton - Cartersville, USGS 1:24,000 series: Cashes Valley - Blue Ridge - Wilscot - Ellijay - Ticknetley - Noontootla. USGS 1:24,000 series for Big Frog: Epworth - Ducktown - Hemp Top - Caney Creek. County Highway Maps: Gilmer - Murray - Fannin - Gordon.*

Fort Mountain State Park

Fort Mountain State Park is located on Fort Mountain, just southwest of the Cohutta Wilderness. The park derives its name from an ancient stone wall, measuring some 855 feet in length, which stands on the highest point of the mountain. Remains of circular depressions made of various sized stones and measuring about 10 feet across, occur in the wall at about 30-foot intervals. The wall ranges in height from two to six feet, although it was probably considerably higher in the past. Archeologists and historians have been unable to solve the puzzle of who, if anyone, built the wall or why or when they built it. There are many theories. A favorite explanation is that the wall was built by the Woodland Indians around 500 A.D. The east-west orientation of its end points would result in alignment at sunrise and sunset at the solar equinox in both spring and fall. The dramatic setting of the wall, offering expansive vistas to the east and west, would add to its religious significance. Ceremonial centers similar to this one were built by the Woodland Indians at Old Stone Fort, Tennessee and Rock Eagle Mound in Putnam County, Georgia. The Woodland Indians occupied the Southeast from several centuries B.C. to about 900 A.D.

A less probable but more romantic theory attributes the wall to a legendary Welsh prince named Medoc. He supposedly sailed into Mobile, Alabama, 500 years ago, then worked his way northward toward the Fort Mountain vicinity. Nothing else is known about Prince Medoc, except that his name is vaguely linked to several petroglyphs found in other parts of the Southeast.

Some geologists believe, and this may be the least romantic explanation of all, that the "wall" is the result of natural weathering of a generally horizontal stratum of a hard caprock of quartzites and conglameratites which produced the present ring of boulders.

In the 1930's the Civilian Conservation Corps built a 38-foot stone observation tower at the mountain's summit 520 feet north of the wall. Its special feature is a heart-shaped stone which lies concealed just above the east window.

Fort Mountain State Park's 1,932 acres were donated to the Federal Government in 1929 by Ivan Allen, Sr. in order for the stone wall to be preserved, and for the public's pleasure. In the 1940's it was turned over to the state of Georgia.

The hiking vistas and natural history are outstanding. The park has a spectacular cascade dropping 400 feet off the cliffs, an old gold mine [(Fig. 11(5)] on streams feeding the lake and an underlay of vast mineral deposits.

The visitor to Fort Mountain may be startled by underground explosions in commercial mines in the bowels of the mountain. Fort Mountain is probably Georgia's leading talc producer. Large companies moved in around 1900. Mines surround the mountain on three sides; two can be seen from the Chatsworth overlook.

Figure 11   FORT MOUNTAIN STATE PARK

Tulip poplar
Liriodendron tulipfera

FACILITIES: *There are fifteen 2-and-3 bedroom cottages; 70 tent and trailer sites; 12 miles of foot trails; swimming beach with bath house; paddle boats; 7 picnic shelters with 117 tables; miniature golf.*
DATES/HOURS: *Open all year round, 7am-10pm; office open 8am-5pm.*
DIRECTIONS: *Located 7.0 miles east of Chatsworth on GA 52. Take exit 136 off I-75.*
ADDITIONAL INFORMATION: *Fort Mountain State Park, Box 7008, Rt. 7, Chatsworth, GA 30705. (404) 695-2621. Or refer to the State Park section in the appendix.*

~FORT MOUNTAIN HIKING TRAILS: Inquire at the park office for detailed directions and a map.

GAHUTI TRAIL. [(Fig. 11(1)] An 8.2-mile loop trail around Fort Mountain. Three limited-use camping sites are located along the trail for backpackers. One orange blaze, which is easy to see, designates the trail. Old logging roads crisscross the trail, and it is easy to mistake one of these for the trail. The first 0.3 mile looks out over the Cohutta Wilderness and is one of the finest views in Georgia. The trail begins at a gravel parking area marked "Cool Springs Overlook" in Fort Mountain State Park.

BIG ROCK NATURE TRAIL. [(Fig. 11(2)] 0.7 mile. This trail provides hikers a glimpse of the rugged and diverse natural habitat found on Fort Mountain. It passes several rocky outcrops which form natural outlooks. One view is of a 400-foot cascade of Gold Mine Creek. Along the creek is ordinary rosebay, with mountain laurel, galax and wild ginger.

LAKE LOOP TRAIL. [(Fig. 11(3)] Approximately 1.1 miles. Follows along the edge of 17-acre Fort Mountain Lake.

OLD FORT TRAILS. [(Fig. 11(4)] 1.3 miles. This trail leads to the ancient stone wall from which Fort Mountain derives its name. The trail passes through a forest of alternating stands of scarlet oak, Virginia pine and knarled white oak. Past the wall there is a stone tower which kids will love. West of the tower, a short trail leads to the Chatsworth Overlook platform.

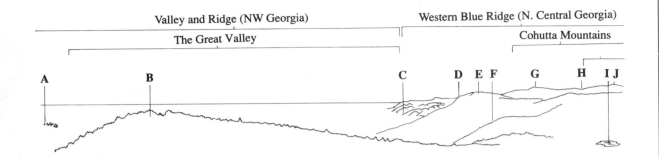

NORTH VISTA
View from Fort Mountain State Park

North View From Fort Mountain State Park

A - Chatsworth
B - NW flank of Cohutta Mountain
C - Cartersville-Great Smoky Fault
D - Chatsworth Overlook
E - Fort Mountain

F - Gold Mine Branch Ravine
G - Grassy Mountain
H - Conasauga Lake
I - Lake on Gold Mine Branch
J - Bald Mountain

NORTH VISTA (Continued)
View from Fort Mountain State Park

G - Grassy Mountain
H - Conasauga Lake
I - Lake on Gold Mine Branch
J - Bald Mountain
K - Cowpen Mountain (unseen)
L - Potato Patch Mountain

M - Flat Top Mountain
N - Cohutta Lodge
O - Cold Springs Mountain
P - Rich Mountain Wilderness
Q - Cold Spring Mountain

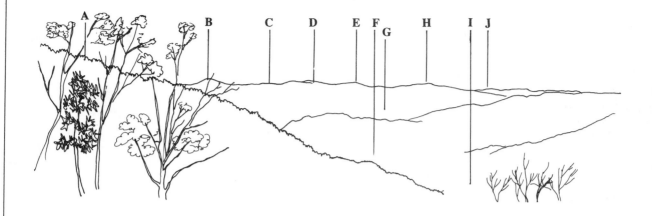

NORTHEAST VISTA
View from Fort Mountain State Park

A - Fort Mountain, E. flank
B - Grassy Mountain
C - Conasauga Lake
D - Bald Mountain
E - Cowpen Mountain
F - Mill Creek Watershed
G - Holly Creek Watershed
H - Potato Patch Mountain
I - Talc mine location
J - Flat Top Mountain

EAST VISTA
View from Fort Mountain State Park

AA - Cold Spring Mountain

65

Hellebore
Veratrum viride

Unlike the smaller "false" hellebore (*V. parviflorum*), which occurs in the upper Piedmont along the Gainesville Ridges, this huge, robust plant (reaching 5 feet) is found in the highest parts of our mountains and under almost bog conditions. All parts are claimed to be poisonous.

Copper Basin

At the junction where east Tennessee, northwest Georgia and southwest North Carolina meet, the Copper Basin stands out in startling contrast to its surroundings -- the epitome of man's disregard for nature. Its denuded red hills shimmer with glowing colors ranging from soft pastels to dark copper and reddish hues, surrounded by a ring of lush green mountains, thus giving the illusion of a bowl or basin. The Blue Ridge Mountains, with elevations reaching 4,200 feet, can be seen in every direction.

Approximately 35,000 acres of rolling hills, the Copper Basin has been described as a moonscape, a red desert or a beloved scar (by people who were born, raised and continue to live in this area) and is damaging testimony to the long-term effect of acid rain. However, unlike present-day acid rain, that which produced the Copper Basin fell close to its point of origin, was highly visible and had an immediate as well as long-range effect. Efforts to reclaim the proper balance of nature have been numerous and reportedly represent the most extensive reclamation project attempted in the United States.

Devastation of the Copper Basin is usually attributed to the copper mining industry. Other factors, however, also contributed. Burning by the Cherokee Indians, followed by early settlers' burning to clear land, established a pattern of land abuse early on. According to Tennessee historian J.B. Killebrew in 1874, the Copper Basin area was "a barren sterile region prior to 1850."

In the mid-1800's, the arrival of the copper mining industry was heralded with exuberance, as it provided much-needed livelihood for the local mountain people. During this period the Copper Basin was a veritable boom area, with people converging from every direction to participate in the mining, as well as the developing railroad. The basin's forests were badly cut over to obtain fuel for copper smelting, then subjected to copper sulfide fumes generated by open-air roasting of copper ore. The fumes—spread further when high smoke stacks were added after 1907—hung close to the ground or mixed with frost, fog or rain, killing nearly every remaining tree, bush, shrub, weed and growing plant in the 35,000-acre area. At that time little thought was given to the effect on the land. Even today, in spite of the ravaged land that remains as a result of copper mining, the people who worked in the mines and their families are fiercely proud of their barren hills. The devastation was two-fold when mining operations ceased. The land was exhausted, as was the morale of the people left with no source of income. Adding insult to injury long after the copper smelting fumes were controlled, Tennessee law permitted open-range cattle grazing. Lowland farmers drove and later trucked cattle up into the basin for free grazing, having burned the land indiscriminately to encourage springtime growth of thin sedge pasturage.

Reclamation began with the help of the Civilian Conservation

Guide To The North Georgia Mountains

Corps in the early 1930's. It has continued through the efforts of at least three copper companies as well as the Tennessee Valley Authority (TVA), the U.S. Soil Conservation Service, U.S. Forest Service, the Tennessee Division of Natural Resources, other state agencies and the Universities of Tennessee, Georgia and North Carolina. The hillsides have been roughly regraded, partially terraced and thickly planted with pines, bush clover, weeping lovegrass, clumps of Japanese knotweed and kudzu. Rock check dams have been built and locust seedlings planted in the accumulated soil above the dams.

The Tennessee Chemical Company still operates a sulfuric acid plant in Copperhill. However, the area's future seems to point to tourism, with the proliferation of whitewater enthusiasts who pass through this area on the way to nearby rapids of the Ocoee River.

The Copper Basin is now listed on the National Register of Historic Places. The Tennessee Chemical Company has given the old abandoned Burra Burra mine, together with seventeen hilltop acres with old buildings, to the Ducktown Basin Museum. In 1988 the state of Tennessee purchased the museum to commemorate the copper mining area as the state's first historical industrial site.

DIRECTIONS: *From Blue Ridge go north on GA 5 for 11 miles to Copperhill, then north on TN 68 to US 64, which bisects the area from east to west.*

MAP REFERENCES: *USGS 1:100,000 series: Cleveland.*

THE GEORGIA CONSERVANCY

68

Alum root
Heuchera villosa

Rich Mountains

The 13,276-acre Rich Mountains are primarily wilderness (9,649 acres) and primitive backcountry (3,627 acres) which is not heavily used. The Rich Mountains are remarkable because many of the peaks and ridges are covered with a deep, black porter's loam, a characteristic shared with the Cohuttas. In the Eastern Blue Ridge such soils are confined to coves. On the Rich Mountains this soil covering results in spectacular wildflower displays. On ridges and slopes alike one finds lush summer herb growth and forests of basswood, ash and black cherry -- trees that occur in the Eastern Blue Ridge mostly in high rich coves. Gaps, at least in the Turniptown area, have populations of the rare columbo, a most unusual plant. There is old-growth timber south of Turniptown Mountain. North-facing coves have boulder fields and rare northern wildflowers at the southern limit of their range. There is a large bear population and one can find "licks" where deer have eaten clay-rich soil.

About 60 inches of rain falls here each year, May usually being the wettest month and April and July the driest.

Sites of old Indian camps can be found along the high ridge lines. Remnants of white settlements dating from about 1910 are just north of Rich Mountain. The largest gold nugget ever found in Georgia came from a creek draining this area. Marble, which is mined at the famous quarries near Tate and Marble Hill, can also be found exposed in the bottom of the syncline.

Elevation varies from approximately 2,000 feet near Little Rock Creek to 4,081 feet on Big Bald Mountain [Fig. 12(1)]. High peaks and lookouts from the Old Road (see below) offer panoramic vistas after leaves fall. Rugged mountain terrain with rock outcrops, and streams with many small waterfalls create a quality scenic resource.

US 76 [Fig. 12(10)] between Ellijay and Blue Ridge, Georgia generally follows the Murphy Syncline, which divides the highly metamorphosed rocks of the Blue Ridge proper-from the moderately metamorphosed rocks of the Cohuttas. This remarkable geologic trough is clearly visible in satellite photographs. It is likely that the uninformed visitor driving up US 76 in the deep gash of the Murphy Syncline would pass the Rich Mountains area by, since the higher peaks and ridges are hardly visible from the road.

Hikers exploring the Rich Mountains area should be experienced and carry topographical maps, compass and other survival gear.

DIRECTIONS: *From the McDonald's Restaurant intersection in East Ellijay on US 76, travel north on US 76 (GA 2 and 5, Appalachian Hwy. 515) for 8.7 miles and turn right at the Rock Creek Baptist Church [Fig. 12(3)]. This road loops in front of the church and immediately onto Rock Creek Road. Turn onto Rock Creek Road, which parallels Little Rock Creek, and proceed 5.0 miles to Stanley*

Figure 12   RICH MOUNTAIN

Wood frog
Rana sylvatica

This animal is found in our Blue Ridge at the extreme southern limits of its range. Its black head patches are characteristic. Key to the survival of this very shy frog is mid-winter breeding which gives it a head start to survive both competition and predation.

Gap [Fig. 12(4)]. The paved road becomes a moderately rough dirt road at 2.1 miles. Stanley Gap is a small parking area on the right at the intersection of an old U.S. Forest Service road.

Alternate access. In addition to the Rock Creek Road access, the Rich Mountains area can be approached on Aska Road and Aaron Mountain and Stanley Gap Roads (FS roads 295 and 338). These roads are passable with 2-wheel-drive vehicles. An old road leaves GA 5 near the gravel quarry at Whitepath and forms the boundary of the area as it winds around Aaron, Bee, Rich, and Little Bald Mountains. Turning north, it forms the northeast boundary of the area as it passes around Big Bald Mountain through Wolfpen Gap and over Stanley Creek to Stanley Gap Road. This boundary road is referred to as the Old Road [Fig. 12(5)]. It is passable with 4-wheel-drive vehicles only.

In order to reach Rich Mountain from Stanley Gap, walk south on an old Forest Service road which starts by the bulletin board and borders the wilderness area to the base of Rich Mountain. From there several primitive, unmarked trails cross through the wilderness and backcountry area. One must be careful in order to avoid getting lost. This is a 7-mile hike with an elevation gain of over 2,000 ft.

~RICH MOUNTAIN TRAIL. [Fig. 12(6)] About 8.8 miles one way. Moderately difficult. The only well-marked trail in the area is the Rich Mountain Trail, designated with rectangular-shaped white blazes.

Begin at Stanley Gap (see directions above) and go north to the shores of Lake Blue Ridge. After about 0.5 mile, intersect with the diamond-shaped-white-blazed Benton MacKaye Trail and share the same route for about the next 2 miles. After that the Benton MacKaye Trail heads straight up the ridge toward Cherry Log, while the Rich Mountain Trail turns right and goes down the side of the ridge toward Lake Blue Ridge.

Alternate Access to Rich Mountain Trail. From Blue Ridge go one mile on US 76 to Aska Road. Turn right and continue four miles to Deep Gap [Fig. 12(7)]. The trail crosses the road at the gap. To reach Stanley Gap, go on Aska Road four additional miles to Stanley Gap Road. Turn right on a gravel road and travel 3.9 miles to the trailhead.

To reach the lakeshore, from US 76 go three miles on the Aska Road and turn left on Campbell Camp Road; travel 2.4 miles to the trailhead.

~AARON MOUNTAIN. [Fig. 12(9)] Has a rounded dome covered with rich, black soil and a wildflower display in spring. An old-timber growth (129 years) lies on the south face of this mountain Horse C2ove. A good boulderfield and northern hardwood forest with some possible record size, second-growth trees, especially silverbell.

~LAKE BLUE RIDGE. The lake shimmers like a sapphire in a green granite setting. Most of the surrounding land is part of the Chattahoochee National Forest, which protects the lake from being overly developed. Except for a few waterskiers, most of the *aficionados* come to camp and fish. It is the only lake in the state where one can battle the mighty muskie, a large game fish of the pike family, although the prime fishing attractions are walleye, bluegill and smallmouth bass. Thirty-five fish attractors—manmade feeding covers—have been scattered around the coves and creeks. Lake Blue Ridge is fed by the north-flowing Toccoa River. The river flows gently for about 15 miles north of the dam, then changes its name to the Ocoee and froths into one of the Southeast's most exhilarating whitewater streams for rafting and kayaking. Call for water level information and power generation schedules which may affect fishing near the dam (800) 251-9242, Mon-Fri 8:30 to 6, weekends 8:30 to 4:30.

ADDITIONAL INFORMATION: *Contact the U.S. Forest Service, East Main St., Blue Ridge, GA 30513. (404) 632-2031 or 632-2032.*

LAKE BLUE RIDGE TRAIL. 0.6 mile. A loop trail that follows the shoreline of Lake Blue Ridge and offers a beautiful view of the lake.

DIRECTIONS: *From Blue Ridge take old US 76 east for 1.5 miles to Dry Branch Road; turn right; go three miles to the entrance to the Blue Ridge Recreation Area. The trail begins and ends in the picnic area.*

LAKE BLUE RIDGE CAMPSITES. 55 campsites in the area, several along the lake; bathrooms and showers; no hookups are provided. For availability around the lake, Memorial Day through Labor Day, contact the U.S. Forest Service, Toccoa Ranger District. (404) 632-3031.

LAKE BLUE RIDGE BOAT RENTAL. Fishing boats can be rented at the Blue Ridge Lake Marina (phone (404) 632-2618) on the northern side, near the dam. It is the only commercial outlet on the lake for gas, food and supplies. It also provides one of several boat-launch ramps. Others are at Morganton Point and the more remote Lake Blue Ridge Recreation Area (also known as Dry Branch or Green Creek). The U.S. Forest Service offers tent camping, swimming beaches and picnic areas at both sites. (404) 632-8331.

LAKE BLUE RIDGE CABIN RENTAL. Most cabins are fully furnished, with fireplaces and decks. Some include breakfast and hot tubs. Contact Bed and Breakfast Hideaway Homes, P.O. Box 300,

Blue Ridge, GA 30513 (404) 632-2411 or contact the Blue Ridge Visitor Center, P.O. Box 875, Blue Ridge, GA 30513, (404) 632-5680.

MORGANTON POINT RECREATION AREA. Located on the shores of Lake Blue Ridge 0.5 mile from the town of Morganton, this campground contains 37 campsites, 8 picnic sites, a designated swimming area with a lifeguard on duty during the summer camping season and a boat-launch ramp. No showers or hiking trails are within this recreation area, and electricity is available only in the bathrooms.

DIRECTIONS: *From Blue Ridge [Fig. 12(11)] take old US 76 east and south of town to Lakewood Junction. Here GA 60 and US 76 join, with GA 60 continuing as the designated main road south and east to Morganton [Fig. 12(12)]. It is approximately 5.0 miles from Blue Ridge to Morganton. The drive is scenic, crossing the TVA dam with a splendid view of Lake Blue Ridge to the southwest. Also between the dam and Lakewood Junction is a U.S. Forest Service boat-launch ramp near Lakewod. At Morganton, look for the white-on-green sign to the recreation area, on the right side of the road just before the road turns east and south.*

~DRIVING TOURS

ASKA ROAD TO NEWPORT ROAD (13.8 MI). Turn left at the dead end onto a paved road to Dial, Georgia [Fig. 12(13)]. This road comes out on GA 60 where one can head for either Dahlonega or Morganton. For a picture postcard alternative, turn right at the dead end onto SR 1010 to Cartecay [Fig. 12(14)]. An unusual side trip is to the Ducktown Tennessee Basin Museum north of Blue Ridge, Georgia, in Greenville, Tenn. Here relics and methods of 100 years of copper mining are preserved at the site of the Burra Burra Mine.

BOARDTOWN ROAD BETWEEN ELLIJAY AND BLUE RIDGE. This 18.6-mile drive between Ellijay and Blue Ridge provides a good look at the intimacy and charm of the north Georgia countryside. Visitors will pass red barns and silver silos, small green fields with silver creeks running through them and cows wandering about, Christmas tree farms, doublewides and cedar homes. Pickup truck drivers will lift an index finger off the steering wheel to say "howdy" as they pass.

DIRECTIONS: *From the town square in the center of Ellijay, take GA 52 and GA 2 west (Dalton Street) to Boardtown Road [Fig. 12(15)], about 0.4 mile from the center of town. There is a road sign, as well as a sign to Sugar Creek Raceway.*

~THE CARTECAY RIVER. [Fig. 12(16)] The Cartecay is a small, intimate river located east of Ellijay. Flowing out of a long valley and past farmlands, it passes over a series of tight drops around upland ridges. It then returns to its more placid nature just prior to its confluence with the Ellijay River, where the two become the Coosawattee. This is a narrow, clear mountain stream with almost continuous Class I and II rapids for the first 5.5 miles of this section. Although level, it is fast-flowing along steep ridges and through shaded tree canopies for the final six miles. This is intermediate to advanced whitewater with one unavoidable Class III rapid. The river requires more skills than do the upper Chattahoochee and Broad Rivers. In places it is comparable to Section III of the Chattooga.

DIRECTIONS: *Put in on a dirt road located 2.5 miles east of Ellijay on GA 52 past Oak Hill Apple House. The dirt road is 1.5 miles from the river [Fig. 12(17)]. Take out at a small roadside park along Ga 52 about two miles east of Ellijay.*

MAP REFERENCES: *For Cohuttas and Rich Mt., USGS 1:100,000 series: Cleveland - Dalton - Cartersville. USGS 1:24,000 series: Cashes Valley - Blue Ridge - Wilscot - Ellijay - Ticknetley - Noontootla. County Highway Maps: Gilmer - Murray - Fannin - Gordon.*

Silverbell
Halesia carolina

Etowah River and Toccoa River Watersheds

The Toccoa River and the Etowah River flow in different directions. The Etowah drains the south side of the Tennessee Valley divide, while the Toccoa drains the north side. In these watersheds, visitors will find the highest waterfall in Georgia, as well as the approach trail for the beginning of the Appalachian Trail. A fish hatchery allows one to see how the hundreds of thousands of rainbow trout that are stocked in Georgia's rivers and streams are raised to catching size. Two fine rivers provide canoeing opportunities for boaters of varying skills and experience.

~AMICALOLA FALLS STATE PARK. [Fig. 13(26)] Amicalola is a Cherokee word meaning "tumbling waters," an appropriate label since the park's beautiful falls [Fig. 13(27)] slide and plunge 729 feet in seven cascades, making it the highest waterfall in Georgia. It tumbles southwest through a cove of Amicalola Mountain and forms part of the Amicalola Creek watershed. This, in turn, feeds into the Etowah, which joins the Oostanaula to form the Coosa near Rome.

The park, nestled along the southernmost edge of the Blue Ridge Mountain chain, consists of more than 900 acres surrounding the waterfall. The forest types include cove hardwood, upland oak-hickory and mixed pine and hardwood.

Both mountain and piedmont flora and fauna can be found here, and most of the species native to this region inhabit the park. Here a small colony of pink lady slippers grows, pileated woodpeckers nest and the eastern milk snake reaches its southernmost range.

All seasons are beautiful at Amicalola Falls. Spring and summer offer an abundance of wildflowers, including dogwood, mountain laurel and rhododendron. Autumn offers brilliant colors in the forest, and the winter months hold a special magic as the deer and other wild animals seek refuge within the park. April and May are ideal times to enjoy the waterfall because of the unusually high volume of water. Little Amicalola Creek flows through the park and provides an opportunity for trout fishing.

FACILITIES: *900 acres; 17 tent and trailer sites; comfort station with hot showers, flush toilets and laundry facilities; 57-room lodge, restaurant and meeting center; 15 cottages, 3 playgrounds, 5 picnic shelters. Walk-in lodge (open 1991) accomodating 40 persons with family style meals; 5-mile hike from park to lodge; 3,000 foot elevation; trail crosses the Appalachian Trail and passes near Cochran's Falls.*
SPECIAL EVENTS: *Jun-Aug, naturalists' programs are provided Thur-Sun on topics dealing with the area's natural, cultural and historical resources. Other programs are scheduled throughout the year. A schedule is available in the park office.*

Figure 13 ETOWAH AND TOCCOA RIVER WATERSHEDS

DATES/HOURS: *Daily 7am-10pm year round. Office open 8-5.*
DIRECTIONS: *15 miles northwest of Dawsonville and 18 miles west of Dahlonega on GA 52.*
ADDITIONAL INFORMATION: *Amicalola Falls State Park, Georgia Department of Natural Resources, Star Route, Box 213, Dawsonville, GA 30534. (404) 265-2885.*

AMICALOLA FALLS HIKING TRAIL. 0.25 mile. The most scenic trail in Amicalola Park leads to the base of Amicalola Falls. The walk follows a rocky path uphill along cascading Amicalola Creek. Several large yellow poplars tower over the trail as it leads through a cove hardwood forest and ends at the lower observation deck.

DIRECTIONS: *The trailhead is in Amicalola Falls State Park near the reflection pool at the end of the main park road. The trail is marked with red blazes.*

WEST RIDGE LOOP TRAIL. A 1.2-mile nature trail within the park. Virginia pine is the dominant tree along much of the trail.

DIRECTIONS: *There are three access points for the trail: 1) across the road and field from the visitor center; 2) to the right on the paved road to the top of the park; and 3) at the turnaround of the main park road, marked with nature trail signs. The access route across from the visitor center is the longest and most scenic, overlooking Amicalola Creek as it winds down the hillside.*

APPALACHIAN TRAIL APPROACH TRAIL. 8.1 miles. Springer Mountain (3,782 feet) [Fig. 13(28)], the southern starting point/terminus for the Appalachian Trail (AT), is reached by this hike from Amicalola Falls State Park. The trail is strenuous, up and down along the peaks and knobs of Amicalola Mountain, and is a good testing ground for those contemplating longer hikes on the AT itself.

DIRECTIONS: *The trailhead begins at the back of the park visitor center.*

THE GEORGIA CONSERVANCY

~AMICALOLA CREEK AND WILDLIFE REFUGE. [Fig. 13(35) South of Amicalola Falls State Park, on Amicalola Creek in the Etowah River Basin, the Georgia Department of Natural Resources operates a 4,700 acre wildlife refuge. Knowledgeable canoeists and naturalists consider the Amicalola to be one of Georgia's most beautiful and exciting waterways. More river than creek in size, the Amicalola was one of the top three candidates in the nationwide search for a river to be designated as the first National Wild River Park. GA Highway 53 crosses the midpoint of the Amicalola approximately seven miles west of Dawsonville. Dawsonville can be reached from GA 400 by traveling west on GA 53.

On the southeast side of the 53 bridge is a guide marker which graphically depicts the river, access points, the more prominent rapids and difficulty ratings. First time users in particular should pay close attention to the information on the marker.

There are several put-in points above the 53 bridge, including Six Mile and Devil's Elbow. Both are state maintained. Some parking is available, camping is allowed and launching is easy. Take-out for above the 53 bridge boating (and put-in for below the 53 bridge boating) is near the DNR ranger's cabin on the northeast side of the bridge. Parking is not allowed at the cabin but adequate parking is available on the shoulders of Hwy 53 at the bridge. There are no access points on the Amicalola below the Hwy 53 bridge until one reaches the Etowah River. Take-out is on the Etowah, two miles below the confluence with Amicalola Creek, at a concrete ramp near Kelley Bridge. Access to Six Mile and Devil's Elbow is reached by proceeding west on 53 approximately one mile and turning north at the first paved road (county road 192). Turn right at the first major intersection to reach Devil's Elbow. Continue north at the intersection and watch for the sign for Six Mile Put-in.

The Highway 53 bridge marks a dividing point in the Amicalola's difficulty. The section above the bridge is ideal for teaching and intermediate canoeing. This section begins as easy water and grows progressively more difficult. Several long "rock gardens," a five foot drop, and a deceptive "roostertail" mark this section. Below the Hwy 53 bridge is the most difficult water on the river. Beginning with the "Edge of the World," a class IV rapid about a half a mile below the bridge, there are several class II-IV rapids which should only be attempted by expert boaters. Low water conditions usually are found after June. A foot trail leads down the east side of the river to "Edge of the World".

The beauty of this river, with its steep banks and gorge-like conditions and mountain vegetation, cannot be overemphasized.

~CANOEING

ETOWAH RIVER CANOEING. The upper section of the Etowah River is an ideal river for beginning canoeists, families and organized groups who want to run a brisk mountain river and also to be close to the scenic and historical attractions of Dahlonega. A 12-mile stretch can be canoed in one day of steady paddling or two leisurely days. (Those opting for the two-day version can break the trip at Castleberry Bridge and camp at the nearby Blackburn Park [Fig. 13(30)] 1.3 miles south of Auraria on GA 9E or go into Dahlonega seven miles south on 9E).

One hazard is Etowah Falls, 1.5 miles from the put-in. The canoeist must land on the rocks on the right bank and portage over or around them. Below Castleberry Bridge [Fig. 13(33)] is an old mine tunnel about seven feet in diameter and about 0.2 mile long. Scout this carefully. Run it only if light is visible at the other end; if the exit light is not clear and bright, the tunnel is likely to be too obstructed with debris and stumps to be safely passable.

DIRECTIONS: *Put in at the bridge on US 19 [Fig. 13(31)]. Castleberry Bridge is a good take-out, or the trip may be continued to the bridge at GA 136.*

TOCCOA RIVER. Some knowledgeable canoeists have described the Toccoa as Georgia's prettiest whitewater stream. It has its headwaters in Union County, flows into Fannin County and becomes the major feeder stream for Lake Blue Ridge. It resumes its flow below Blue Ridge and travels into Tennessee, where it is known as the Ocoee.

The stream's first couple of miles provide a startling contrast between undisturbed river banks and those touched by human hand. In apparent efforts to squeeze a little more yield from flood plains, some farmers have cleared to the edge of the water, removing vegetation which holds the soil. The unhappy consequence is that the banks are rapidly eroding, dumping silt and any remaining vegetation into the water.

The river offers a variety of interesting forms of vegetation for each season. Early spring brings bluets in the moss, then azalea, laurel and -- all around Deep Hole Campground -- wild strawberries. In late spring abundant rhododendron garnishes the banks. Summer offers the richness of mature hardwood stands in full leaf. When autumn comes the hardwoods take on an incredible glow. Alternate leaf dogwood and deciduous holly sport their bright red berries right on into winter. When upper-story trees provide enough shade, galax carpets the banks, the waxy leaves dark green until December, then thriving coppery as pennies for the winter months. Galax is gathered frequently for use in floral arrangements. Sadly, this has led to its near-extinction in many areas.

The most beautiful section of the Toccoa River lies behind Toonowee Mountain. Small rapids, hemlocks trailing in the water and the beautifully clear stream itself combine to saturate the senses.

DIRECTIONS: *Put in for the upper section is at Deep Hole [Fig. 13(19)], a U.S. Forest Service campground on GA 60, 27 miles north of Dahlonega. Driving from Deep Hole, continue north on GA 60 for 4.5 miles and then left onto an unmarked, paved road that goes between two buildings and looks at first like a driveway. Continue on mixed gravel/paved roads to Dial [Fig. 13(13)], where there are 2 bridges. On the way is the Chastain House, the oldest home in Fannin County. The old bridge at Dial is blocked to traffic and is the take-out, or if running the lower section, the put-in. If the put-in is at Dial, the take-out is at the Shallow Ford Bridge, reached on the east side of the river by continuing on the gravel road along the river and bearing left at a fork about midway; or, cross the Dial Bridge to the west side of the river. Continue on the paved road to the first road on the right, turn right and continue until reaching the Shallow Ford Bridge [Fig. 13(20)].*

~**WATERFALLS**

LONG CREEK FALLS. Picturesque falls and trail. Requires a 20-30 minute walk in each direction.

DIRECTIONS: *From Blue Ridge follow old US 76 to Aska Road across from Harmony Church. Turn south and go 13.8 miles to the end of the road. Turn right on Newport Road, go 4.3 miles to the end of the road. Turn left, cross bridge over Noontootla Creek, continue on gravel road. Pass cemetery and come to intersection 0.6 mile from bridge. Turn hard right on FS 58 and go southeast into forest along this road 6.6 miles to Three Forks [Fig. 13(21)]. Hike to the northeast up Long Creek to the falls. The trail corridor has an assortment of blazes designating three major hiking trails: the Appalachian (white vertical 2"x 6"), the Duncan Ridge National Recreational Trail (blue vertical 2"x 6") and the Benton MacKaye Trail (white diamond 5"x 7"). The distance to the falls is 1.1 miles, ascending gradually along the way. A side trail to the falls is indicated with vertical blue blazes.*

FALL BRANCH FALLS. [Fig. 13(22)] A fine double waterfall.

DIRECTIONS: *From Blue Ridge follow old US 76 to Aska Road. Turn south and go approximately 8.2 miles to intersection with Stanley Creek Road, entering from the right. Turn right onto Stanley Creek Road, and go 3.2 miles to small parking area just beyond an* *interesting farm owned by long-time Forest Service fire warden Garfield Stanley. Cross a wooden bridge over Fall Branch and park on right. Hike up hill on Benton MacKaye Trail to double falls [Fig. 13(22)] on right. There is a small picnic and/or camping spot 30 yards above the waterfall.*

SEA CREEK FALLS.

DIRECTIONS: *From Blue Ridge follow old US 76 east 5.0 miles to intersection with GA 60 South at Lakewood Junction. Continue 14.7 miles south on GA 60 through the small town of Morganton, past entrance to Deep Hole Recreation Area to junction with FS 4, entering from left. Follow FS 4 an additional 3.3 miles to right-hand curve in road just inside U.S. Forest Service boundary. Road to immediate left before curve is access to falls. Park in area at end of this spur (about 0.3 mile) and walk upstream 150 feet to view falls.*

LITTLE ROCK CREEK FALLS. [Fig. 13(24)] There is a series of small falls just before reaching the main one. The walk is strenuous along a footpath leading along the left side of the creek and going only part of the way to the falls. There is not a footpath up the side of the main falls because of the dangerous slippery rocks in the area. Use extreme caution.

DIRECTIONS: *From Blue Ridge follow the directions above for Sea Creek Falls, but only as far as the crossing of Skeenah Creek on GA 60 south. Skeenah Creek is located about 11.3 miles south of Morganton. There is an old but still operational mill on the northeast side of the highway. A commercial campground is also located on this site. After crossing Skeenah Creek, continue south on GA 60 another 3.1 miles to intersection with FS 69, Fish Hatchery Road, coming from right. Turn onto this road and go about three miles to where the road crosses Little Rock Creek [Fig. 13(24)]. There is a bridge and a small pull-out area here.*

~THE CHATTAHOOCHEE FOREST NATIONAL FISH HATCHERY. [Fig. 13(25)] The hatchery produces rainbow trout for stocking in rivers, streams and lakes of the Chattahoochee National Forest and other areas of north Georgia. While spawning operations are not conducted at this hatchery, fertilized eggs are shipped here and incubated under controlled conditions. Eggs hatch within three to four weeks, and the young fry are soon placed on a specially formulated dry feed. Upon reaching two to three inches in size, the fingerlings are moved to outside raceways for rearing to catchable size. The hatchery turns out about 850,000 trout each year. These fish are harvested from the raceways and distributed by truck for stocking into streams, lakes and reservoirs of north Georgia in cooperation with the State Game and Fish Department. There are signs located throughout the grounds to explain the hatchery and its operations, and there is a sheltered exhibit.

There is fishing in Rock Creek by the hatchery, and nearby Cooper Creek is an angler's paradise for trout fishing.

FACILITIES: *Group tours by arrangement, handicapped access, restrooms.*
DATES/HOURS: *7:30-4:30 daily.*
DIRECTIONS: *Located 5 miles off Ga 60, 26 miles south of Blue Ridge. Direction signs are posted near the Hatchery road.*
ADDITIONAL INFORMATION: *U.S. Fish and Wildlife Service, Fish Hatchery Road (FS 69), Suches, GA 30572. (404) 838-4723.*

~FRANK GROSS CAMPGROUND. [Fig. 13(34)] A small campground located along Rock Creek near the Chattahoochee National Fish Hatchery. Fishing is allowed (at no charge) in the adjacent Rock Creek and also in the 13-1/2-acre Rock Creek Lake 1.7 miles further west on the right side of Fish Hatchery Road. The lake is managed by the National Fish Hatchery, and the creek and lake are stocked periodically with nine-inch rainbow trout.

FACILITIES: *11 campsites with picnic tables, drinking water and two chemical toilets. Trailers up to 22 feet can be accommodated.*
DATES/HOURS: *Late spring to early fall.*
FEES: *$5 per night.*
DIRECTIONS: *Take GA 60 north from Dahlonega for 27 miles; turn left (south) and go 5 miles on the Fish Hatchery Road (FS 69).*
ADDITIONAL INFORMATION: *Frank Gross Campground, U.S. Forest Service, Toccoa Ranger District, E. Main St., Box 1839, Blue Ridge, GA 30513. (404) 632-3031.*

~DEEP HOLE RECREATION AREA. [Fig. 13(19)] A small campground located in an attractive mountain setting on a bend of the Toccoa River just north of the fish hatchery. Its name comes from a deep hole in the river by the campground. This is an excellent canoe launch for the Toccoa River.

FACILITIES: *Eight campsites suitable for tents or small trailers; restrooms; drinking water.*
DATES/HOURS: *Open late spring through early fall.*
FEES: *$5 per night.*
DIRECTIONS: *27 miles north of Dahlonega on GA 60.*
ADDITIONAL INFORMATION: *Deep Hole Recreation Area, U.S. Forest Service, Toccoa Ranger District, E. Main St., Box 1839, Blue Ridge, GA 30513. (404) 632-3031.*

~DAHLONEGA GOLD RUSH MUSEUM. [Fig. 13(29)] America's first gold rush took place not in California, but in the southern Blue Ridge Mountains in the vicinity of Dahlonega during the late 1820's. The town's name, in fact, comes from the Cherokee word for gold, *talonega,* which translates literally as "precious yellow color." Gold was first discovered by white men near Dahlonega in 1828. Four years later, large discoveries of the precious metal were made in nearby Auraria. It was not until 1848 that gold was discovered in California and that gold rush occured. From 1837 until 1861, the U.S. government operated a mint in Dahlonega which manufactured a total of $6 million worth of gold coins from locally-mined ore. Samples of the precious metal, scale models showing old mining techniques and other relics of Dahlonega's golden era are on display in the museum. Constructed in 1836, the museum is Georgia's oldest public building.

DATES/HOURS: *Mon-Sat 9-5, Sun. 10-5.*
FEES: *Adults $1.50, 12 and under $.75, 5 and under free; group rates with advanced notice.*
DIRECTIONS: *On the town square in Dahlonega.*
ADDITIONAL INFORMATION: *(404) 864-2257.*

MAP REFERENCES: *USGS 1:100,000 series: Dalton - Toccoa*

The Eastern Blue Ridge

The Blue Ridge Mountains were formed some 235 million years ago, during a geologic age of mountain building, when the North American and European and African continents collided, a process called "plate tectonics." The movement of two continents against each other produced an intense pressure from the direction of what is now Southeastern Georgia. The process was something like a deck of cards being bent end to end. As the rocks folded, forming mountains and ridges, they also melted, creating a kind of protective "shingle" effect. Over millions of years the forces of nature have worn as much as five miles off the mountains, shaping them into the peaks, cliffsides and valleys we see today.

The changes that have gone on for millions of centuries continue today. For example, the Eastern Continental Divide that runs through much of Georgia, separating the waters that flow into the Gulf of Mexico from those that flow into the Atlantic, is currently moving northward at the rate of 3,000 feet every million years. Rivers continue to change course. Until recently (in geological terms) the Chattooga River, which originates in North Carolina and flows along the border between Georgia and South Carolina, was part of the headwaters of the Chattahoochee River and flowed into the Gulf of Mexico. The Savannah River, gradually cutting a path northward, eventually intersected with the Chattooga and diverted its flow southeastward into the Savannah and eventually into the Atlantic. This "river capture," one of the most interesting and easily visualized phenomenon of geological history, has occurred a number of times in Georgia and is an ongoing process. Topsoil -- the thin, fragile covering of the hard gneiss and schist rock of the Blue Ridge -- is forming at the rate of about one inch every 50 to 100 years. Visitors to the foot of Toxaway Dam can see how the flood of 1916 wiped away the topsoil down to bare rock in a matter of minutes.

Georgia's Blue Ridge Mountains, with their rich geological history and diverse recreational opportunities, are surprisingly undiscovered. When visiting the mountains, most of us stick to the main highways; towns such as Helen, Clayton and Dahlonega are familiar names. But few people have discovered the upper portions of the wild and scenic Chattooga River, much less explored the hundreds of scenic logging roads or, even less, walked the unmarked hiking trails known mostly to hunters and fishermen. The information on the Blue Ridge in the following pages is designed to help readers get off the main roads and onto the backroads and trails and to discover the diversity, beauty -- and surprising fragility -- of these ageless mountains.

Cooper Creek Scenic Area

The 1,240-acre Cooper Creek Scenic Area [Fig. 14(1)], which ranges between 2,000 and 2,500 feet in elevation, is surrounded by more than 34,000 acres of the Cooper Creek Water Management Area and the slightly larger, overlapping Cooper Creek Wildlife Management Area. Within the latter are two U.S. Forest Service campgrounds, Cooper Creek [Fig. 14(2)] and Mulky [Fig. 14(3)] Recreation Areas. Cooper Creek scenic area is roughly a mile and a half long by one mile wide. Cooper Creek [Fig. 14(5)], a cold mountain trout stream, runs approximately two miles down the center of the scenic area. Numerous small branches join Cooper Creek. Two of these, Stillhouse Branch and Deep Cove Branch, are completely contained within the boundaries of the scenic area. Bryant Creek [Fig. 14(4)], a larger tributary with its headwaters on the south face of Duncan Ridge, parallels the eastern boundary. There are stands of large hemlock and white pine, reaching three and four feet in diameter, along Cooper Creek (and to some extent, Bryant Creek) and a short way up its tributaries. These are of special interest because this is close to the southern geographical limit of the hemlock/white pine community. The only evidence of human occupation in the scenic area is a few rock piles on Deep Cove Branch, a possible former cabin site.

Cherry may have been cut for furniture manufacture in the past, and some dead chestnut was removed from among the giant poplars in the southeast corner. Otherwise, it is believed that the scenic area represents original untouched forest. Fire has apparently only rarely touched the hemlock/white pine habitat. Dense growth of uniformly-aged white pine on Chestnut Ridge and the ridge along the south boundary may attest to severe burns there in times past. The U.S. Army holds training exercises in Cooper Creek Wildlife Management Area, so the solitude and quiet may be occasionally shattered.

DIRECTIONS: *Take GA 60 north from Dahlonega for 26 miles, turn east (right) onto FS Road 4 [Fig. 14(6)] and go six miles.*
ADDITIONAL INFORMATION: *U.S. Forest Service, Chestatee Ranger District, 1015 Tipton Dr., Dahlonega, GA 30533. (404) 864-6173.*

~**MULKY CAMPGROUND.** [Fig. 14(3)] A small campground with 10 campsites. Camping is usually from the last Saturday in March through mid-October. There are sanitary facilities, drinking water, tent pads and picnic tables.

DIRECTIONS: *Same as for Cooper Creek, above. Once on FS 4, continue on this dirt/gravel road entering and leaving National Forest property once before reentering just before the campground sign.*

Hemlock
Tsuga canadensis

The hemlock is a mountain species and our most attractive evergreen. Huge old hemlocks were once cut solely for the tannic acid in the bark. Along with rosebay rhododendron, it forms the hemlock-heath environment that protects and cools the streamside zone of our mountain trout streams.

Figure 14   COOPER CREEK SCENIC AREA

~COOPER CREEK RECREATION AREA. [Fig. 14(2)] Located along the banks of sparkling mountain streams stocked with trout, adjacent to the Cooper Creek Scenic Area. The 20 campsites can accommodate either tents or trailers up to 22 feet. There are sanitary facilities and drinking water. The Mill Shoals Trail originates in the Recreation Area and the Yellow Mountain Trail is nearby.

DIRECTIONS: *Same as for Cooper Creek and Mulky Campground, above. Continue less than a mile through the Mulky Campground to intersection with FS 236 entering from right. The recreation area is immediately ahead on this road.*

~HIKING TRAILS

HEMLOCK AND WHITE PINE STANDS. A suggested walking route to see the streamside stands of hemlock-heath and white pine begins at the bridge over Cooper Creek on Cavender Gap Road, FS 236 [Fig. 14(7)], and follows the right (south) bank to at least the second small feeder branch coming in on the right side. Here there is a rough trail made by fishermen. It passes through a grove of white pines, then under an almost solid canopy of rhododendron and mountain laurel. After a 0.25 mile one begins to encounter the large hemlocks and white pines. At the second branch is another intriguing grove in the tiny valley of the feeder stream. Farther up these small branch streams are cove hardwoods, oak, buckeye, hickory, cucumber tree and yellow poplar.

VIRGIN OLD-GROWTH HIKE. [Fig. 14(8)] About 1.0 mile. Park at a low gap about 0.4 mile from the end of the pavement going east on FS 33. There will be an old road pitching steeply north, the first road to the left after leaving the pavement. Park along FS 33. Walk down this road and take the first left hand log road just before the Turkey Creek ford. This nearly level log road passes through several moist coves with wildflower displays. Across Cooper Creek is a 6-acre bottomland that has been continuously in cultivation since early settler times and probably even in Indian days. After passing two small coves, watch for the first place that a vehicle could be turned around (the turn-around is on a ridge which leads down to a fine pool at the mouth of Bryant Creek [Fig. 14(4)]). From the turn-around ridge the first of the big trees is only several hundred yards along the old log road. The old-growth forest has widely spaced specimens of large white and northern red oak and black birch, but the largest trees are giant tulip poplars with circumferences of up to 17 feet. Storms through the ages have broken the tops out of many of them. While many big trees can be seen from the log road, others must be searched for above and below the road. The log road continues, crosses a white pine ridge and in about 0.25 mile reaches the "valley of the giants" where the largest poplars grow. The trail continues to parallel Cooper Creek for an undetermined distance.

MILL SHOALS TRAIL. [Fig. 14(2)] This trail is approximately two miles one way and considered moderate to strenuous. It is nearly impossible to follow without a map and detailed instructions. The starting point is well marked with a sign opposite the first entrance to the recreation area, but after that there are neither blazes nor signs. Stay to the right when entering the trail. It climbs steeply to a ridgetop, then descends through hardwoods to a jeep road, turns right onto the jeep road for 15 or 20 paces, then narrows and drops toward a stream on the left. It winds through an area with tall hemlock, white pine and dense vegetation, crosses three small streams, turns right on an old road and in about 50 feet turns left. At Duncan Ridge Road [Fig. 14(9)] it turns right, stays on the road for 350-400 yards and then continues on the left of the road. Leaving the roadside, it slowly goes up the side of a dry ridge on which one can see bracken fern, then goes straight and ends at the next jeep road.

YELLOW MOUNTAIN TRAIL. [Fig. 14(11)] This is mainly a ridge trail. It is 1.6 miles one way and is considered moderate. The trail entrance is marked by a yellow post on the northeast side of Cavender Gap Road, FS 236. The trail is marked with yellow blazes. At the start of the trail, one passes through a shady grove of hemlock on a hillside above a small stream; later there are several large remnant oaks. The trail gently ascends a ridge, which forms the northern boundary of Cooper Creek Scenic Area, for 1.2 miles to the top of Yellow Mountain [Fig. 14(10)]. Short leaf pine are common along the route. The trail then descends through an area scorched by fire and ends at the first dirt road.

~SCENIC DRIVES: There are three scenic drives which can be made through the area. Each drive begins at the entrance sign to Cooper Creek on FS 4.

MULKY GAP. [Fig. 14(12)] The first drive continues on FS 4 north across Mulky Gap. It goes up along Mulky Creek, with a beautiful streamside zone of hemlock-heath. Soon after the gap, one can either turn right on FS 40, a dead end road which in May and June will reward the visitor with a display of mountain laurel in bloom, or continue on FS 4, which winds down to US 76 west of Blairsville.

FANNY GAP DRIVE. [Fig. 14(13)] Turn right (east) from FS 4

New York fern
Thelypteris noveboracensis

onto FS 39. It passes Fanny Gap before turning sharply to follow Duncan Ridge past Buckeye Knob, Coosa Bald (4271 feet) and Wildcat Knob. The road ends at GA 180 [Fig. 14(14)], which goes east to Vogel State Park [Fig. 14(15)] and US 19/129 past Sosebee Cove Scenic Area, or goes west past beautiful trout-stocked Lake Winfield Scott [Fig. 14(16)] to GA 60 at Suches.

THE LOOP DRIVE. Turn right (south) near the Cooper Creek Recreation Area [Fig. 14(2)] onto the dirt Cavender Gap Road (FS 236) [Fig. 14(7)] which winds through a forest of large eastern white pine, eastern hemlock, oak, hickory and poplar and ends at paved FS 33, Turkey Creek Road [Fig. 14(17)]. Turn left (east) and proceed until the pavement ends after approximately two miles. Go on the gravel road for 0.4 mile to a low gap (Two Mile Gap) where a narrow road dips steeply at the left. This is the main entrance to the east end of the scenic area and the starting point for the short hike to the virgin old-growth area (see above). The gravel road continues to the point where FS 33 makes a hairpin curve to the right. Here go straight ahead onto FS 33A [Fig. 14(18)], which crosses Cooper Creek, Addis Gap and Bryant Creek before ending at FS 39. Turn left and go to the juncture with FS 4; turn left again and return to the starting point.

~A CANOEING GUIDE TO COOPER CREEK. Cooper Creek flows from the base of the dam on Lake Winfield Scott [Fig. 14(16)]. The dam is 14.5 miles south of Blairsville on GA 180. From its beginning, Cooper Creek twists and flows out of the mountains for 15 miles before it joins the Toccoa River along GA 60. The creek runs through three federally protected areas: the Chattahoochee National Forest and two areas within—Cooper Creek Game Management Area and Cooper Creek Scenic Area. Cooper Creek has long been a popular trout-fishing stream and could well become one of Georgia's most popular canoeing streams as well.

The first four miles of Cooper Creek are too narrow and shallow to canoe, and the final four miles flow mostly through flat, privately-owned farmland. The seven-mile stretch in between, however, is as interesting a run of Class II whitewater as Georgia has to offer. The average gradient of Cooper Creek is a steep 40-plus feet per mile, which puts it in the "gradient class" with such mighty rivers as the Chattooga Section IV (45 feet per mile) and Alabama's Little River Canyon (31 feet per mile). However, because Cooper Creek has a smaller watershed area and a lower level of water, it is less difficult to canoe than either of these rivers. Cooper Creek is within the Class II-III difficulty range. Nevertheless, the creek is a steep little stream that requires experience and skill to negotiate. There are two waterfalls -- one drops five feet and the other eight feet -- which are good Class III runs. A long slide of twisting channels and barrier rocks, which descends more than five feet, is, in high water, a Class

III run as well.

DIRECTIONS: *To reach the put-in on Cooper Creek, go north out of Dahlonega for nine miles on US 19/GA 60 to the point where the two roads separate. Bear left on GA 60, go seven miles to Suches and turn right (north) onto GA 180. Go north on 180 for 4.4 miles to Lake Winfield Scott Recreation Area. Turn left on FS 33 and go five miles. An access path leading down to the edge of the creek branches off FS 33 at the five-mile point. Limited but adequate parking space is provided at this put-in. To reach the take-out, go west from the put-in on FS 33 for 1.4 miles to an intersection. (A right turn at this intersection and a 0.1 mile drive will lead to the Bryant Creek Road Bridge. The bridge offers a good view of the river and could serve as an alternate put-in, shortening the canoe trip by 1.7 miles.) At the intersection turn left and continue on FS 33 for 3.5 miles to where it meets FS 236; turn right (north) on FS 236 and drive for 2.3 miles to the Cooper Creek Scenic Area and the Tom Jones Creek Bridge over Cooper Creek; drive over the bridge and continue for 0.5 mile through the campground; turn left (west) on FS 4; drive another 0.5 mile to Mulky Creek Campground [Fig. 14(3)]. The total distance from put-in to take-out is about seven miles.*

MAP REFERENCES: *1:24,000 series: Suches - Neels Gap - Mulky Gap - Coosa Bald.*

Blood Mountain

Blood Mountain is the highest peak on Georgia's portion of the Appalachian Trail. Some believe the name came from a bloody battle between the Cherokee and Creek Indians long before white men arrived in the area. The name more likely is derived from the red lichens growing on rocks at the summit. At 4,450 feet, it overlooks an area rich in streams, hiking trails and scenic recreation spots, one of which -- Sosebee Cove [Fig. 15(2)] -- is probably Georgia's only north-facing cove traversed by a paved road at such high elevation. It has an accessible boulderfield, northern hardwoods and large buckeyes and provides an example of how tulip poplar takes over following too-thorough logging of cove hardwood forests.

~VOGEL STATE PARK. [Fig. 15(3)] One of the prettiest state parks in all of Georgia. It is over 2,500 feet in elevation, usually affording cool temperatures even during hot summer months. The park can be crowded in summer, and campsites fill up quickly. There are short hiking trails in the park as well as the trailhead for the challenging 12.5-mile Coosa Backcountry Trail (see below).

FACILITIES: *36 cottages, 95 tent or trailer sites with water and electrical hookups (15 sites without), picnic shelters and tables, grills, restrooms, hot showers, stocked trout lake, swimming beach, paddle boats for rent, playground, miniature golf. Maps are available at the visitor center near the entrance.*
DATES/HOURS: *Open year round 7am-10 pm, swimming Jun 1 - Labor Day except on Mondays; office open 8-5.*
DIRECTIONS: *11 miles south of Blairsville on US 19/129.*
ADDITIONAL INFORMATION: *Vogel State Park, Rt. 1, Box 1230, Blairsville, GA 30512. (404) 745-2628.*

~BEAR HAIR TRAIL. [Fig. 15(4)] 4 miles. This orange-blaze-marked loop trail is ideal for family hikes. It is of moderate difficulty, beginning and ending in Vogel State Park.

DIRECTIONS: *Follow directions to Vogel State Park, above. The trail begins behind the Visitor Center.*

~COOSA BACKCOUNTRY TRAIL. [Fig. 15(23)] 12.5 miles. This difficult trail is marked with yellow blazes and signs and for the most part is easy to follow. It fords streams on its lower part and traverses the high Duncan Ridge, including Coosa Bald [Fig. 15(5)] at over 4,000 feet. It is recommended that hikers take more than one day to hike the entire route, although it can be done in one long day, particularly during the longer daylight hours of spring and summer. A permit is required and is available free, together with a

Figure 15   BLOOD MOUNTAIN

Dutchman's breeches
Dicentra cucullaria

This and squirrel corn (*D. canadensis*) look very much alike and both are indicators of moist, rich high elevation north-facing coves and boulderfields. They may be seen above the road at Sosebee Cove. Their delicate filigreed foliage is distinctive.

trail map, at the Vogel State Park Visitor Center.

DIRECTIONS: *The trail begins in Vogel State Park (see directions above).*

~**SOSEBEE COVE SCENIC AREA AND HIKING TRAIL.** [Fig. 15(6)] This 175-acre tract of prize hardwood timber is a memorial to Arthur Woody, who served as a Forest Service Ranger from 1911 to 1945. Ranger Woody, the "Barefoot Ranger," loved this peaceful cove and negotiated its purchase by the Forest Service. Rare and beautiful wildflowers and ferns abound. In the boulderfield above the road, there are the rare yellowwood tree and representative northern hardwoods such as yellow birch, and a salamander-rich branch flows down the cove. There are several large buckeyes below the road along with a stand of second-growth yellow poplar that followed heavy logging and destroyed the diversity of the cove forest. A 0.5-mile loop trail circles the area.

Woody, with his own funds, brought the first deer back into the mountains after they had been extirpated in 1895. He always claimed his father killed the last deer in north Georgia in that year

DIRECTIONS: *Take US 129 south from Blairsville for 9.5 miles; turn right (west) on GA 180 and go 2.0 miles to the Sosebee Cove Parking area [Fig. 15(2)] on the right.*

~**DOCKERY LAKE RECREATION AREA.** [Fig. 15(7)] Dockery Lake (2,388 feet), nestled within a large cove surrounded by ridgetops and small valleys, offers the forest visitor a wide variety of natural and scenic beauty. Deer and grouse are common sights. Purple rhododendron blooms in May at higher elevations, while the white variety blooms in mid-June at lower elevations. Native trees such as dogwood, sourwood, locust and laurel add more color to spring and brilliance to the fall leaf season. Trout fishing is available along the Pigeon Roost Creek and nearby Waters Creek, as well as in the six-acre Dockery Lake, which is stocked on a regular basis.

FACILITIES: *11 campsites (no electrical or water hookups or showers), restrooms, drinking water, fishing, hiking, 6 picnic sites.*
DATES/HOURS: *For picnicking and fishing, from the last Sat in Mar-Nov 30; overnight camping usually extends from around May 1 through the end of Oct.*
FEES: *Campsite $5 per night.*
DIRECTIONS: *Follow GA 60 for 12.3 miles north of Dahlonega and turn right onto FS Road 654 opposite the Dockery Lake sign [Fig. 15(8)].*
ADDITIONAL INFORMATION: *Dockery Lake, U.S. Forest Service, Toccoa Ranger District, E. Main St., Box 1839, Blue Ridge, GA 30513. (404) 632-3031.*

~DOCKERY LAKE TRAIL. [Fig. 15(9)] 3.4 miles. This trail provides access to the Appalachian Trail. It winds north 3 miles over an old logging road and terminates at Miller Gap [Fig. 15(10)]. The trail parallels a portion of Pigeon Roost Creek and provides scenic views of nearby mountain ridges and peaks. Twelve streams either parallel or cross the trail. Stands of hemlock, white pine, hickory, black walnut and magnolia cling to the mountain slopes of granite and milky quartz. Delicate mosses and colorful lichens adorn the boulders bordering much of the trail. In spring, the trail comes alive with blooming magnolias and wildflowers including wild iris, trillium, bloodroot and fleabane.

DIRECTIONS: *Follow the directions for Dockery Lake Recreation, above. The trail begins at the parking lot.*

~LAKESHORE TRAIL. [Fig. 15(7)] 0.5 mile. This trail encircles Dockery Lake and is accessible to the handicapped. Footpaths provide access to fishing areas around the Lake.

DIRECTIONS: *Follow directions for Dockery Lake Recreation Area, above. The trail begins at the parking lot.*

~LAKE WINFIELD SCOTT. [Fig. 15(11)] This lovely, clear, 18-acre mountain lake, which is owned and managed by the U.S. Forest Service, is the source of Cooper Creek and contains a large population of rainbow trout. A nice hiking trail circles the lake.

FACILITIES: *Camping, picnicking, swimming, boating (electric motors only), fishing and hiking.*
DIRECTIONS: *Take US 19 south from Blairsville 9.5 miles; turn right (west) on GA 180 and go 7 miles.*

~JARRARD GAP TRAIL [FIG. 15(12)] AND SLAUGHTER CREEK TRAIL [FIG. 15(13)]. 1.0 mile and 2.7 miles, respectively. These two trails provide access to the Appalachian Trail from Lake Winfield Scott Recreation Area. The Jarrard Gap Trail follows an old logging road through cove hardwoods.

DIRECTIONS: *Follow directions to Lake Winfield Scott, above. The trails begin at the main bulletin board near the head of the lake and share the same path for a short distance. Parking is available near the campground host's cabin.*

~DESOTO FALLS SCENIC RECREATION AREA AND TRAIL. [Fig. 15(14)] DeSoto Falls was named for the Spanish explorer DeSoto because a piece of armor attributed to his expedition was supposedly

Bloodroot
Sanguinaria canadensis

One of the earliest spring wildflowers, its characteristic large round leaf with irregular edge persists into summer. The tuberous red roots produce an orange dye that can color both skin and cloth.

found in the area. The scenic area is located in rugged mountainous country with exceptional views. Elevations in this 650-acre area of clear streams feeding Frogtown Creek vary between 2,000 and 3,400 feet. Visitors can hike to view five waterfalls.

FACILITIES: *Parking, restrooms, camping, picnicking, fishing, hiking.*
DATES/HOURS: *Open late spring to early fall.*
FEES: *Campsite $5 per night.*
DIRECTIONS: *Take US 129 north from Cleveland 15 miles.*
ADDITIONAL INFORMATION: *DeSoto Falls Scenic and Recreation Area, U.S. Forest Service, Chestatee Ranger District, 200 W. Main, P.O. Box 2080, Dahlonega, GA 30533. (404) 864-6173.*

~DESOTO FALLS CAMPGROUND. [Fig. 15(15)] Rugged, mountainous country with exceptional views and several beautiful waterfalls. Adjacent to DeSoto Falls Scenic Area (see above).

FACILITIES: *24 campsites, 6 picnic sites, restrooms with cold showers, streams for wading and fishing.*
DIRECTIONS: *Take US 129 north from Cleveland 15 miles.*

~DESOTO FALLS TRAIL. [Fig. 15(14)] Three miles. The lower 0.8 mile of the trail passes by the two lower cascades of DeSoto Falls [Fig. 15(16) and is relatively easy. The last 2.2 miles leading to the uppermost falls on Frogtown Creek [Fig. 15(17)] are much steeper. The trailhead is in the Desoto Falls Recreation Area.

DIRECTIONS: *Follow the directions to DeSoto Falls Scenic Area (above). The trail begins at the bridge in the lower camping loop of DeSoto Falls Recreation Area.*

~CHESTATEE OVERLOOK. [Fig. 15(18)] The overlook offers a scenic vista of Blood Mountain Cove. There are hiking trails in the area (see below). The watershed in the foreground is the famous Waters Creek trophy trout stream [Fig. 15(19)].

FACILITIES: *Three picnic tables.*
DIRECTIONS: *Take GA 60 north from Dahlonega 12 miles.*

~WOODY GAP. [Fig. 15(20)] The gap, with scenic vistas of Yahoola Valley, is marked with a large wooden sign. This is where the white-blazed Appalachian Trail crosses GA 60. A moderate one-mile hike to the north leads to a rock-outcrop overlook on the rocky face of Big Cedar Mountain (3,737 feet). A 1.5-mile hike to the south leads to a southerly view of the Yahoola Valley from atop Ramrock Mountain (3,200 feet). Both of these trail sections offer a pretty display of spring wildflowers on this richly wooded Blue

Ridge Mountain range.

FACILITIES: *Large parking area with chemical toilets and trash cans; picnicking areas with 10 tables located on both sides of the road.*
DIRECTIONS: *14 miles north of Dahlonega on GA 60.*

~WALASI-YI INTERPRETIVE CENTER. [Fig. 15(21)] The beautiful stone center was built from 1934 to 1938 of native rock by the Civilian Conservation Corps. It was placed on the National Register of Historic Places in 1977. In the breezeway here is the only place where the 2,135-mile-long Appalachian Trail (AT) goes through a man-made structure. There is a store here with outdoor books, mountain crafts, gifts, maps, clothing and camping equipment.

DIRECTIONS: *At Neel's Gap on US 19 and 129, approximately 18 miles north of Cleveland and 21 miles north of Dahlonega.*

~NEEL'S GAP TO BLOOD MOUNTAIN HIKE. [Fig. 15(1)] About two miles. An enjoyable day trip with many scenic vistas is a climb up Blood Mountain (4,461 feet). The trail is generally steep and rocky in many places but easy to follow. Near the summit hikers will be rewarded with several picnic rocks and superb vistas from rock outcrops, including views of Mount Yonah, Tray Mountain, Lake Winfield Scott and Slaughter Mountain. An old stone cabin, built by the Civilian Conservation Corps in the 1930's as an Appalachian Trail shelter and listed on the National Register of Historic Places, sits near the top. This is the highest point on the Appalachian Trail in Georgia. It is perhaps the state's most-hiked portion of the Appalachian Trail.

DIRECTIONS: *To reach the trailhead follow directions to the Walasi-Yi Center, above. Parking for day hikers is 0.5 mile north of the center. Follow the blue blazes from the parking area along the Reece Access Trail. After about 0.3 mile the trail intersects with the white-blazed Appalachian Trail at Flatrock Gap (a 420-foot increase in elevation). Turn right onto the AT and proceed about 1.5 miles to the top of Blood Mountain.*

~WATERS CREEK RECREATION AREA. [Fig. 15(22) Located along a beautiful mountain stream. The headwaters is a trophy trout stream.

FACILITIES: *Camping, picnicking, hiking and fishing.*
DIRECTIONS: *Take US 19 north from Dahlonega 12 miles, turn left (northwest) onto FS 34 [Fig. 15(22)] and go 1 mile.*

~BLOOD MOUNTAIN FALLS. [Fig. 15(26)] This waterfall is located on the Blood Mountain Creek, which flows approximately 20 feet

© M. FUNDERBURK

Umbrella leaf
Diphylleia cymosa

This plant bears some of the largest leaves of any mountain plant. Resembling a giant mayapple, it grows only in very moist situations along tiny streams and seeps at higher elevations, rarely below 3000 feet, in north-facing coves. As with many other of our native plants and animals, its closest relatives are in temperate eastern Asia.

through a rock cut, creating a churning sluice of water. An unmaintained footpath leads to the falls. Picnic facilities are available at the Waters Creek Recreation Area (above).

DIRECTIONS: *Follow the directions to Waters Creek Recreation Area, above. After passing the game warden station the road narrows; go 2.5 miles to the Blood Mountain Stream. The falls are located on the right.*

~DUNCAN RIDGE TRAIL. [Fig. 15(24)] On this trail, one can traverse the longest contiguous ridge line leading off the main Blue Ridge. Trail begins at Blood Mountain [Fig. 15(1)], crosses northwest through Slaughter Gap [Fig. 15(13)], Wolfpen Gap [Fig. 15(25)], Coosa Bald [Fig. 15(5)], then goes westward to Mulky Gap (Cooper Creek Section) and intersects with Benton Mackaye Trail (Long Trails Section).

MAP REFERENCES: *USGS 1:24,000 series: Neels Gap - Coosa Bald.*

Raven
Corvus corax

The subject of Edgar Allen Poe's famous poem, this very large black bird, twice the size of a crow, sticks to the highest parts of the Georgia Blue Ridge above 3000 feet where it nests in cliffs. A hoarse, croaking call is usually the only evidence of ravens in the vicinity.

Raven Cliffs

Raven Cliffs Wilderness Area is located northwest of Cleveland. A number of trails with beautiful mountain streams and waterfalls, mountaintops, a wide variety of natural community types, rock outcrops and scenic vistas abound throughout the area.

~DUKE'S CREEK FALLS HIKE. [Fig. 16(1)] About one mile. The large falls seen from the trail and parking lot [Fig. 16(4)] is called Duke's Creek Falls even though it is on Davis Creek. There are several smaller waterfalls in the area. The trail ends at the confluence of Davis Creek and Duke's Creek. Duke's Creek is a beautiful mountain waterway with large boulders and splashing water around foaming pools and riffles. Spray from the falls, which is about 250 feet high, cools the area and provides a pleasant relief for the hiker.

Careful observers will notice the small wildflowers growing along the banks of the trail. Water seeps out of this bank at scattered locations and, with broken patches of sunlight, provides excellent habitat for a variety of flora. This is a west-facing slope with patches of mountain laurel and rhododendron all along the way. The upper part of the slope is drier, with mixed hardwoods, especially oaks, hickories and tulip poplar forming a tree canopy about 50 feet high. Toward the bottom of the trail and along Duke's Creek, a cove forest of young hemlock and white pine is developing. Several large hemlocks provide an accent along the stream bank.

DIRECTIONS: *Take Ga 75 north from Helen for 1.5 miles; turn left on GA 356 (75 Alt); go 2.3 miles to the Richard Russell Scenic Highway; turn right and go 2 miles to the Duke's Creek Falls parking area [Fig. 16(4)]. An alternate access is to go approximately 1.0 mile further north on Richard Russell Scenic Highway to a Forest Service road which intersects the highway [Fig. 16(3)] to the southwest and travel along the southern boundary of the Raven Cliffs Wilderness Area. If the gate is open, one can drive 0.6 mile, park and then follow an unmarked trail over a small ridge and down to the top of Duke's Creek Falls. The falls can be clearly heard from the FS Road, and the hike is only about 1,200 feet from the road.*

~RAVEN CLIFFS FALLS. [Fig. 16(5)] About 2.5 miles. Marked with blue blazes. Dodd's Creek is one of the most beautiful mountain streams which is easily accesible in north Georgia. It splashes and winds along through the mountain valley with an abundance of whitewater, riffles and pools, moss-covered seepages and overhanging tangles of laurel. At numerous points along the trail the hiker can approach the stream for a closer view. There are five or six lesser falls to observe along the way, and one of these is

Figure 16 RAVEN CLIFFS

102

impressive enough to make many visitors think it is Raven Cliffs Falls itself. Near the falls the trail climbs about 40 feet and moves a little away from Dodd's Creek, then returns at Raven Cliffs. Directly ahead, the visitor encounters a massive cliff face of solid rock that rises vertically from the landscape about 80-90 feet. The cliff appears from the trail as two large blocks with a narrow crevasse between. Raven Cliff Falls results from the water of Dodd's creek falling straight down between the blocks back inside the crevasse and into a dark pool at the bottom. Although the water flow is not great this high in the drainage basin, the sound of it is amplified by the cliff face and gives the visitor an overall impression of the powerful forces at work sculpting the mountain landscape.

Even though no signs identify the trail, it is a heavily visited area. On a November weekend, for example, 42 vehicles were parked at the trailhead and six camps were in use nearby. At Raven Cliffs, two mountain climbers were rappelling from the cliff face and several persons were sitting on top of the cliff. In spite of such a level of activity, this is one of the best trails anywhere for a great hiking experience with the whole family.

DIRECTIONS: *Take Ga 75 north from Helen 1.5 miles; turn left on GA 356 (75 Alt) and go 2.3 miles to the Richard Russell Scenic Highway; turn right and go 2.8 miles to the trailhead and parking area [Fig. 16(6)].*

~WILDCAT MOUNTAIN, WHITLY GAP TRAIL. [Fig. 16(7)] Whitly Gap Trail is about 1.1 miles long; if the visitor wants to visit Adams Bald [Fig. 16(8)], another 0.5 mile is added to the trip. However, the best part of the trail is to the top of Wildcat Mountain, which is only about 0.5 mile. The climb up the north slope is about 300 feet. This trail is fun for children and adults alike. It ascends from the road first through a stand of sweet birch and some hardwoods and then through a laurel thicket of rhododendron and mountain laurel. This type of heath growth is typical on the north-facing slope of higher peaks in this area. Whitly Gap Trail is an easily accessible example of this fairyland growth form. Children are amazed by this natural community type. Everything is their size and everything is green and pretty. Rocks along the trail are moss-covered, and there are ferns and wildflowers along the way. Small gnarled limbs of the laurel thicket arch over the path, making it a small secret passageway. The trail emerges from the evergreen thicket near the ridgetop of Wildcat Mountain at an elevation just under 3,800 feet. This is the highest peak in the vicinity and provides an outstanding scenic view in all directions, especially west and south. The fairyland theme continues on the Wildcat Mountain ridgeline. White oaks, chestnut oaks, scarlet oaks and several sweet birch, which normally grow into tall dominant trees, are gnarled and stunted on the mountaintop. Limbs start about 2 feet from the ground and

Solomon's seal
(Polygonatum biflorum)

The two-foot-long fronds of these plants are common in the herb layer of most cover forests. The false Solomon's seal (Smilacina racemosa) has flowers borne on the end of the stalk rather than dangling from the axils of each set of leaves, as in the Solomon's seal.

children can't resist climbing them to get an adult's view of the surrounding mountain ranges.

DIRECTIONS: *About 7.0 miles northwest of the junction of the Richard Russell Scenic Highway and GA 75 Alt. The Appalachian Trail crosses Richard Russell Scenic Highway at Hogpen Gap. Whitly Gap Trail branches off the AT on the north slope of Wildcat Mountain. A parking area [Fig. 16(9)] on the north side of the Russell Highway provides convenient access to Wildcat Mountain.*

~LOGAN TURNPIKE. [Fig. 16(11)] About two miles. The Logan Turnpike is an abandoned toll road which was privately maintained and used during horse-and-buggy days as a corridor through the mountains. It is difficult to imagine anyone pulling an empty wagon, much less a fully loaded one, straight up this steep trail through Tesnatee Gap [Fig. 16(10)]. About 1,200 feet down the trail and near the bottom of the steep part of the slope, one of the most interesting aspects of this trail begins to appear. Here is an excellent location to observe firsthand the formation of a natural stream in the forest. Tiny springs of water begin to appear along the lower slopes to the right and left of Logan Turnpike. Crystal clear water seeps up from points along the ground and flows so gently that it does not push aside the leaf litter to make a visible path. These small trickles would go unnoticed in the woods except that several coalesce and travel along the trail underfoot. Eventually, the small trickles join others, making small but noisy brooks less than a foot wide. Several of these turn and run along the trail before crossing it to the west side and forming the beginning of Town Creek. The beautiful stream which results contains clear, cold water with moss-covered rocks through the stream bed and no silt to be found. Contrast this with the striking difference seen in an urban/suburban community where after a rain, the warm muddy water rushes along gullies from the roadside and fills the streams first with a torrent of erosive force and then with mud and silt as the storm water subsides. The trail extends 2.6 miles almost due south from the trailhead and drops about 1,270 feet in that distance—700 feet in the first half-mile, a part of the trail that is steep and rocky.

DIRECTIONS: *At the highest point on the Richard Russell Scenic Highway, 7.6 miles from the junction with GA 75 Alt., the scenic drive passes close to Tesnatee Gap, then turns due north. The Logan Turnpike goes south through Tesnatee Gap [Fig. 16(10)]. There is a marker here for the Gap. A parking area provided on the south side of the Russell Highway provides easy access. The Logan Turnpike begins on the east side of the parking lot and goes south down the draw. To reach the southern trailhead for the turnpike, take US 19 north from Dahlonega for 13.5 miles to Turners Corner; turn right and proceed south on US 129 for 2.8 miles; turn left on Town Creek*

Trailing arbutus
Epigaea repens

Road (gravel road) and go 2.5 miles; park off the road and walk 0.2 mile to the trailhead. The trail begins at the junction of the county road and the Forest Service property line. A historical marker on the approach road to the trailhead designates the tollkeeper's house.

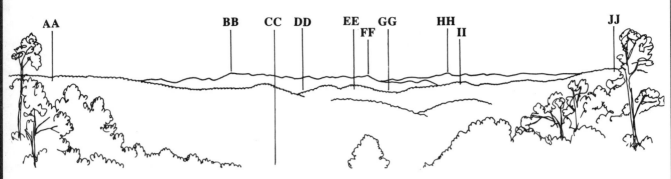

EAST VISTA

View from Richard Russell Highway, 4.1 miles

AA - Locust Log Ridge
BB - Tray
CC - Bear Den Creek Valley
DD - Little Low Gap
EE - Blue Knob
FF - Chimney
GG - Saddle Gap
HH - Tallulah Mountains
II - Little Blue Knob
JJ - Stoney Knob

4.1 miles looking right

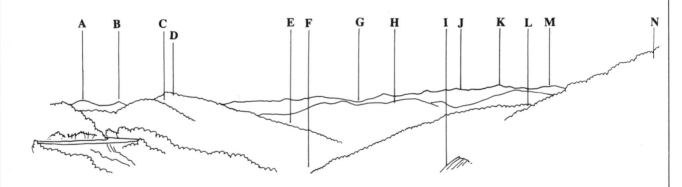

NORTH VISTA

View from Richard Russell Highway, 7.0 miles

A - Slaughter
B - Coosa Bald
C - Turkey Pen Flats
D - Double Poplar Top
E - Nottely River Valley
F - Lordamercy Cove
G - Trackrock Gap

H - Cass Mountains
I - Cliff
J - Arkaqua Ridge
K - Brasstown Bald
L - Grassy Ridge
M - Sheep Rock Top
N - Wolden Stamp

7.0 miles looking north

SOUTH VISTA
View from Richard Russell Highway, 6.0 miles

A - Piney
B - Blue Ridge Front
C - Stony
D - Hickory Nut
E - Little Hickory Nut
F - Dodd's Creek
G - Currahee

H - Sal
I - Piedmont
J - Dukes Creek Falls
K - Yonah
L - Allison Ridge
M - Pink
N - Ridge to Adams Bald

6.0 miles looking south

~RICHARD RUSSELL SCENIC HIGHWAY. [Fig. 16(2)] This scenic route crosses the Blue Ridge and provides gravelled and paved vistas. It forms the northern boundary of the eastern half of the Raven Cliffs Wilderness. It gives access to Raven Cliffs' trails, Duke's Creek Falls and the Appalachian Trail at two places.

DIRECTIONS: *Take 356 (75 Alt) out of Helen 2.3 miles. Watch for 348 turning west where it deadends into 356. Set the odometer on zero. The first overlook is at 1.4 miles. The entrance to Duke's Creek Falls parking is 0.8 miles farther, and the trail to Raven Cliffs about a mile beyond that. One encounters white pines about mile 2.4; it is a common tree until mile 4.7, when deciduous (oak-hickory) forest continues to the gap. The road begins to climb steeply at 3.2 miles.*

The Tray Mountain vista (see vista) is to the right at 4.1 miles. The foreground ridge bears white pine mixed with hardwoods, while red maples grow close below the parking area. At mile 4.2 the road bank has a remarkable covering of Christmas fern and primitive club moss. Vistas to the left, such as at miles 5.1, 6.0 and 6.7, overlook the Raven Cliffs Wilderness. One is able to gaze across the flat Dahlonega Gold Belt to Yonah Mountain (see vista) and the distant Piedmont. At milepost 6.0 one begins to see in the road cuts the structure of the most common rock making up the eastern Blue Ridge, a banded gneiss. This rock becomes more noticeable at mile 6.3 and at the Hogpen Gap [Fig. 16(19)], just beyond the crossing of the Appalachian Trail. Here, at 7.0 miles, the large cut on the left offers a study in the wavy banding of dark and light that characterizes metamorphic rock (see vista). Starting down the colder north slope of the Blue Ridge there is parking at 7.5 miles and close access to the Appalachian Trail at Testnatee Gap [Fig. 16(10)]. At this point one crosses the old Logan Turnpike, which came through Tesnatee Gap, one of the earliest crossings of the Blue Ridge by the early settlers. From this point the highway parallels the old Logan Turnpike, descending rapidly down the Nottely River headwaters -- in this case, Lordamercy Cove. At 8.9 miles one encounters a hemlock-heath community along the creek, and at 9.4 miles in the floodplain south of the highway is a white pine—tulip-poplar forest indicating the site of an abandoned field. One should anticipate a settlement ahead, and after passing through a mix of white pine and Virginia pine, one reaches the first house at 10.5 miles. At mile 10.8, by looking across the floodplain, one can see the extent of former hillside pastures so common in the early days of settlement. Note how the growth of white pines in the old pasture is sharply delineated from the hardwoods above it. Highway 348 deadends into 180 at 13.6 miles. Turn east on 180. In about 4.0 miles the road enters the ring of ultrabasic rock surrounding Brasstown Bald and in which Indian carvings are preserved at Trackrock Gap nearby. Continue and cross Jack's Gap where the Jack's Gap Trail crosses and the road to Brasstown begins its very steep ascent. Dropping down the east side from the gap, one descends Soapstone Creek, leaving the soapstone and other peculiar rocks at the Owl Creek road turnoff. Continue on, deadend into highway 17 and turn south. Almost immediately the High Shoals Falls Scenic Area road turns east, and in another mile the very steep road to Indian Grave Gap and Tray Mountain (FS 283) also turns east. Continuing on 17, one should reach Unicoi Gap in approximately 3.0 more miles. Unicoi Gap was the boundary between Indian and white lands until the Dahlongea Gold rush. It was one of the first gaps crossed by a highway. Continuing down the south side of the Blue Ridge, watch for the sign marking Andrews Cove on the left. Here Andrews Creek follows the westernmost part of the famed geologic anomaly, the Warwoman Shear, which cuts across Lake Burton to the Chattooga River country. Past Andrew's Cove one descends to the Chattahoochee headwaters and the starting point at Helen.

MAP REFERENCES: *USGS 1:24,000 series: Cowrock - Neel's Gap.*

Gray treefrog
Hyla versicolor

Following the mid-winter calls of the wood frog and the shrill cries of the spring peeper, the hoarser calls of the gray treefrog come in late May and June from areas near standing water.

Helen And The Upper Chattahoochee

The north Georgia town of Helen [Fig. 17(1)] developed around the Byrd-Matthews Sawmill, which was built in 1912. The town was named for the daughter of John McCombs, a prominent citizen of that era, who was part owner of the mill and of the newly built railroad through the valley. The sawmill operated continuously until the late 1920's, when the virgin pines and hardwoods, once plentiful here, had been cut down and run through its blades. It was subsequently demolished. For the next 40 years Helen's fortunes declined. Bypassed by the major transportation routes through the mountains, it got little benefit from the steady increase in tourism that the mountain region as a whole experienced during that period, and the town's few citizens found jobs scarce. A new women's apparel plant, Orbit Manufacturing, opened in the early 1960's run by a man named Jim Wilkins, and a few people were hired. But the town was almost a ghost town in 1968, when the business district consisted of one run-down motel and 16 concrete block buildings, nine of them empty. Then things began to change.

Three men were the prime movers behind born-again Helen. One of them was Jim Wilkins, the founder of Orbit Manufacturing, who owned most of the west side of the business district. Another was Pete Hodkinson, who lived in nearby Clarkesville worked with Wilkins in the management of Orbit and also owned land in Helen. They added their ideas and resources to those of the third member of the triumvirate, John Kollock, an artist who lived nearby and who had a passion for the architecture and landscape of the Bavarian Alps. Within a week of their first meeting, these three drew up the initial plan for putting a new face on Helen -- one calculated to be alluring to the mountain tourists. Kollock drew a series of sketches depicting his vision of what the town would look like after its projected transformation, and the other two wasted no time in convincing their fellow businessmen and property owners in town to cooperate with the effort. Hodkinson was later killed in 1976 in an accident while hot air ballooning, a sport he brought to Helen and which later developed into one of the area's major promotional attractions as the Helen-to-the-Atlantic Balloon Race.

In the years since, Helen has developed into a major north Georgia tourist attraction, drawing visitors from Atlanta as well as from all over the Southeast. Outside entrepreneurs have opened new businesses, all in keeping with the Bavarian Alpine theme, and have bought up slices of the surrounding woodlands for development as second home sites. Visitors to Helen can wander through the Alpine style shops to browse for antiques, brownies, books, Indian jewelry, cigars, backpacks and Christmas ornaments or sit on a restaurant deck overloooking the Chattahoochee to dine on anything from pizza to knockwurst.

Figure 17   HELEN AND THE UPPER CHATTAHOOCHEE

Showy orchis
Orchis spectabilis

The attractive lavender and white flowers of the showy orchis are the crowning glory of spring wild flower displays. This orchid is neither rare, small, nor inconspicuous. It spreads its charm on moist and shady slopes and in coves and ravines.

~NACOOCHEE VALLEY. [Fig. 17(2)] Just north of the junction of GA 75 and GA 17, the Nacoochee Valley extends to the east. In the foreground is the Nacoochee Indian Mound, rising from the flat pastureland and crowned with a white latticework gazebo. A much larger, wooded mound stands in the floodplain to the east. At the time of the first European contact with this area -- Hernando de Soto's 1540 expedition in search of gold -- this was the center of civilization in the region, a Cherokee town called Guasili, or Guaxale. The mound, however, predates even the Cherokees; it was built by their predecessors in this valley, the Uchee Indians (the name "Nacoochee," in fact, comes from the Uchee word for this small temple mound, *Nagutsi*).

~WEST END. [Fig. 17(2)] Just north of the GA 75/17 junction is the impressive Italianate Victorian house known as West End. One of the oldest surviving structures in the valley, it was built in 1870 for retired Confederate Colonel John Nichols and was later occupied by Lamartine Griffin Hardman, Georgia governor from 1927 to 1931.

~CANOEING THE UPPER CHATTAHOOCHEE. The section of the Chattahoochee River above Helen is a tight, difficult and rapidly descending mountain river [Fig. 17(3)]. It should be run by experts only. Water levels vary almost hourly and this section can usually be run only after a rain.

On reaching the valley, the river calms into steady Class I water and stays that way through Helen down to Nora Mill, where a portage is necessary.

The Nacoochee Valley is a nice float through mostly open farmland, but downed trees can often cause canoeists problems.

Near the end of the valley, Sautee Creek [Fig. 17(4)] enters from the left. Many paddlers put their boats into Sautee Creek on Lynch Mountain Road, an unpaved county road next to the GA 17 bridge over the creek. The float down the creek is only a hundred yards to the main stream of the Chattahoochee.

As noted in *North Georgia Canoeing* by Bob Sehlinger and Don Otey, from the Sautee creek junction down to GA 255 [Fig. 17(5)] is one of the longest undisturbed stretches of the river. The terrain is heavily forested with large white pines and frequent rock outcroppings. Rapids are fairly frequent, but are of the mild Class I and II category.

The section between GA 255 and GA 115 [Fig. 17(6)] contains some Class III water. From GA 115 to Duncan Bridge [Fig. 17(7)] is the section most appealing to whitewater buffs. None of the rapids is particularly difficult; but combined, they provide interesting and challenging canoeing.

DIRECTIONS: *For the put-in above Helen, go north out of Helen on*

GA 75 for approximately 1.5 miles, turn left on GA 356; cross the bridge; immediately turn back right on a dirt road on the west side of the river. Follow this road past a ranger station (3.5 miles) and on to where the road crosses Jasus Creek. Put in here [Fig. 17(3)]. In Helen there is a take-out point across from the Wildwood Outfitters. There is a put-in spot where Sautee Creek enters the river from the northeast. One can put in to Sautee Creek on Lynch Mountain Road, an unpaved county road next to the GA 17 bridge over the creek. Other put-in, take-out points: 1) The GA 255 bridge, on the left or Habersham County side of the river only. The property owner on the right side should not be disturbed. Use the public highway right-of-way. 2) The GA 115 bridge. Enter on the White County side at the small county park on the left side of the highway, as one approaches the river from Cleveland. 3) Duncan Bridge. The distance from Jasus Creek to Helen is about eight river miles and approximately six hours should be allowed for the run. From Helen to the GA 255 bridge is approximately 13 miles; from the GA 255 bridge to the GA 115 bridge is 4.2 miles, and from there to Duncan bridge is some four miles.

~UNICOI STATE PARK. Just two miles north of Helen, Unicoi is a 1,081-acre park with a beautiful 100-room lodge plus a wide range of other accommodations and a buffet style restaurant.

FACILITIES: *100-room lodge and conference center, 30 cottages, 80 tent and trailer sites, 53-acre lake and beach, 4 lighted tennis courts, buffet style restaurant.*

Popular activities include hiking on 12 miles of trails, group camping and walk-in tent campsites, mountain culture programs and craft shop in lodge.

SPECIAL EVENTS: *Fireside Arts and Crafts Show-Feb, Mountain Eatin's & Squeezin's-Jul.*

DATES/HOURS: *Park, 7am-10pm; office 8-5.*

DIRECTIONS: *Located 2 miles northeast of Helen via GA 356.*

ADDITIONAL INFORMATION: *Unicoi State Park, P.O.Box 849, Helen, GA 30545. (404) 878-2201 (office and group reservations), 878-2824 (lodge and cottage reservations), 878-3366 (campground and shelter reservations).*

~UNICOI LAKE TRAIL. 2.4-mile loop trail around Unicoi Lake, across the dam and returning to the information center.

DIRECTIONS: *Follow directions to Unicoi State Park (above). The trail begins at the information center.*

~BOTTOMS LOOP TRAIL. 2.1 miles. A pleasant trail past streams, fields, low ridges and wildflower displays.

DIRECTIONS: *Follow directions to Unicoi State Park (above). The trail begins near the lodge and conference center.*

MAP REFERENCES: *USGS 1:100,000 series*: Toccoa

Tray Mountain

This is rugged back country combined with some fine state parks and easy-to-reach waterfalls and hikes. The Appalachian Trail goes all the way through this area. Access is available to most parts of this area by car. The Tray Mountain area, while not classified as wilderness, includes unique sites such as the incomparable Ramp Cove, with the finest stand of giant buckeyes in Georgia (if not the Southeast) and a wildflower paradise. Exciting boulderfields are common here just under the Appalachian Trail (AT) and off the Kelly Ridge. The Kelly Ridge spur provides a superb hike similar to the great Duncan Ridge in the Blood Mountain area. The huge rock outcrop at the Mill Creek Roughs is worth exploring. Tray Mountain itself, with its superlative boulderfield, is one of the major overlooks in the Georgia Blue Ridge.

~TRAY MOUNTAIN. [Fig. 18(50)] Tray ranks among Georgia's highest peaks (4,398 feet). Because of its elevation and the fact that it stands as a sentinel in a great sweeping arc of the Appalachian Trail from west to north, Tray Mountain is a magnificent grandstand from which to view the Nantahalas and the Georgia Blue Ridge. Southward one can see the Piedmont. On clear days it is said that even Kennesaw and Stone Mountain are visible. Closer is the flat terrain of the Dahlonega Gold Belt, bordered on the west by the Hayesville Fault, from which the mountains of the Raven Cliff Wilderness rise abruptly. In the foreground, also, is the lovely peak of Yonah Mountain. Yonah's abrupt cliffs provide the best easily-accessible area for rock climbing in the Georgia mountains.

~MAIN ACCESS ROUTES TO TRAY MOUNTAIN. The first is to take SR 356 east from Robertstown (one mile north of Helen) for five miles. Turn left at Bethel Church onto Chimney Mountain Road and follow it for two miles to FS 79. This is Tray Mountain Road, which is maintained for four-wheel-drive vehicles and pickup trucks. Travel FS 79 north for seven miles to Tray Mountain Gap at the intersection of FS 698 and the AT crossing.

The second route, a steep incline with switchbacks, is to take GA 75 north from Robertstown for one mile. Turn right on FS 79 across from the Hooch Trading Post. Travel in a northerly direction 6.5 miles to a fork. The left fork goes to a landmark called Indian Grave Gap [Fig. 18(52)], a high wide saddle between Rocky Mountain (4,017 feet) and Tray. On either side are "hanging valleys" of great scenic beauty. Also crossing here are the trails up High Shoals Creek [Fig. 18(53)] and from Andrews Cove [Fig. 18(54)]. Here the last remnant of the great gash of Warwoman Shear [Fig. 18(56)] makes its final appearance, lining up the head of High Shoals Creek [Fig. 18(55)] with Andrews Creek. The right

Figure 18   TRAY MOUNTAIN

fork goes past the little meadow [Fig. 18(61)] called "Cheese Dairy," the former site of a goat cheese factory. There is a spring here at this popular camping spot. Continue to Tray Gap (intersection of FS 698 and the AT). The trail to Tray Mountain begins here at Tray Gap.

The third route, the shortest, is to take GA 75 north from Helen for 11 miles (two miles north of Unicoi Gap). Turn right on FS 283. Follow that in a southerly direction for about four miles. At the junction with FS 79 go east on 79 two miles to arrive at the intersection of 698 and the AT crossing. At 1.3 miles you will pass the High Shoals trailhead [Fig. 18(58)] to a bridge over High Shoals and a trail down to two sets of exceptional falls where, because of several deaths, viewing platforms [Fig. 18(59)] have been built.

~APPALACHIAN TRAIL. It is an exhilarating experience to hike the 0.9-mile portion of the Appalachian Trail that climbs 600 feet to the summit of Tray Mountain. The ridges at Tray Gap and upward bear red oak ridge forest; near the summit, the oaks become dwarfed and gnarled. There are patches of lily of the valley and other interesting plants on the way. Near the top, there is a veritable garden of purple, or Catawba, rhododendron which—unlike the common or rosebay—blooms in spring rather than summer. It surrounds rock outcrops on which grow patches of high-altitude spike moss.

Just below the top of Tray on the north side is one of the best-developed boulderfields in north Georgia [Fig. 18(62)]. It is hazardous walking, but one can drop down through it to the Corbin Creek Road [Fig. 18(37)] or go up the third cove [Fig. 18(63)] two miles or more north of Tray Gap. It is characterized by two high-altitude maples—striped and mountain—together with holly and Catawba rhododendron. Two herbs here—the beautiful rosy twisted stalk and an elderberry—are at their southernmost limits. Just down the AT, north from the top a few hundred yards, there is a side trail to the south leading to an exceptional overlook [Fig. 18(64)] of the southern part of the Tray Mountain area and the headwaters of the Soque River.

~SWALLOW CREEK. The northern portion of the Tray Mountain area is largely the watershed of Swallow Creek and was recommended for inclusion in the national wilderness system. It has two outstanding high ridges—the Blue Ridge (from Dick's Gap to Kelly Knob—4,276 feet) and the Kelly Ridge. The walking along both is easy, and the scenery is rewarding. This area, tucked away in the Blue Ridge, is hardly known at all. There is a high cove of huge old-growth buckeyes (Ramp Cove) [Fig. 18(6)] and the heaviest growth of the fabled mountain garlic (ramps) in Georgia. The abundant north-facing coves offer boulderfields and wildflower assemblages. The beauty of this area is that one can hike up one creek, hit the ridge, go around and down another creek and arrive back at the starting point, creating a hike suited to individual desires.

DIRECTIONS: *The basic approach to the area is by turning off US 76, two miles east of where GA 17/75 dead end into it. Turning here [Fig. 18(1)] at the lower Hightower Church, one drives several miles to the end of the pavement to park [Fig. 18(3)]. If the gate straight ahead is open, one may proceed another mile or so. Most visitors park at the end of the pavement [Fig. 18(3)]. Of the two dirt roads to the right, select the left-hand (a jeep can drive another 0.25 mile on FS 300, but it is not recommended.) From the end of the pavement, go up the dirt road and take the first old road to the right that fords the creek [Fig. 18(4)] (there are two old roads; take the one most traveled). Follow this old logging road, which shortly climbs a long ravine [Fig. 18(5)]. High up in this ravine, one finds smooth-barked, black and crooked trunks of the rare yellowwood tree. Cross a flat area, follow the road on up and soon enter what may be the grandest old-growth forest in the mountains [Fig. 18(6)]. The buckeyes here reach four feet in diameter and exceed those in Sosebee Cove. Moreover, the herbaceous ground is extremely rich in species, including abundant ramps for which the cove is named. The soil is rich black Porter's loam. One can continue up to the top of Kelly Ridge [Fig. 18(7)], walk around and come down Stroud [Fig. 18(8)], or Dismal [Fig. 18(9)] Coves (note that Stroud and Dismal are not marked on the ground and can be difficult to locate) or take the AT to Moreland Gap and come down Swallow Creek itself [Fig. 18(10)]. There are a series of small falls and cascades along Stroud Creek [Fig. 18(11)]. Kelly Knob itself is a high scenic point [Fig. 18(12)]. As one walks east along Kelly Ridge and on the AT, almost every cove has a boulderfield at its head [Fig. 18(13)]. Some can be seen from the AT.*

One obvious, easy way to reach Kelly Ridge is from Dick's Gap on US 76, which cuts out some of the climbing. West on Kelly Ridge one can drop off to a parking area on SR 88 [Fig. 18(14)]. Normally, one could drop off at Schoolhouse Gap [Fig. 18(18)], but a clearcut presently blocks the way. Another access to Kelly Ridge is by way of the Cynth Creek [Fig. 18(15)] Road which turns east at the first bridge over the Hiawassee River south of the GA 17/US 76 junction. This road [Fig. 18(17)] passes around one of the Dyer Family's four trout-rearing stations [Fig. 18(16)], which sell trout for stocking and as bait for striped bass in Lakes Burton and Lanier.

South of Kelly Ridge is an area of interest. The western access is by the Mill Creek Road [Fig. 18(19)], which is 3.5 miles north of Indian Grove Gap Road or 3.4 miles south of the junction of GA 17 and US 76. The pavement ends above the Dyer Trout Farm on Mill Creek [Fig. 18(20)]. The road climbs through nice oak-hickory slope forest and passes a trailhead for Sassafras Creek [Fig. 18(21)] and a north-turning gated road [Fig. 18(22)] which can lead the hiker to Kelly Ridge. About 0.25 mile before a locked gate (9.1 miles from

Yellowwood
Cladrastis lutea

This very rare tree grows in a few ravines and boulderfields on the north face of our higher peaks and ridges. Its leaves and flowers resemble black locust but the trunk is often twisted and the bark smooth and almost black, quite different from the deeply furrowed gray locust bark. It occurs in Sosebee Cove, Ramp Cove and a large population in Loggy Branch Cove on Hightower Bald.

GA 17)] on the main road one crosses three small branches at the Mill Creek Roughs [Fig. 18(23)]. Just below the juncture of the last two branches is a beautiful waterfall [Fig. 18(24)]. Up the tiny branches are about a quarter of a mile of "flats" ideal for picnicking. At the head of the flats, one encounters the "roughs" [Fig. 18(25)], and trails cease. A dense, unbanded rock outcrops here near the surface over many acres. Streams cascade off it through rhododendron thickets. The huge area of rough is most unusual in northern Georgia. Soil has difficulty forming over this immense outcrop. Because of its roughness, it has not been logged since horse-logging days—and then perhaps sparingly. Some old trees might reward exploration.

~ADDIS GAP. [Fig. 18(26)] The gap cannot be reached by vehicle. The old road has been gated. The gap was named for the Addis Family who farmed the rocky slopes 0.25 mile east of the gap [Fig. 18(27)].

DIRECTIONS: Addis Gap is reached from the east by the Wildcat Creek Road (26-1) [Fig. 18(28)], which turns off GA 197 1 mile north of LaPrades or 1.5 miles south of Moccasin Creek State Park (also GA 197). It is the first left road past Wildcat Creek going north on 197. It is marked FS 26. Just north of the old Addis homestead a gated Forest Service road (675) [Fig. 18(29)] serves as a trail at least as far as White Oak Stamp [Fig. 18(30)] on the head of Chastain Creek. There is an easy connection with the AT at Deep Gap [Fig. 18(31)], where the trail up an old logging road also terminates.

~TRAILS. At [Fig. 18(32)] the Park's Gap to Dick's Creek Road begins [Fig. 18(33)]. A gated road, it can be hiked to the Dick's Creek Watershed. Down a short distance, the trail down Moccasin Creek [Fig. 18(34)] by the Moccasin Creek Falls begins. At Fuller Gap [Fig. 18(35)] another "trail," really an old log road, joins this one at the vicinity of the Moccasin Creek Falls. The Moccasin Creek "trail" is a renowned hike of great beauty. It is actually the roadbed of the old railroad by which the watershed was logged in the early 1900's. Hiking up from Moccasin Fish Hatchery to the high falls located between Falls Mountain and Pig Pen Ridge takes about one hour. There is a smaller set of falls below the large one. Exploration of these falls can be dangerous.

Some four miles back down the Wildcat Creek road [Fig. 18(36)], a gated log road runs up Wildcat Branch.

DIRECTIONS: Northern Access. The principal access to the northern half of the Tray Mountain area from the west is the Corbin Creek Road which turns east off GA 17/75 about 1 mile south of the Mill Creek Road. Take this gravel road (698) 4.2 miles to where it crosses Miller Branch. One can park here and walk a gated log road

(FS 698-A) [Fig. 18(38)] to Tripp Gap. There is a trail here that turns right up the ridge towards High Top, passing it to the north and continuing into and around the head of Sassafras Branch Cove [Fig. 18(40)]. On the northwest face of High Top is a very fragmented rock outcrop [Fig. 18(41)] with much lichen growth and with occasional seeps with sphagnum moss and saxifrage. The flat on the south side [Fig. 18(42)] is a white-oak forest. Many of the trees are quite old. On the north slope between the two tops of Dismal Mountain is a poorly developed boulderfield with some yellow birch [Fig. 18(43)]. About 0.5 mile south from Miller Branch, one encounters the terminus [Fig. 18(44)] of the old road up Corbin Creek [Fig. 18(45)]. The other end begins as a gravel road about 0.5 mile south of the main Corbin Creek Road.

The next trail of consequence goes up the Double Branch [Fig. 18(46)] to Steeltrap Gap.

~Spring Cove area. [Fig. 18(47)] Spring Cove has a nice spring surrounded by stately older (80-year) forest with ash, buckeye and hemlocks with diameters up to 36 inches. It is reached on foot along a blocked log road [Fig. 18(48)] or where Corbin Creek Road crosses Corbin Creek, or by a trail up the ridge [Fig. 18(49)].

~The Head of the Soque River and Chimney Mountain. The wilderness south of the AT is rough and steep terrain. It is not well known at all. Private land [Fig. 18(65)] currently blocks easy access up the Soque River. The most interesting hike is to the top of Chimney Mountain [Fig. 18(66)], reached by the ridgeline [Fig. 18(67)] from a gap [Fig. 18(68)] and an access trail up the Rich Cove [Fig. 18(69)]. To get to this trailhead, one either comes down 4.4 miles on FS 79 east out of Tray Gap or up a similar distance from GA 356. The views from Chimney Mountain (3,357 feet) are exceptional. The trail to the top passes through high-quality pitch pine and scarlet oak ridge forest and is very pleasant walking. The south and west faces of Chimney Mountain have extensive rock outcrops. The southern outcrop is surrounded by red cedar which appears to be quite old. It is unusual for red cedar to appear on mountaintops. The summit is a flat lichen/sedge-covered outcrop. There are three rather hollow rock cairns about four feet high on the summit of Chimney Mountain. They are of unknown origin.

The other access to this portion of the wilderness is by way of the Skelton Branch Road [Fig. 18(70)], reached by taking GA 197 to the first left turn after GA 356 deadends into it. Go two miles on paved road and take the first main (gravel) road to the left for 0.5 mile; there, take the right fork; then the first road to the left should be Skelton Branch. The best trail [Fig. 18(71)] crosses Wolf Pen Branch and strikes the north prong of the Soque, from which point one can go up the left prong to Deep Gap [Fig. 18(68)] or down the left fork to two waterfalls [Fig. 18(73)]. There is no verification of

Pitch pine
Pinus rigida

This is the common mountain ridgetop pine at moderate elevations. At higher elevations it is often replaced by the table mountain pine, especially in the Rabun Bald area and on the Highlands Plateau. Oddly, it sometimes grows in bogs over deep peat. It is easily seen on the ridge west of Patterson Gap (Southern Nantahalas, eastern sector).

the trail [Fig. 18(76)], but it is marked on 1957 topographical sheets. The old-timers ranged cattle on the Wolfpen Ridge [Fig. 18(74)]. There was an old tram railroad up the Soque [Fig. 18(75)] during the early logging era. While one can find occasional large trees in the Soque watershed, most of the timber is young (around 30 years), owing to the disastrous Hickory Nut Ridge fire that swept 10,000 acres of the basin in 1953. Another fire ravaged the Wildcat watershed in 1958. Fortunately, the wetter north side of the Blue Ridge did not burn. There is one road one should not attempt without four-wheel drive and perhaps a chain saw; that is FS 690 [Fig. 18(77)] south to Unicoi Park.

~HIGH SHOALS TRAIL. 1.2 miles. High Shoals Scenic Area is comprised of 170 acres with five waterfalls, luxuriant banks of rhododendron and laurel and sparkling mountain streams. The only way to see the two major attractions, Blue Hole and High Shoals Falls, is to hike the steep, moderately difficult 1.2-mile trail [Fig. 18(58)]. The trail, marked by blue blazes, is in good condition, but reaching the trailhead can be difficult. The road is rough, and fording the stream may cause trouble. When the road is frozen or very muddy, only a four-wheel-drive vehicle can negotiate it.

The trail descends from 2,880 feet to 2,560 feet by many switchbacks through a predominantly hardwood forest. After reaching the bottom, the trail follows High Shoals Creek downstream, crosses the water on a wooden bridge, then descends steeply more than 300 feet as the creek cascades downward in a series of five waterfalls. Side trails lead to two observation decks [Fig. 18(59)]. The first deck overlooks Blue Hole, a pool more than 20 feet deep created by the churning of the water and rock falling from 30 feet above. Farther downstream is the grander High Shoals Falls, which tumbles more than 100 feet over jagged rocks, splashing and spraying water into the air.

DIRECTIONS: *Go 11 miles north of Helen on GA 75 to the dirt and gravel Indian Grave Gap Road, FS 283 (the first road to the right after Unicoi Gap) [Fig. 18(57)]; make a sharp right turn (east); proceed ahead, ford the usually shallow stream and continue up the hill. Parking for the trail is approximately 1.3 miles from GA 75.*

~ANNA RUBY FALLS SCENIC AREA. [Fig. 18(80)] Anna Ruby Falls, high on the slopes of Tray Mountain, is formed at the junction of Curtis and York Creeks. Both creeks originate atop Tray Mountain and are fed by underground springs, rain and snow. Curtis Creek then drops 153 feet, and York Creek drops 50 feet, forming the double falls. At the base of the falls, where there is an observation deck, the water becomes Smith Creek and tumbles downhill to Unicoi Lake. The U.S. Forest Service purchased the land surrounding the falls in 1925. The 1600-acre Scenic Area adjacent to and surrounding part of Unicoi State Park was established in 1964. The falls were named for Anna Ruby Nichols, the only daughter of Col. John H. Nichols, who purchased the surrounding land in 1869. His Victorian-style mansion, "West End," still stands at the junction of GA 17 and 75. He also built Crescent Hill Baptist Church and the gazebo atop the Indian Mound, both of which are still standing along GA 17.

A paved 0.4-mile trail leads from the parking lot to the foot of the falls.

FACILITIES: *Picnicking, drinking water, restrooms, trails, fishing, parking, group tours by arrangement, vending machines, information.*
FEES: *Parking - cars $2, buses $4.*
DATES/HOURS: *9-8 daily.*
DIRECTIONS: *Take GA 75 north from Helen for 1 mile; turn right on Ga 356 for 1.5 miles; then turn left at the entrance to the falls; follow this road 3.6 miles to the parking area, which accommodates 140 cars and two tour buses.*
ADDITIONAL INFORMATION: *Anna Ruby Falls Scenic Area, U.S. Forest Service, Chattooga Ranger District, Burton Road, Hwy 197, Clarkesville, GA 30523. (404) 754-6221.*

~SMITH CREEK TRAIL. [Fig. 18(80)] 4.6 miles. This trail provides hikers with a nice walk through dense patches of rhododendron, mountain laurel, hemlock and ferns. The trail goes up and over Hickory Nut Ridge through hardwood stands and crosses several small mountain streams before ending at Unicoi State Park Campground.

DIRECTIONS: *Follow the directions to Anna Ruby Falls. The trail begins at the right of the observation bridge.*

~DESOTO FALLS SCENIC RECREATION AREA AND TRAIL. See Blood Mountain Section.

~UNICOI STATE PARK. See Helen and Upper Chattahoochee Section.

~ANDREWS COVE RECREATION AREA. [Fig. 18(54)] This recreation area is located along a beautiful mountain stream in a heavily wooded area. It is two miles from Andrews Cove to the Appalachian Trail over an easy to moderate trail.

FACILITIES: *Toilets, drinking water pump, camping, hiking.*
DATES/HOURS: *Apr 1-Nov 1, 7am-10pm.*
DIRECTIONS: *On Ga 75, five miles north of Helen and 14 miles north of Cleveland.*
ADDITIONAL INFORMATION: *Andrews Cove Recreation Area, U.S.*

Forest Service, Chattooga Ranger District, P.O. Box 196, Burton Road, Clarkesville, GA 30523. (404)754-6221.

Map References: *USGS 1:24,000 series: Macedonia - Tray Mountain.*

WEST VISTA
View from Brasstown Bald

A - Yonah	**G** - Chimney Top
B - Pink	**H** - Track Rock Gap
C - Blood	**I** - Cohuttas
D - Slaughter	**J** - Big Frog
E - Duncan Ridge	**K** - Lake Nottely
F - Arkaqua Ridge	

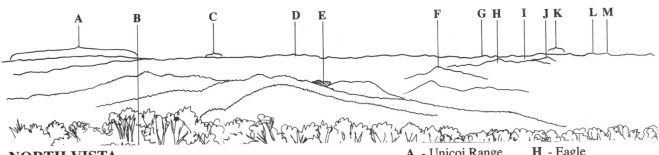

NORTH VISTA
View from Brasstown Bald

A - Unicoi Range	**H** - Eagle
B - Wolfpen Ridge	**I** - Yellow
C - Snowbirds	**J** - Hightower
D - Tusquitee Bald	**K** - Standing Indian
E - Lake Chatuge	**L** - Little Bald
F - Bell	**M** - Ridgepole
G - Kimsey Bald	

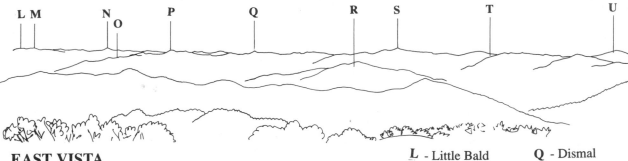

EAST VISTA
View from Brasstown Bald

L - Little Bald	**Q** - Dismal
M - Ridgepole	**R** - Spaniard
N - Rabun Bald	**S** - Tray
O - Kelly Ridge	**T** - Unicoi Gap
P - Kelly Knob	**U** - Yonah

THE GEORGIA CONSERVANCY

Brasstown Wilderness

Brasstown Bald is Georgia's highest mountain. From its summit at 4,784 feet there are breathtaking views of four states. On a clear day it is possible to see as far south as Atlanta.

In 1986, 11,405 acres within the Chattahoochee National Forest were designated by Congress as the Brasstown Bald Wilderness Area. The bald itself is only three-quarters of an acre. A narrow ring of ultrabasic rocks (soapstone, dunite and olivine) completely surrounds Brasstown Bald and the ridges leading to it. This is the southernmost habitat for many northern plant and animal species, including the red-back vole. A northern hardwood "cloud forest" of huge, old birches covers the north face. Rhododendron and mountain laurel are among the few shrubs that can survive on these thin, cold soils. The wildflower displays are particularly outstanding in the north-facing coves and down the east side of Wolfpen, one of the longest, highest ridges in Georgia.

Brasstown Bald was so named because of confusion between the Cherokee words *itse-yi,* meaning "new green place," and *untsaiyi,* meaning "brass."

Cherokee legend described a horrible, sharp-clawed, winged beast who attempted to steal and eat the Indian children. The Cherokees cleared the forest to capture the monster and prayed to their Great Spirit, who killed the beast, restored the children and has kept the mountaintop clear of trees ever since.

A steep, paved 0.5-mile trail leads from the parking area [Fig. 19(1)] to the visitor center [Fig. 19(2)] on the Bald. For a fee, a shuttle bus carries visitors from the parking area to the visitor center.

The access trail to the summit [Fig. 19(2)] is well worth walking down. From a shrub bald with the red-berried mountain ash and other unique mountaintop species such as dwarf willow, one enters a dwarfed red oak and white oak forest where the trees are very old, twisted and limby. As one descends, the trees gradually get taller. At first, purple rhododendron is the major heath shrub. Rosebay rhododendron appears as one nears the parking lot. Just before the bottom, one crosses the old wagon road [Fig. 19(3)] to Young Harris, which leads east then north into the fantastic "cloud forest" [Fig. 19(12)] of northern hardwoods on the north side of the mountain, below the visitor center. The huge old yellow birch are festooned with old man's beard lichen because of the continuous moisture from cloud condensation.

~THE VISITOR CENTER COMPLEX. The center, built of stone, offers interpretive programs, including the exhibit "Man and the Mountain," tracing human and natural history of the Southern Appalachian region. The Mountaintop Theater features continuous video programs. An outside observation deck provides a 360-degree

Figure 19   BRASSTOWN WILDERNESS

128

view of the surrounding area. Here visitors may be awed by the view but unprotected from the wind. Because of its height, Brasstown Bald gets much weather that misses the valleys. Strong wind, rain and lower temperatures are not uncommon. In winter there is usually snow and ice. The fire lookout tower is not open to the public.

FACILITIES: *video show, picnicking, bookstore and gift shop, hiking, parking ($1.00 fee), restrooms, exhibits, observation deck, brochures, concessions.*
DATES/HOURS: *10-5:30 daily Memorial Day-Oct, weekends in early spring (depending on the weather); parking lot, observation deck and trails are open year-round.*
DIRECTIONS: *From Cleveland take GA 75 north through Helen to GA 180; turn left (west) onto GA 180 (also GA 66) [Fig. 19(4)]; go 6 miles; turn right onto GA 180 spur [Fig. 19(5)]; continue 3 miles to Brasstown Bald parking lot [Fig. 19(1)].*
ADDITIONAL INFORMATION: *Brasstown Bald, U.S. Forest Service, Brasstown Ranger District, Highway 129/19 South, Blairsville, GA 30512. (404) 745-6928.*

~HIKING TRAILS FROM BRASSTOWN BALD. There are four hiking trails, including the paved summit-access trail. All start from the parking area at the bald, but only three of the trails are marked with signs. No trail maps are available other than the stylized plan drawn on the Forest Service Brasstown Bald brochure. The 1:24,000 scale topographical maps of the area (Hiawassee Quadrangle and Jack's Gap Quadrangle) show only two of the trails— Arkaquah and Wagon Train Trail.

JACK'S KNOB TRAIL. [Fig. 19(6)] About 4.5 miles. Built in the 1930's by the Civilian Conservation Corps and reconstructed in the 1980's by the Forest Service, Jack's Knob Trail is limited to foot traffic. Descending southward from the parking lot along a ridge following the boundary of Towns and Union Counties, it crosses GA 180 in Jack's Gap [Fig. 19(13)] at an elevation of 3,000 feet and ascends Hiawassee Ridge past Jack's Knob [Fig. 19(7)], elevation 3,805 feet. Jack's Knob Trail joins the Appalachian Trail in Chattahoochee Gap near the source of the Chattahoochee River [Fig. 19(8)].

ARKAQUAH TRAIL. [Fig. 19(9)] About 5.5 miles. There is a difference of 2,500 feet in elevation as the trail descends westward along a ridgetop from its beginning in the Brasstown Bald parking area to its end at Track Rock Gap Archeological Area [Fig. 19(10)]. With a difficulty rating of moderate to strenuous, this is not considered a beginner's trail. Blue Bluff overlook [Fig. 19(14)] is on the trail. Hikers pass Chimney Top Mountain and will be able to see Rocky Knob to the south. Plott Cove Research Natural Area [Fig. 19(15)], which is rich in herbs, wildflowers and northern hardwoods, is north of the trail at Cove Gap. To reach the western end of the trail on Track Rock Gap, go east of Blairsville on US 76 for six miles, turn right onto Track Rock Road and go three miles.

WAGON TRAIN TRAIL. [Fig. 19(3)] This trail is unmarked at both beginning and end. To find it, go between the bookstore and the concession stand located in the parking area. Take the paved trail and turn right (east) onto a dirt road. This trail is a wide path originally intended to be GA 66, and on some state maps still shown as such. It is an easy seven-mile walk with fine views. Near the summit, the trail passes remarkable cliffs and goes through boulder fields [Fig. 19(12)] where rock tripe, lichens, reindeer moss, old man's beard and club moss flourish. In early spring, silverbells, service berry, mountain buttercups, white saxifrage, toothwort, cinquefoil, bluets, hi-bush and low-bush blueberries, white and purple violets, Solomon's seal and plume, pussytoes and four varieties of trillium were seen blooming along the trail. The trail ends behind the women's dormitory on the Young Harris College campus.

~TRACK ROCK ARCHEOLOGICAL SITE. [Fig. 19(10)] Like the Mayan hieroglyphics of southern Mexico and Central America, the ancient petroglyphs carved into three large soapstone boulders on the west side of the road here have resisted translation. Referred to by the Cherokees who inhabited the area at the time of the white settlement as *degayelunha*, or "printed place," the rocks have been enclosed in metal cages to protect them from vandals and graffiti scrawlers. Though the stones are weathered, their mysterious inscriptions are still discernible to travelers who take time to stop here at the foot of Brasstown Bald. Similar examples of ancient picture writing can occasionally be found on rocks and on very old beech trees in the Southern Appalachians.

DIRECTIONS: *On Track Rock Road off US 76, six miles southwest of Young Harris.*

MAP REFERENCES: *USGS 1:24,000 series: Jack's Gap - Hiawassee - Blairsville.*

Painted trillium
Trillium undulatum

This species likes acid soils at high elevations often associated with rhododendron and hemlock. The flowers, with reddish markings near the center, distinguish it from all other trilliums.

Hightower Area of Southern Nantahala Wilderness

As one drives US 76 between Hiawassee and Dick's Creek Gap, the east-west trending high ridge or lead to the north is the western portion of the Southern Nantahala Wilderness. Visible are the cliffs near the top of Hightower Bald (4,568 feet), the highest peak in the area. This long, high ridge links a series of peaks with stunning views both north and south. It is an area for the backcountry hiker and explorer. Getting up on the high lead involves considerable climbing, beginning at the head of deep coves and flats.

On the northern approach there is a wealth of logging roads by which one can hike up to the edge of boulderfields in both Loggy Branch and Giesky Creek watersheds. The western approach up Sim's Branch passes east of the prominent Bell Knob, with its landmark quartz mine on top, visible for miles around. Of the eight access approaches, six are through private lands whose owners have been friendly to hikers and campers (though not necessarily to hunters), providing they are courteous and considerate. Always ask permission.

This area is not well known, and the old settler trails across Skut and Lemon Gap are hard to find, but sometimes that is half the fun. There is little evidence of logging roads above 4,000 feet in the zone of northern hardwoods.

~LOGGY BRANCH AND HIGHTOWER BALD. The easiest approach to Hightower Bald is the Loggy Branch access [Fig. 20(3)]. How far to drive on these rough roads will be a matter of personal judgement. A jeep road turns and goes south up the hillside west of Loggy Branch, swings right and passes by an enormous red maple at the foot of a large boulderfield [Fig. 20(5)]. Nearby there is a government corner marked in red paint. The road then extends to Loggy Branch [Fig. 20(4)] a short distance below the wilderness boundary. If so inclined, one can locate the famous Montgomery Corner and/or 30-mile post where the state line takes a large jog north and south.

Loggy Branch Cove itself is a botanical paradise. According to Georgia's eminent botanist Wilbur Duncan, it compares favorably with anything in the Smokies. Up and down Loggy Branch, one can find the black, twisted trunks of the rare yellowwood tree. This is Georgia's largest colony, and one of the largest aggregations of yellowwood in the Blue Ridge. Most of this area is privately owned.

Higher up in the cove, one encounters a northern hardwood forest of beech, sugar maple and yellow birch. In mountain gaps and below them can be found the southern limit of the "Beech Gap" phase of this community, where high altitude varieties of beech predominate. On the cold, high side of Hightower [Fig. 20(6)] just

Figure 20 HIGHTOWER RIDGE/SOUTHERN NANTAHALAS

Red-back vole
Clethrionomys gapperi

A creature of the alpine tundra and the deep spruce-fir forests, this animal can survive only on our higher peaks and ridges and in a few deep gorges such as that of Beech Creek (Tallulah River sector). It has been taken as far south as Brasstown Bald and is rare in any trapline.

under the top, there is a refuge for two plants normally associated with the spruce-fir forest: a beautiful viburnum and a type of oxalis clover. This is the only place in Georgia where this particular viburnum (*Viburnum alnitolium*) is known to grow.

The 150-foot cliffs on the south side [Fig. 20(7)] are dominated by moss and lichen, primitive rock spike moss, the rare Blue Ridge St. John's wort and the federally listed and very rare Biltmore sedge. The boreal red-back vole, another Pleistocene relic, has been found here. On top is a dwarf oak forest of white and red oak with a remarkably extensive growth of beaked hazelnut which, with mountain raspberry, dominates the understory. Large hawthorn trees grow here and there. One can climb a dwarfed oak, as if walking up a ladder, and see some fine views.

The ridgeline is supported by massive gneiss and amphibolite. A walk west down the ridge to Tom's Gap is rewarding; after a climb up a little cliff just west of Tom's Gap, one gets excellent vistas of the Hightower Cliffs and the watershed below. Dwarf willow grows here in abundance on the cliff edge, and purple rhododendron is common.

The most difficult section of the ridgeline is between Shooting Creek Bald (4,317 feet) [Fig. 20(9)] and along the High Cove Ridge [Fig. 20(10)], an almost continuous series of rock outcrops, cliffs and rhododendron. One can walk around under the cliffs; bear hunters prefer to burrow along the top. There is extensive rhododendron on the north face of Rattlesnake Knob. Otherwise the ridge is a fairly easy walk all the way to Eagle Mountain. Oak ridge forests to the east of Skut Gap [Fig. 20(15)] are dominated by northern red oak; those west, by white oak. Just south of Egypt Gap [Fig. 20(16)], a series of small cliffs is covered with marginal wood fern, alum root, rock cap fern and, nearby, monkshood. The Sassafras Knob Cliffs [Fig. 20(14)] have bush honeysuckle. The coves, especially lower Owensby Cove [Fig. 20(34)] and Loggy Branch [Fig. 20(4)], often have beautiful open stands of oak-hickory slope forest or poplar, waterfalls and wildflower assemblages.

Much is to be learned from this relatively unexplored area. Early settlers lived remarkably high and far back in the mountain coves. On the Loggy Branch Road a family named Davenport lived on rocky soil at about 3,000 feet. It is said that sled loads of mayapple (for medicinal purposes) selling for two cents a pound came out of Loggy Branch Cove. There are reported Indian petroglyphs on a rock on the trail to Lemon Gap [Fig. 20(32)].

~ACCESS ROUTES

LOGGY BRANCH COVE ACCESS. Northern access to Loggy Branch Cove, Hightower Bald and eastern part of the wilderness. On old US 64 east, pass Bethabara Road [Fig. 20(19)] 0.4 mile; turn right at a sign on paved Eagle Fork Creek Road [Fig. 20(33)]; go 2.1 miles to the third bridge; turn left on a dirt road just before the bridge. (At 0.4 mile a gated road turns left. Continue straight for this is a very rough jeep road. If the left road is chosen, take all other right turns and eventually reach Bly Gap on the Appalachian Trail. The gate opens Nov. 1.) Continuing straight, go about two miles from the paved road, following the most developed road through some private lands, to reach a U.S. Forest Service sign. Do not cross the branch but turn up the ridge following an old logging road which goes by a huge red maple and on to Loggy Branch [Fig. 20(3)], well up in the cove. Whether four-wheel drive is needed will depend on logging activities and rain. Certainly past the government boundary, one will need four-wheel drive, but at that point the short distance to the lower cove [Fig. 20(4)] can be hiked.

NORTHERN ACCESS. To Beech Flats, Lemon Gap and the central part of the wilderness. From Hwy 75 north out of Hiawassee, dead end at old US 64; turn east for four miles; turn south at the sign Bethabara Road (1166) [Fig. 20(19)]; go two miles; take the last road (dirt) to the right (west) just before the bridge; go about 0.4 mile through an apple orchard; turn left; ford a creek and park [Fig. 20(20)]. Continue south about 0.6 mile to where the road is blocked at a branch. Walk up the road on the left side of the branch. The wilderness boundary is very close. Climb southeast through Beech Flats until coming to the ridgeline where, with luck, one will find oneself in the vicinity of Rattlesnake Knob [Fig. 20(11)]. To dodge difficult cliffs [Fig. 20(10)] of High Cove Ridge, avoid striking the ridge east of Lemon Gap. It is said that an old trail to, or close to, Skut Gap [Fig. 20(15)] leaves the entrance road (turns south) just past the last house after one has forded the creek.

OLD SKUT GAP TRAIL. Northern access to Old Skut Gap Trail and western part of wilderness. From the junction of Hwy 75 north, turn east on old US 64; go 3.2 miles to the Giesky Creek sign (1165); turn right (south); at 2.4 miles reach bridge over Nattie Branch in U-shaped curve. The landowner here, John Robbins, lives just north of the bridge and says to park on the west side of the branch where the old log road follows the route of the old trail to Skut Gap by way of Burnt Cabin Cove.

EAGLE MOUNTAIN ACCESS. [Fig. 20(17)] The western end of the wilderness. Off GA 75 north of Hiawassee, turn east on Upper Bell Creek Road (Rd 9) just before a bridge crosses an arm of Lake Chatuge; go 1.2 miles; turn right (south) on road 78. At about 1.6 miles stop at a gate [Fig. 20(18)]; hike up the log road past Ben Gap (1.3 miles); reach another gate at 2 miles; walk up switchbacks to Eagle Mountain summit [Fig. 20(17)] (about 3.2 miles total from the

Beaked hazlenut
Corylus cornuta

While the American hazlenut occurs statewide, the beaked hazlenut is confined to the higher mountain ridges beneath the dwarfed red oak. It forms thickets on top of Hightower Bald. The nuts are sweet and relished by wildlife. Along with the chinquapin and beech, it contributes to the smaller "mast" supplementing the fruits of the oaks and hickories.

parking area).

SCATAWAY CREEK ACCESS. Southern entrance to the wilderness. Go north on GA 17/75 from Helen; turn right on US 76 and go 3.2 miles; turn north on a paved road (SR 100). At 1.2 miles a paved road (SR 101) to the left goes up Jack Hooper Branch. It is possible to hike up to Eagle Mountain [Fig. 20(17)] by this route, but there is no trail over the last mile of very steep terrain. The right fork [Fig. 20(SR 100) continues towards the Southern Access Trail to Skut Gap. After leaving the pavement, park and hike up an old log road trail [Fig. 20(21)] which does not follow the creek, but in 0.5 mile turns east up the slope and enters a clearcut. Instead, head steeply uphill (north) through a small stand of pine trees, coming to an old road. This road climbs steeply, rounds the end of a ridge and joins a more open road. Approximately 1.2 miles from the U.S. Forest Service boundary, a trail turns right and probably goes southeast to the top of Bluff Cove Cliffs [Fig. 20(22)]. The old trail to Skut Gap [Fig. 20(15)] continues but is grown up and extremely hard to follow.

HALL CREEK ACCESS. Southern entrance to the central ridge of the wilderness. Go two miles east along US 76; turn north on paved upper Hightower Road (SR 105); take the first paved left (1.4 miles); pass a lake on the right (almost 1.2 miles) and go through the Hall Creek Falls subdivision [Fig. 20(24)]. There is a nice waterfall upstream, where one crosses the Shook Branch [Fig. 20(25)]. As soon as the branch is crossed, look for an unmarked dirt [Fig. 20(26)] road that turns left. After a short distance one reaches the wilderness boundary. (The subdivision owners are sensitive about hunters but not about hikers.) Park at wilderness boundary [Fig. 20(23)]. About one mile up the trail which follows Shook Branch, the Shoal Creek Trail forks east to Eller Gap [Fig. 20(27)]. The "trail" up the Owensby Cove [Fig. 20(34)] to Lemon Gap may be indistinct. These are not official trails and are not clearly marked or maintained. A route with far less climbing but more walking is the eastern approach to Hightower Bald [Fig. 20(6)] via the Appalachian Trail. About two miles past the Mt. Pleasant Church (above), the pavement ends. Continue on the gravel road, but bear right at a fork [Fig. 20(30)]; go 1.2 miles to reach Blue Ridge Gap [Fig. 20(31)] (four-wheel drive recommended). At either Rich Knob [Fig. 20(2)] or Bly Gap [Fig. 20(1)], pick up the main ridge west to Hightower Bald.

MAP REFERENCES: *USGS 1:24,000 series: Shooting Creek - Macedonia - Rainbow Springs - Hightower Bald.*

White Oak Stamp

White Oak Stamp, together with Buck Creek and Chunky Gal Mountain (next section) is so unique that parts of this area are classified and protected as "special interest areas" by the U.S. Forest Service. White Oak Stamp and adjacent areas of Chunky Gal and the Buck Creek watershed offer not only one of the very best examples of old-growth, high-altitude forest areas to explore, but also vistas as exciting as any area within the scope of this book.

It is rare to find a large "flat" area such as White Oak Stamp at high elevations along the Blue Ridge. Most of the land above 4,200 feet is virgin old-growth. A good part of it, especially on slopes and ridges, is high-altitude northern red oak forest [Fig. 21(56)], with many trees exceeding two feet in diameter. Shrubs here include flame azalea, several viburnums and three species of blueberry. Mixed northern red oak-white oak forest occurs in certain areas [Fig. 21(76)]. Perhaps the most exciting environment is the area of northern hardwoods [Fig. 21(57)], especially in the Big Laurel cove heads, through which the Buck Creek access trail [Fig. 21(64)] passes. Here are giant old yellow birch between two and three feet in diameter. Subdominants are buckeye and beech, the latter predominating on slight ridges with a rare pure beech forest lower down [Fig. 21(77)]. Just above it is a large stand of rare chokeberry.[Fig. 21(78)].

The trail bisects one of the strikingly beautiful gneissic boulderfields. The northern herb/wildflower display is outstanding, with perhaps the largest display of the edible ramp and the poisonous large hellebore that visitors will ever see. This forest continues on the east side of Chunky Gal as far as Bear Gap [Fig. 21(72)].

In a low area not far from the Appalachian Trail [Fig. 21(58)] lies a remarkable high-altitude heath bog on the head of Muskrat Branch [Fig. 21(53)]. While the dominant shrubs are rosebay rhododendron and mountain laurel, purple rhododendron does occur. This thicket is difficult to penetrate, but bears love it and native brook trout are common in the tiny crystal clear streams. Yellow birch, hemlock and red maple make up a scattered overstory. The rare bog turtle may be present. Two small areas are open sedge marshes with cinnamon fern. Approaching the bog from the north is an old "burl road" [Fig. 21(54)] formerly used to haul out rhododendron root burls. These burls were used in the manufacture of pipe bowls when supplies from the Mediterranean were cut off during World War II.

There is a spring at the Muskrat Creek shelter [Fig. 21(50)] on the Appalachian Trail. Not far south of it are two clifftop vistas (no trails) which overlook the Tallulah Watershed [Fig. 21(66 and 69)].

Hikers who walk west on the ridge opposite the shelter and are able to find the old cattle and pig trail [Fig. 21(67)] can follow it down and around and north of a little top, then back out southeastward to the top of Raven Rock Cliff [Fig. 21(68)], which

Bog turtle
Clemmys muhlenbergii

This palm-sized turtle is the smallest of our mountain turtles, is now extremely rare and lives only in bogs, which themselves are endangered environments. Bog turtles, like wood frogs, seem to occur only on the north side of the Georgia Blue Ridge. An orange temple patch is characteristic.

Figure 21   WHITE OAK STAMP

has fine vistas.

DIRECTIONS: *Four trails converge at White Oak Stamp. The easiest access may be from Deep Gap [Fig. 21(59)] via the old AT loop south of Yellow Mountain. Deep Gap road is reached off old US 64, which is paved and turns off New US 64. Those who relish the exertion of a two-hour climb can come up the Holden Cove Trail [Fig. 21(48)].*

MAP REFERENCES: *USGS 1:24,000 series: Rainbow springs*

Buck Creek and Chunky Gal Mountain

Buck Creek and Chunky Gal Mountain together with White Oak Stamp (previous section), are so unique that parts of them are classified and protected as "special interest areas" by the U.S. Forest Service. Buck Creek is a renowned site of ultrabasic rocks of great interest to those interested in minerals, gems or botany. Chunky Gal Mountain gets its name from the Cherokee legend of a plump Indian maiden who fell in love with a brave and followed him over this mountain after her parents had banished him from camp. With its long ridgetop scenic trail and noteworthy Riley Knob botanical area, Chunky Gal is considered by conservationists to be worthy of Wilderness Area designation.

~CHUNKY GAL MOUNTAIN. Chunky Gal is a long (eight miles), high and remote ridgelike mountain connecting the Blue Ridge and the Appalachian Trail with the Tusquitee and Fires Creek ranges. For hikers going north, there is a scenic overlook to the west from a cliff said to contain garnets and olivine. This is about 1.5 miles before Bear Gap. The trail's end south of Bear Gap [Fig. 22(72)] has most interesting vegetation in a near-original state. At Grassy Gap [Fig. 22(75)], a cove forest reaches the trail with a lush herb flora including monkshood and purple-fringed orchid. A rare plant—wolfsmilk—occurs as far south as Grassy Gap, the southern limit of its growing range in the United States. Grassy Gap apparently was the crossing of the old Macon Trail [Fig. 22(90)] used by the Indians and was also a horseback mail route before the construction of US 64. It was a "short cut" from Shooting Creek to the headwaters of the Nantahala River. Accessible from Muskrat Creek [Fig. 22(60)], it may, nevertheless, be difficult to find.

~THE RILEY KNOB/CHUNKY GAL SPECIAL INTEREST AREA. [Fig. 22(62)] The area covers 215 acres between 3,600 and 4,400 feet and is an outstanding example of an extensive old-growth, high-altitude white oak forest. There is some cove forest and red oak ridge forest. Much of the rock in the Riley Knob area is amphibolite, which supports a rich herb flora. The knob and the Chunky Gal Ridge Trail are reached from US 64 at Riley Cove [Fig. 22(74)] or at a blue-blazed trail [Fig. 22(71)] from Glade Gap access point [Fig. 22(73)].

From this latter point, according to Allen de Hart's trail guide, one can cross US 64, turn left on old US 64, then right at 0.2 mile from Glade Gap on an old jeep road. Eventually one reaches Boteler Peak (also called Shooting Creek Bald, 5,010 feet) [Fig. 22(80)] at about 2.8 miles from Glade Gap. Here a blue-blazed trail descends northward to Perry Gap and continues on to link with the Rim Trail on the east rim of the Fires Creek Basin, a noted bear

Figure   22   BUCK CREEK/CHUNKY GAL MOUNTAIN

refuge.

~THE BUCK CREEK PINE BARRENS. The Buck Creek pine barrens are both geologically and botanically unique. Basic magnesium-rich rocks such as olivine and dunite [Fig. 22(83)] predominate. At the first little creek [Fig. 22(84)], about 0.5 mile past the bridge [Fig. 22(82)], one is treated to an assortment of unusual rocks. The creek bed is littered with pieces of olivine, gabbro, chlorite schist, talc (with which one can write) and other mineral specimens -- a smorgasbord of basic and ultrabasic rock. The Buck Creek barrens contain the largest single outcrop of dunite in the entire Georgia and North Carolina olivine belt.

Back 0.1 mile is a pullout by Buck Creek, a good place to picnic. Across the Creek is a "tailings pile" or mine dump. The old corundum mine shaft [Fig. 22(85)] is above it in an area of dunite rock [Fig. 22(83)]. In the late 1800's, mining for the abrasive corundum, which has a hardness next to the diamond's, was carried out throughout the corundum belt. Old roads [Fig. 22(86)] go back to Corundum Knob [Fig. 22(87)], where corundum was also mined. Here it is possible to find tiny rubies in a matrix of green stone, a type of amphibole called "smaragdite."

Because of the unique plant life here, 103 of the 346 acres in the Buck Creek barrens have been proposed as a botanical preserve. Before leaving US 64, note the presence of a normal montane deciduous forest [Fig. 22(65)]. After crossing the bridge [Fig. 22(82)], one almost immediately enters an area dominated by pitch pine with scrubby, scattered white oak. The soil moisture and temperature are such that some prairie grasses have become established. The Forest Service recognizes three unique plant communities here: 1) pitch pine/witherod, 2) the only location of pitch pine bluestem grass and prairie dropseed south of Pennsylvania and 3) one of two sites for pitch pine/little bluestem grass in North Carolina. Two unusual wild flowers are big-leaf grass of parnassus and fringed gentian.

The weird rocks, the unusual vegetation and the chance of panning a piece of ruby corundum out of Buck Creek make this area a prized one. After passing through the mineralized zone, one quickly reaches a fork [Fig. 22(81)]. The left-hand turn goes 2.8 miles west to the Perry Gap Trailhead [Fig. 22(79)], the right-hand turn is into what was the old Buck Creek Lodge, which is still private property. After a return to New US 64, it is 2.3 miles to the Shooting Creek Overlook [Fig. 22(89)] (with picnic tables). The next gated road on the left goes only a short distance up Muskrat Branch [Fig. 22(60)] where, with luck, one can locate the old Macon Trail [Fig. 22(90)].

MAP REFERENCES: *USGS 1:24,000 series: Rainbow Springs - Shooting Creek.*

Nantahala Basin

Rivers in the Tallulah and the Nantahala Basins, separated from each other by the Eastern Continental Divide, run in opposite directions. Water flowing north in the Nantahala follows a much longer path via the Mississippi to the Gulf of Mexico, while water in the Tallulah Basin reaches the Atlantic via the Savannah River. Because the route to the Atlantic is a shorter, steeper one, downcutting is heavier on the south side of the Blue Ridge. This may be one reason why the Tallulah River is nearly 1,000 feet lower than the bed of the Nantahala River.

At 3,000 feet, Nantahala Lake, into which the Nantahala River flows, is one of the highest large lakes in the mountains. Because of the coldness of Nantahala Lake, the Nantahala River experiences two fish-spawning runs—a run of Kokanee salmon in the fall (stocked by Bob Humphries in the early 1960's) and a run of large rainbow trout (steelhead) in the winter. The river may be the only one in the Southeast experiencing a salmon run.

The Nantahala watershed has an extensive system of trails of different lengths and varying degrees of difficulty. There are at least three horse trails and a special horse camp. There are fascinating plant communities, including bogs and some virgin forest.

Because of its soils and elevation, the Nantahala watershed had original timber of a size and density which brought visitors from as far away as Asheville, even when virgin timber was widespread.

The area was logged until the 1920's. Ritter Lumber Company had its logging camp where the main campground for the area is today [Fig. 23(5)] and at Rainbow Springs [Fig. 23(40)], Ritter had a band-saw mill to saw the huge trees. Narrow-gauge railroads ran up and down the Nantahala River and went up its tributaries until stopped by waterfalls. The route of the dismantled railroad is marked on topographic sheets (Rainbow Springs Quadrangle).

The Nantahala is known for large brown trout, and its headwaters still support native brook trout populations. It has also been a black-bear refuge for years.

DIRECTIONS: *Go north on US 441 to Franklin, NC; turn left onto US 64; go 12 miles and turn left onto old US 64; go 1.8 miles to Wallace Gap [Fig. 23(1)] and turn right onto FS Road 67/1, which is the road into the basin.*

~A DRIVING TOUR OF THE BASIN. For those interested in combining driving and short walks, there is a marvelous tour of the area to see an immense poplar tree, two waterfalls and vistas from Pickens' Nose.

DIRECTIONS: *From the turnoff at Wallace Gap (above), go 0.4 mile*

145

Figure 23 NANTAHALA BASIN/STANDING INDIAN MOUNTAIN

to a parking area on the left [Fig. 23(3)]. It is directly adjacent to the Appalachian Trail (AT), so that one can park here for walks in either direction on the AT. This is also the trailhead for the short (1.4-mile round-trip) walk on a graded trail to the John Wasilik Memorial Tree [Fig. 23(4)], which is the second largest yellow poplar in the United States. It is eight feet in diameter, 25 feet in circumference and was 135 feet tall until topped by a storm. The tree is in one of a series of north-facing coves, called the Runaway Knob Special Interest Area [Fig. 23(38)], where over 100 plant species have been identified. Lying between 3,200 and 4,400 feet, the 140-acre area is the location of an exceptionally beautiful spring wildflower display. The forest below the Wasilik poplar contains North Carolina's largest reproducing population of the rare yellowwood tree, which occurs in only a few localities in Georgia and North Carolina.

Continue on FS 67/1 [Fig. 23(2)] to a fork at about 1.1 miles; take the left fork, FS Road 67/2, about 0.2 mile to Backcountry Information site [Fig. 23(7)]; (In the valley upstream are flat areas of flood plain and alluvial fill with some open areas [Fig. 23(20)]. Some of these are wildlife openings and others are rare wetland bogs—some as large as 20 acres, lying between 3,400 and 3,500 feet in elevation. This is the second largest bog complex in western North Carolina and the subject of paleobotanical studies of the peat underlying them. The bogs should not be entered.)

Continue 4.7 miles on FS 67/2 to the parking area for Big Laurel Falls [Fig. 23(26)] (1.2 miles round trip) [Fig. 23(25)], an easy hike for the whole family.

Continue on FS 67/2 for 0.8 mile to the pull off area for Mooney Falls. The trail is a 0.2-mile round trip to the falls [Fig. 23(28)].

Continue on FS 67/2 until its intersection with FS 83 [Fig. 23(30)]. Turn right and continue past Mooney Gap [Fig. 23(39)], a station for acid rain studies by University of Georgia students, and crossing of the Appalachian Trail. At 0.7 mile past Mooney Gap, park on the north and walk south one mile to Pickens' Nose (5,000 feet). Vistas are to the east, west, and south into the Betty Creek Basin. An optional walk is to Albert Mountain. Backtrack on Forest Service Road 83 as far as it will go north, then hike up to the Albert Mountain fire tower [Fig. 23(32)] which provides an exceptional 360-degree view. (Pickens' Nose and Albert Mountain can also be reached by Buck Creek Road through the Coweeta Hydrologic Laboratory off US 441 north of the GA/NC state line.)

~KILBY CREEK. The best virgin timber in the area lies above the falls of Kilby Creek [Fig. 23(24)], a challenge for wild-country addicts. This is largely cove hardwood with big hemlock-rhododendron forests along the streams. Above the falls there are eastern brook trout, the only native species.

This is wild and rough country, a true wilderness. Visitors to it should take no chances.

~STANDING INDIAN. [Fig. 23(10)] At 5,499 feet this is the highest peak in the Nantahala Mountains. Its Indian name translates literally, "the place where man stood." Cherokee mythology relates the story of a winged monster that stole a child and carried him to the cliffs on top of the mountain [Fig. 23(11)]. The Indians prayed to the Great Spirit, who answered their prayers by sending a lightning bolt that destroyed the monster and the trees on the summit, but also killed a lone Indian sentry and turned him to stone.

The easiest way to reach the summit is via US 64 and FS 71 [Fig. 23(8)], a long gravel road to Deep Gap [Fig. 23(59)]. Along this road is a dense roadside growth of an extremely primitive plant, a species of horsetail or scouring rush, whose silica content was useful to the early settlers for scrubbing pots. From Deep Gap it is a 2.5-mile walk to the summit, climbing 1,200 feet and passing a good spring and shelter about one-third of the way up. The first large northern loop of this trail [Fig. 23(9)] goes over and around a flat, wet, sheltered ridge with a deep stable soil, which may explain the white oak ridge forest here with flame azalea and fern understory. It also shows the effect of exposure. The white oak goes downslope only 30 feet to the east, but it goes down the western slope 120 feet. The summit of Standing Indian is heath or shrub bald, principally of purple rhododendron. Formerly, a fire tower stood here and a telephone wire ran up from the Tallulah Valley. The Fraser fir nearby were planted. There are two springs northeast of the summit. South of the ridgeline in the ridge forest (not on the Appalachian Trail) are some pits [Fig. 23(12)], relics of the period when mica was mined in the area. These may be discovered by diligent explorers. The Appalachian Trail here tunnels through rhododendron and flame azalea and is quite dramatic in early summer. Traveling on down the 1.5-mile ridgeline, one sees Little Bald directly south and passes through several environments, principally red oak ridge forest and areas of shrub bald vegetation [Fig. 23(13)] dominated by mountain laurel, with some purple rhododendron. Some drier areas have grasses, while other almost-bare-soil areas are covered with a rare tundra species—the three-leaved cinquefoil, a threatened species at the southern periphery of its range. The effects on the soil of ice heavage—that is, the repeated freezing and thawing of the earth—and the results of wind shear on the shrubs are evident. There has been much scientific debate on the origin of balds such as this which cap many of the Appalachians' highest peaks. Here on the southwest slope, one can see the "bald" area grading into dwarf northern red oak-evergreen heath, which within several hundred feet grades into northern red oak-deciduous heath (azaleas and blueberries). On the opposite side (the northeast slope) the bald areas grade into a beautiful northern red oak—fern community that in turn grades into a northern hardwood forest.

Galax
Galax aphylla

Galax, or coltsfoot, is widespread in the mountains on dry, acid soils. It is evergreen but may turn purple or bronze in winter. It has been used as a Christmas decoration.

To the west lies Big Scaly (5,200 feet) [Fig. 23(42)] in the immediate foreground. The Girl Scouts had a connector trail [Fig. 23(41)] leading down to Beech Creek through the rhododendron and virgin red oak ridge forest with flame azalea understory, but the entrance is difficult to find. There are two other accesses to Beech Creek—one an old log road, the other a steep trail (see Tallulah Basin)—both beginning at Beech Gap.

The upper portion of the Big Indian Loop horse trail [Fig. 23(21)] passes through a succession of cove hardwoods, northern hardwoods and boulder fields.

Loop trail possibilities are numerous. If two vehicles are available, a shuttle can be set up. For example, one vehicle may be left at Deep Gap [Fig. 23(59)] and another at either White Oak Bottoms Campground [Fig. 23(5)] or at the Beech Gap Trail junction with FS 67. Then one could hike to the summit of Standing Indian and down the Lower Ridge Trail [Fig. 23(34)], or down the long spine of Standing Indian to Beech Gap [Fig. 23(22)] and down the Beech Gap Trail [Fig. 23(23)], with a side visit to the Kilby Creek virgin forest [Fig. 23(24)].

~HIKING TRAILS IN THE AREA. There are seven trails from the valley up to the Appalachian Trail (AT). They can be combined in a number of ways to create interesting loop hikes. One warning: the weather here can change rapidly. In particular, the hiker should beware afternoon thunderstorms on the high ridges and peaks in the summer months.

KIMSEY CREEK TRAIL TO STANDING INDIAN. 10 miles roundtrip. One favorite hike is to walk to Standing Indian Mountain starting from the Back Country Information site on the Kimsey Creek Trail [Fig. 23(35)], a wonderfully varied trail along creeks and through wildlife meadows with many wildflowers. The trail connects with the AT at Deep Gap [Fig. 23(59)]. Follow the AT to the top of Standing Indian, which is a strenuous climb. There is a junction at which one spur goes from the AT to the top for a vista. Return to the AT and continue a very short distance (10 yards or so) to Lower Ridge Trail [Fig. 23(34)], which returns to Back Country Information site in four miles.

LOOP TRAIL. 10.9 miles roundtrip. Another loop might be to hike up the AT on the Long Branch Trail [Fig. 23(18)] from the Back Country Information site (1.9 miles). Hike south (to the right) on the AT to the Albert Mountain Lookout Tower (5,280 feet) [Fig. 23(32)] for views in all directions (3.1 miles). Continue on AT for 0.3 mile to Bearpen Gap Trail [Fig. 23(31)]; descend 2.4 miles on Bearpen Gap Trail to FS 67/2; turn right and walk 3.2 miles back to the Back Country Information site.

~OTHER TRAIL POSSIBILITIES. Many other combinations are possible using the following trails in conjunction with the Appalachian Trail: Kimsey Creek Trail [Fig. 23(35)], Lower Ridge Trail [Fig. 23(34)], Long Branch Trail [Fig. 23(18)] and Beech Gap Trail [Fig. 23(23)].

PARK CREEK AND PARK RIDGE TRAILS. 10-mile loop. An interesting 10-mile loop away from the AT, which means it is less crowded, combines the Park Creek [Fig. 23(37)] and Park Ridge Trails [Fig. 23(36)]. One begins at the Back Country Information site. The beginning of the trail is the same as for the Lower Ridge Trail and the Kimsey Creek Trail. After about 0.5 mile from the bridge in the campground, the Park Ridge Trail goes left up the ridge and climbs to Park Gap [Fig. 23(43)] at FS 71-1. Cross the road and descend on Park Creek Trail along a lovely stream to the Nantahala River; turn right and walk about 1.5 miles to the junction with Park Ridge Trail and retrace the path to Back Country Information site.

~ACCESS TO DAY HIKES. Another access to day-hike trailheads is from FS 71-1. Take US 64 west from Franklin, past the turn-off at 12 miles onto old US 64; go about 2.5 miles and turn left onto FS 71; go about 2.5 to 3 miles to reach Park Gap [Fig. 23(43)]; park in this area and walk the Park Ridge and Park Creek loop trail. By driving past this parking area for another 3 miles, one can reach the end of the road at Deep Gap. Here one has access to the Kimsey Creek Trail, the AT east to Standing Indian Mountain (2.8 miles one way), a primitive trail south to the Tallulah River and the AT west to White Oak Stamp and Bly Gap.

THREE-DAY WALK. 24 miles. A good backpacking trip is to start at the Back Country Information site, taking the Long Branch Trail [Fig. 23(18)] to the AT. Turn right (south) on the AT and follow it over Albert Mountain [Fig. 23(32)], through Bear Pen Gap, over Big Butt, down to Mooney Gap [Fig. 23(39)], passing Carter Gap and Beech Gap [Fig. 23(22)], climbing Standing Indian Mountain and descending to Deep Gap [Fig. 23(59)]. Turn right on Kimsey Creek Trail and return to Back Country Information site. This is a pleasant three-day (24 mile) walk. There are shelters at Big Spring Gap, Carter Gap and Standing Indian (near Deep Gap). This is a popular loop, so shelters may be filled. Walked in early June, the stretch up Standing Indian Mountain is a botanical garden. The Catawba rhododendron and mountain laurel arch over the trail to make a floral tunnel.

ADDITIONAL INFORMATION: *The U.S. Forest Service has prepared a Recreational Opportunities Guide (which they refer to as ROG) in which many of the hiking trails in the area are summarized along with directions to the trailheads. The public may view this guide at the Wayah Ranger District Forest Service office or order copies of the pages of the guide for the cost of copying and mailing. Topographical maps of the area are also available here. 8 Sloan Road, Franklin, NC 28734. (704) 524-6441 or 524-4410.2*

MAP REFERENCES: *USGS 1:24,000 series: Prentiss - Rainbow Springs.*

Tallulah Basin

Until the turn of the 19th century, Tallulah Falls and Tallulah Gorge were relatively unchanged by man. Formed by the mighty Tallulah River, which joined the Chattooga River just below the canyon, they were protected from outsiders by the rugged mountain terrain. For centuries only the Cherokee Indians inhabited the area, and few whites penetrated the wilderness. The few white hunters and traders who wandered through the area told stories about the gorge and its mysterious thundering waters. Even the Cherokees seldom ventured into the gorge, believing it to be inhabited by a strange race of "little people" who were alleged to live in the nooks and crannies of the cliffs overlooking the falls. The Cherokees also believed that one of the caves in the gorge was the entrance to the Happy Hunting Grounds; if an Indian ever entered, he would never return.

After the Cherokees were driven out in 1819, white adventurers began to explore the region. Unhindered by the Indians' fears about the gorge, they probed its depths. When they returned to civilization, they said that they understood the Indians' awe and wonder regarding the falls and gorge. Within a year of the Cherokees' departure, spectacular accounts were circulated concerning this natural wonder in the northeast Georgia mountains. Newspapers printed the stories, and knowledge of the existence of Tallulah Falls and Tallulah Gorge spread like a prairie fire. Although great stamina was required to make the trip, tourists began forging their ways through the mountains to see this curiosity of nature. Clarkesville was the closest point where pack horses could be obtained to begin the 12-mile trek through the mountains to the gorge.

Interest in Tallulah Falls and Gorge had spread beyond Georgia. During the 1830's and 1840's foreign and American dignitaries began to make pilgrimages to the region, including Vice-President John C. Calhoun; John Howard Payne, composer of "Home Sweet Home"; and Georgian Joseph LeConte, who would later become one of the founders of the University of California and of the Sierra Club. The area's attraction was not hard to understand. The gorge itself is a three-mile-long gash in the earth that reaches a depth of almost 600 feet, bordered by rocky, vertical walls. The Tallulah River carries runoff from a watershed area of over 200 square miles. In those days this mighty river roared into the gorge over a series of spectacular cataracts, creating a continuous thundering sound that echoed through the gorge day and night.

At the head of the gorge, the bed of the Tallulah River suddenly became narrow, creating a swift current headed toward the first falls. Tourists named this narrow bed Indian Arrow Rapids. The first of the great falls over which the Tallulah poured into the gorge was named Ladore; then came the 76-foot-high Tempesta Falls; then, the 96-foot Hurricane Falls. The fourth of the great falls was named Oseana. Next was Bridal Veil Falls, with a drop of 17 feet. And

Pigmy shrew
Microsorex hoyi

One of the world's smallest mammals, this tiny shrew barely enters Georgia in the headwaters of the Tallulah River. Even here it is rare and difficult to trap.

Figure 24   UPPER TALLULAH BASIN

last was Sweet Sixteen Falls, with a 16-foot drop. Beyond the falls, deep in the canyon, was a great bend in the river called Horseshoe Bend, from which visitors liked to gaze upward to guess the height of the towering cliffs. Many streams and creeks poured over the canyon rim into the gorge below and were given appropriate names—no one knows exactly by whom. Everything was named. The pool at the bottom of Ladore Falls was named Hawthorne Pool, in memory of a man who fell to his death there. A natural water slide on the side of the gorge was named Hank's Sliding Place, in memory of a native of the region who slipped and fell more than 100 feet into the raging river below and lived to tell about it. The thundering waters beneath an overhanging rock reminded someone of the voice of Satan, so that rock was named Devil's Pulpit—probably the most popular tourist site at the gorge, then and now. An outcropping that reminded someone of a profile was given the name Witch's Head and was a popular spot for photographers in the 19th century.

As tourists grew impatient with making the long trek from Clarkesville and with having to camp at the gorge, inns sprang up near the attraction. Although the Civil War interrupted tourism for a while, lodges right on the rim of the gorge were in operation soon after the end of that conflict. Fine hotels were built, able to accommodate as many as 300 guests. Tallulah Gorge became a mecca for summer vacationers, offering cool temperatures, great views and accommodations for rich and poor. Georgians were proud of Tallulah Gorge, whose natural attractions were made available to the public without being damaged.

The editor of the *Atlanta News* said in 1905 that "every foot of the scenery which surrounds Tallulah is superior to that of Niagara, and the state should buy that magnificent domain of scenery and make it the most beautiful park and reservation this side of Yellowstone." The mention of Niagara Falls was not accidental. Business interests had long had their eyes on the Niagara River, desiring to divert its flow in order to generate electric power. They were also considering the Tallulah River with the same idea in mind. Colonel John H. Estil, editor of the *Savannah Morning News*, wrote in 1906, "To commercialism there is nothing beautiful except the machine that grinds out dollars, unless it possibly be the power that actuates the machine. Imagine Bridal Veil Falls sawing logs, or majestic Tempesta ginning cotton. Think of Horseshoe Bend as a mill site and the magnificent cliff across the rim covered with patent-medicine signs. There is only one Tallulah, and if it is spoiled, the loss will be immeasurable."

In 1905, the State Legislature made an effort to buy and preserve the land around Tallulah Gorge. Unfortunately, the Legislature could not come up with the $100,000 needed to make the purchase. Three years later, what was to become Georgia Power Company was organized by E. Elmer Smith of York, Pennsylvania, and Eugene

Ashley of Glens Falls, New York. In 1909 these two men made a trip to explore Tallulah Falls. They were impressed with what they saw and obtained the $108,960 necessary to purchase the strategic tract of land around the head of the gorge. By late 1910 they had completed the necessary contracts with construction companies to build dams, tunnels and power plants along the Tallulah River and in the gorge.

Efforts were made to rescue the Tallulah River and Gorge from development. In the first large environmental battle in the state's history, a group of citizens led by the widow of Confederate General James Longstreet appealed to officials of Rabun County, to the State Legislature, to the Governor, to the Georgia Supreme Court and even to President Taft. But it was too late. Work on Tallulah Dam began.

Throngs of people came to the gorge area to watch this remarkable engineering feat. But more came in 1912 to view Tallulah Falls for the last time. The editor of the *Toccoa Record* wrote, "The men and women with sentiment have taken their last look at the falls as they loved them. Both Georgia and the United States had a chance to save this unparalleled natural wonder, but we've waited too late."

In September of 1913, with the dam at the head of the gorge completed and the river diverted through its powerhouses, electricity flowed for the first time over the wires to Atlanta—to run the city's trolley cars. The "terrible" Tallulah River, as the Cherokees had called it, had been tamed and reduced to a trickle, dripping through Tallulah Gorge.

The decline of Tallulah Gorge as a tourist attraction was rapid thereafter. Many hotels closed. Others were burned in a fire of 1922 that almost destroyed the little tourist town of Tallulah Falls. Two years later, the construction of US 441 bypassed Tallulah Falls altogether.

The moaning of the wind is the only sound that comes from the gorge now, although the place has enjoyed a few brief moments of notoriety, such as when Karl Walenda walked on a wire strung across the gorge in 1970, and in 1972 when a few scenes from the movie *Deliverance* were shot in the canyon.

From its mile-high beginnings on the southwest slopes of Standing Indian Mountain in North Carolina, the Tallulah bounded southward through the north Georgia mountains, falling more than 4,700 feet during the 46-mile journey to its confluence with the Chattooga beyond the end of Tallulah Gorge, at the South Carolina border. Its last four miles, beginning at the falls, were the most dramatic. Over these falls the river plunged downward a total of 600 feet in less than a mile.

What remains of the once terrible Tallulah? Although the river and the lakes which now impound it are nothing like the scene of 100 years ago, the Tallulah today is an exciting and unusual experience. The destinations below, whether reached by car, canoe, foot or a combination thereof, provide a rare opportunity for visitors to view the mountains from scenic lakes, run the rapids of what remains of the Tallulah Gorge and pay tribute to what was once one of the mightiest rivers in Georgia.

~THE HEADWATERS OF THE TALLULAH RIVER. If one had to select a national park site in Georgia, this land of gorges, waterfalls and scenic splendor would be it. It has been a hunting ground for bear and hog hunters for years. Only now are horseback riders and hikers discovering this watershed and its myriad trails, many of them connecting with the Appalachian Trail. There was no easy way for the early settlers to reach the remote valley called Tate City, a pastoral setting rimmed by a great northward flex of the Blue Ridge. Tate City was once a busy corundum mining community and later a logging town with stores and churches. Now only two churches and a handful of homes remain. Most of the original mountain people who lived by subsistence agriculture are gone. The bears and perhaps even the cougar have returned.

~TALLULAH RIVER SCENIC DRIVE. [Fig. 24(2)] FS 70 dead ends in the heart of the wilderness. The major access point for the Tallulah River basin, it follows beside the Tallulah through the three-mile-long Rock Mountain Gorge [Fig. 24(6)] to [Fig. 24(8)] on the old railroad bed which was blasted out of solid rock by the lumber company logging the valley in virgin timber days. This lovely road crosses the Tallulah four times. The picturesque gorge has been the site of television commercials and postcard vistas. One can picnic on the rocks or fish the pools stocked weekly with eating-size rainbow trout. In the gorge grow a number of the beautiful and rare flowering tree, the mountain camellia or *stewartia*. The best place to see it is in a stand at a wide place in the road at the extreme southern end of the Tate Branch Campground [Fig. 24(49)]. At Line Branch one can look back, high up at the Flat Branch Falls [Fig. 24(7)]. Just below the Tate Branch Campground the Charlie's Creek Road fords the river [Fig. 24(10)]. When this road emerges on a flat near the AT, a north-turning fork [Fig. 24(44)] leads one to the main Charlie's Creek. Across the creek and up the road a few hundred yards there is bare dirt and a trail up to an amethyst mine [Fig. 24(12)] that has produced some of the finest gem amethysts in the United States.

~THE BEECH CREEK - CHIMNEY ROCK LOOP. [Fig. 24(16)] A 12-mile loop. This hike has been a favorite of scout groups for many years. Skirting private property, the lower trailhead is at the "Glory Patch" [Fig. 24(16)] and crosses a low gap in Scaly Ridge before descending to the Beech Creek log road trail at an old homesite. Shortly thereafter, this main road crosses Bull Cove

Branch (a striking cliff and falls, with rich herb growth, lies just out of sight upstream) [Fig. 24(18)] and fords the creek to enter [Fig. 24(17)] the stunningly beautiful Beech Creek Gorge [Fig. 24(20)] (a trail to the left [Fig. 24(19)] leads to Bear Creek Falls). In about two miles the log road trail reaches an old ore-crusher foundation of packed rock [Fig. 24(21)] and begins switchbacks up through the vast cliffs [Fig. 24(22)] on the face of Big Scaly Mountain [Fig. 24(25)]. At about the second switchback left, a prominent trail goes off east and down to the creek, where it reaches beautiful High Falls [Fig. 24(24)], probably 200 feet high. Trail length is less than 0.25 mile. The old Tate Corundum mine is high in the cliffs [Fig. 24(23)], and the remains of the old oxen haul road (with dead-packed, or mortarless, rock) up to the mine may be found to the left (west) at about the third switchback to the east. If one goes west through the cliffs, there is perhaps 50 acres of virgin slope forest. It is possible to hike through this to Chimney Rock. Bears raise and den in these cliffs [Fig. 24(22)] and are often seen in the gorge below if the visitor can remain quiet. After gaining the "top" of the cliffs on the main road, one enters an incredibly long "flat" [Fig. 24(46)]. After 1.5 miles one arrives at the Beech Creek spring [Fig. 24(28)], once the site of an Adirondack shelter. Approaching the spring on the left, one passes through an unusual climax variety of northern hardwood forest of beech with yellow birch and hop-hornbeam [Fig. 24(41)]. This is possibly a relict Ice-Age forest of the Pleistocene era 15,000 to 20,000 years ago. At this point the hiker is about 4,600 feet above sea level. Upslope, at about 4,700 feet, one enters a totally different environment—a high-altitude or northern oak ridge forest which can best be experienced on the trail [Fig. 24(26)] to the top of Big Scaly. Near Beech Creek Spring, the forest of rich black soil was once principally northern red oaks. Trees were wide apart, and the area resembled an orchard. Trunks were short and limby. One can find a few of these ancient specimens missed by loggers. There are numerous small chestnut sprouts. Fraser's fir are also here, planted, as they are on top of Standing Indian [Fig. 24(30)]. The Beech Creek Flat [Fig. 24(46)] is a mecca for wildflower lovers. The highly prized ramps or "mountain garlic" grow in profusion and are found down nearly to Bear Creek Falls in the gorge below.

Just north of the spring is an area of naked red earth, clay-rich soil which deer eat. This is the "Indian Stomp Ground" [Fig. 24(27)]. It is certainly possible that the Indians danced here, but early settlers may have invented this name as an explanation for the naked ground. Several hundred yards beyond, a log road turns left. Here a gentle nature trail [Fig. 24(26)] leads through virgin northern red oak ridge forest to the rocky summit of Big Scaly [Fig. 24(25)] (5,200 feet), surrounded by dense purple rhododendron and yielding magnificent vistas to the northwest and southwest.

One can take the very steep and poorly marked Appalachain Trail connector trail [Fig. 24(14)] to the AT, where one will find areas of

Ramp
Allium tricoccum

This wild garlic-type onion is found only above 3000 feet and then usually only in north facing coves and on sites with deep-rich soils. When its leaves first appear in the spring, ramps are gathered and eaten by mountain people. This spring ritual, a celebration of nature, has developed into ramp "festivals," drawing even presidents. By summer both leaves and flowers are gone and no trace remains.

shrub bald [Fig. 24(31)]. To the left (north) is Standing Indian Mountain (5,499 feet) [Fig. 24(30)]. To the right (south) is Little Bald (5,015 feet) [Fig. 24(38)], which one can also reach from the loop trail [Fig. 24(16)]. Just south of Little Bald is Dicks Knob [Fig. 24(39)], the third highest peak in Georgia. Just before Case Knife Gap, a few feet past the turnoffs of the Big Scaly and AT connector trails, the north-facing cove to the right has a boulder field [Fig. 24(29)] with some northern hardwoods (go down past a spring and follow the small branch). Down the loop road and through Case Knife Gap is the Chimney Rock watershed. This section is not nearly as steep as the Beech Creek section. As one goes down, one should watch carefully the ridgeline that comes down westerly from Big Scaly. Sticking slightly above it will be Chimney Rock [Fig. 24(32)]—a climbable (with great care) rock formation that affords a tremendous view of the watershed and is reached by a short (less than 0.25-mile), indistinct trail winding up through huge scenic rocks. The trail turns south in a flat about 200 yards below the last fork of Chimney Rock Branch that is forded. The main log road trail continues down, passing through a gap [Fig. 24(43)] overlooking the Waterspout watershed and then meeting the Deep Gap Trail in a serene pasture. The Girl Scouts' primitive camping area was located there [Fig. 24(33)]. Thomas Falls is located to the west of the Deep Gap Trail [Fig. 24(34)].

FACILITIES: *Three campgrounds are located on the upper Tallulah River: Tallulah [Fig. 24(4)], 17 campsites ($7.00 fee); Sandy Bottom [Fig. 24(11)], 12 campsites ($5.00 fee); and Tate Branch [Fig. 24(9)], 19 campsites and 10 picnic shelters ($6.00 fee).*

~WATERFALLS. Many of the streams entering the Tate City Valley have waterfalls.

DENTON CREEK FALLS. [Fig. 24(15)] A sheer drop easily reached about 0.25 mile upstream from the first ford (where the road is blocked).

FALL BRANCH FALLS. [Fig. 24(13)] Best visited from the top by way of the Bly Gap Trail [Fig. 24(47)], a long trail which at Bly Gap [Fig. 24(45)] intersects both the Appalachian Trail and a road down into the Shooting Creek Valley. Park at the trailhead [Fig. 24(P)].

~THE HOLDEN COVE TRAIL. [Fig. 24(48)] This trail offers a number of smaller falls. Generally moderate, it is difficult in one place. Halfway up, a logging road intercepts the trail, making the rest of the climb easy and providing a view of Chimney Rocks [Fig. 24(36)], the formidable Brushy Mountain cliff [Fig. 24(37)] and rhododendron slicks. It proceeds to intersect both the AT and the Chunky Gal Trail at White Oak Stamp [Fig. 24(42)].

~COLEMAN RIVER ROAD. [Fig. 24(1)] Wilderness access and scenic area [Fig. 24(5)].

A Canoeing Guide and Driving Tour of the Tallulah River Basin.

The guide [Fig. 25] which follows provides directions for canoeing 31.5 miles of the Tallulah River, including its scenic impounded lakes and sections of the river where Class I-IV rapids provide hints of what the river once was. The trip can be divided into six parts or done as one long trip. The driving directions to put-ins and take-outs provide an opportunity for visitors to see much of the same terrain by car.

THE FIRST TEN MILES. Although the first ten miles of the Tallulah are uncanoeable, driving streamside is worthwhile for the mountain scenery alone. See directions for the scenic drive in the previous section.

THE UPPER TALLULAH—SECTION I. This section begins 10 miles from the source of the river and offers miles of Class I-III whitewater paddling on a relatively untouched area of the river beside the Coleman River Wildlife Management Area and two miles of paddling on the backwaters of Lake Burton.

DIRECTIONS: *The put-in for Section I is at the Tallulah River Recreation Area Campground [Fig. 25(a)]. Put in either at the campground or just up the road at the Coleman River Bridge. The take-out is on US 76, 9.2 miles west of Clayton on Jones Bridge over the Tallulah River finger of Lake Burton. The best take-out point is not at Jones Bridge itself, but 0.2 mile up Vickers Road [Fig. 25(h)], which starts at the northwest corner of the bridge.*

LAKE BURTON—SECTION II. Lake Burton, the largest of the five reservoir lakes on this trip, impounds almost ten miles of the Tallulah River in its 2,775 acres. A many-fingered mountain lake with 62 miles of shoreline, Burton serves as a reservoir, controlling the water flow to Lakes Seed, Rabun, Tallulah and Tugalo below. It is a favorite spot for fishermen. Impounded in 1919 upon completion of Burton Dam, it was named after the town of Burton, which once occupied the site on which the lake now stands. Lake Burton is a large, deep lake, and canoeists must be alert for rapidly rising winds and thunderstorms. Paddling near the banks is recommended. Follow the map carefully to avoid making a wrong turn into one of its dead-end fingers.

DIRECTIONS: *This section is a 4.5-mile paddle down the lake's main Tallulah River channel, from the Jones Bridge put-in [Fig. 25(h)] to the Murray Cove take-out [Fig. 25(i)], the nearest public landing to Burton Dam. To reach Murray Cove from Jones Bridge, go east on*

Map Guide

Numbers on our map indicate river and lake mileage. Letters indicate points of interest.

Section One: Upper Tallulah River

a. Put in at Tallulah River Park.
b. Rocky rapids (mile 1).
c. Shoals (mile 2).
d. Sharp turn with strong current under bridge (mile 3).
e. Portage over wooden bridge (mile 4).
f. Plum Orchard Rd. bridge with gauge (mile 4.3).
g. Backwaters of Lake Burton (mile 5).
h. Take out on Vickers Rd beside Jones Bridge (mile 7).

Section 2: Lake Burton

h. Put in on Vickers Rd beside Jones Bridge (mile 7).
i. Take out at Murry Cove Landing (mile 11.5).
j. Burton Dam (mile 12.7).

Section 3: Seed Lake

k. Put in at base of Burton Dam (mile 12.7).
l. Take out at Seed Lake Boat Launch (mile 16.2).
m. Dam on Seed Lake (mile 17.4).

Section 4: Lake Rabun

n. Put in at base of dam on Seed Lake (mile 17.4).
o. Rabun Beach Recreation Area (mile 18.5).
p. Hall's Boat House on Lake Rabun (mile 24.5).
q. Take out at top of Mathis Dam (mile 25.4).
r. Mathis Dam (mile 25.4).

Section 5: Tallulah River and Lake

s. Put in at Tallulah River bridge (mile 26.5).
t. Loop in river, with Class II & III shoals (miles 29–30).
u. Terrora Generating Plant, with Class IV rapids (mile 30.8).
v. Tallulah Lake take out (mile 32).
w. Tallulah Dam at the top of Tallulah Gorge (mile 32.3).

Section 6: Tallulah Gorge and Tugalo Lake

x. Tallulah Gorge (mile 33).
y. West fork of Tugalo Lake (miles 34–35).
z. Put in and take out at Tugalo Dam (mile 36).

Figure 25   TALLULAH RIVER CANOEING GUIDE

162

US 76 for 2.2 miles and turn right (south) onto paved Charlie Mountain Road. Follow this road for 3.5 miles and turn right onto paved Bridge Creek Road. Go 0.3 mile and turn right onto Murray Cove Road.

LAKE SEED—SECTION III. Lake Seed, sometimes called Lake Nacoochee, offers a canoeing experience entirely different from that offered by Lake Burton. Burton's wide and many-fingered layout provides breathtaking views of distant mountains. Seed, on the other hand, is tight and narrow and follows the original bed of the Tallulah River quite closely. Seed is 4.5 miles long, impounded by the 75-foot-high Nacoochee Dam completed in 1926. The lake has a 13-mile shoreline. The canoe route goes 3.5 miles from the put-in at the base of Burton Dam [Fig. 25(k)] to the public boat ramp on Lake Seed [Fig. 25(l)].

DIRECTIONS: *Put-in for this 3.5-mile trip is at the base of Burton Dam [Fig. 25(k)] (mile 12.7 on the map). Take Murray Cove Road to its intersection with Bridge Creek Road, turn right and go 1.6 miles to Lake Rabun Road. Turn right (west) and go 0.5 mile to the bridge over the Tallulah River at the base of Burton Dam.*

LAKE RABUN—SECTION IV. Lake Rabun has been a most popular recreation area for many years. Houses and cottages were built on its shores as early as the 1930's, and today its 25-mile shoreline is dotted with homes. Georgia Power Company, which owns most of the shoreline and leases land for homes, limits development, so sprawling motel complexes are not present. This eight-mile trip is winding and scenic, offering a stop at the popular Rabun Beach Recreation Area [Fig. 25(o)] located just off Lake Rabun Road. On the lake, stick close to shore to avoid heavy motorboat traffic. The Nacoochee Park Recreation Area [Fig. 25(n)] offers picnic tables and restrooms.

DIRECTIONS: *Put-in for Lake Rabun is at the base of the dam on Lake Seed at the Nacoochee Park Recreation Area [Fig. 25(n)] just off Lake Rabun Road. Take-out is at Hall's Boat House in the little town of Lakemont [Fig. 25(p)].*

TALLULAH RIVER AND LAKE TALLULAH—SECTION V. The special feature of this 5.5-mile stretch is that it follows for 4 miles the original bed of the Tallulah River, offering significant rapids including a Class IV. The final 1.5 miles are on a lake complete with waterfalls and mountain streams trickling along its banks. This small lake, only 63 acres, is impounded by the 130-foot-tall Tallulah Dam. Completed in 1912, it was the first dam built on the Tallulah River. Its construction on the rim of Tallulah Gorge cut off most of the water for Tallulah Falls. Unlike its sister lakes, it is full of yellow perch.

DIRECTIONS: *The take-out for this stretch is in Terrora Park behind the Terrora Visitor Center [Fig. 25(v)] off US 441 at Tallulah Dam [Fig. 25(w)]. To reach the put-in, leave Terrora Park, turn left onto old US 441 and go 4.0 miles to the put-in bridge. At 1.6 miles into the shuttle, old US 441 joins the current US 441 for about 100 yards; turn left at this intersection. Stay on old 441, which leaves the new road at the signs pointing to Lake Rabun. The put-in, located 1.0 mile downstream from Mathis Dam at the junction of the Tallulah River and Tiger Creek [Fig. 25(s)], is steep. Best access is at the northwest corner of the bridge.*

To scout the river, take the road that leads across the river to the Terrora Generating Station [Fig. 25(u)] 0.8 mile from Terrora Park, and to a bridge over the Tallulah River 0.9 mile beyond the park. These are good places from which to scout the four dangerous rapids in this section, one of them rated Class IV.

TALLULAH GORGE AND LAKE TUGALO—SECTION VI. The last two miles of canoeable water on the Tallulah River are in Tallulah Gorge, on the west finger of Lake Tugalo [Fig. 26(60)]. This section is canoed as a four-mile round trip, using the same point as put-in and take-out. The Tugaloo River begins where the Tallulah and Chattooga Rivers meet, and its name, in Cherokee, means "fork of a stream." Lake Tugalo was formed with the completion of the Tugalo Dam [Fig. 26(63)] and Hydroelectric Plant on the Tugaloo River in 1922.

Lake Tugalo covers 597 acres and has 18 miles of shoreline. The property around the lake is undeveloped. Tugalo is surrounded by a mixed pine-and-hardwood forest that has been relatively undisturbed by logging because of its steep shoreline.

Tugalo is a beautiful lake for both fisherman and canoeist. Catfish and bass fishing are good. Tugalo is one of the few lakes in Georgia where canoeing and slow boat traffic are the norm. On a leisurely day's paddle around the lake a canoeist can explore many spots only accessible by water. Paddling up the Tallulah River arm of the lake leads into the Tallulah Gorge; paddling on the eastern side leads into the Chattooga Gorge [Fig. 26 & 31(61)]. Waterfalls cascade into the lake at several points, and spring and summer wildflowers are abundant. Wildlife in the area include deer and turkey. There are plenty of places to stop along the shore to stretch, have a picnic or explore. Fires and camping are allowed only in Tugalo Park.

On the South Carolina side the ramp [Fig. 26&31(31)] is very steep and difficult to navigate with a big boat and trailer. The parking lot here is often full during rafting season, this being a popular take-out point for rafters completing Section IV of the

Chattooga River. There are no restroom facilities at the parking area.

Tugalo Park [Fig. 26(62)] has primitive campsites level and big enough for a tent or small trailer. There is no reservation system. The boat ramp in the park is level and graveled, giving access to the northern end of Lake Yonah.

FACILITIES: *Primitive camping, picnic tables, non-flush restrooms, boat ramps, parking.*

DATES/HOURS: *Check with the Georgia Power office at Terrora Park, (404) 754-6036 for date of opening of Tugalo Park. It will be closed for construction during 1990.*

DIRECTIONS: *Access to Lake Tugalo from the South Carolina side is at Long Creek, SC. Take US 76 east from Clayton approximately 10.7 miles to Long Creek; go south on Orchard Road (S37-538) for 2.6 miles to Battlecreek Road; turn right and go 2.5 miles to Damascus Church Road; turn right again. Just past Damascus Church (1.2 miles) turn right on Tugalo Lake Road (gravel); go 3.9 miles (the last mile is paved) to the boat landing on Lake Tugalo below the Chattooga River [Fig. 26&31(31)].*

For directions and a U.S. Forest Service map of the Chattooga River Corridor ($2), stop at the Chattooga Whitewater Shop on US 76 in Long Creek.

ADDITIONAL INFORMATION: *Georgia Power Company, Terrora Park, US 23/441, P.O. Box 9, Tallulah Falls, GA 30573. (404) 754-6036.*

Figure 26   LOWER TALLULAH BASIN/PANTHER CREEK

Fraser's magnolia
Magnolia fraseri

The magnolia is a primitive tree and a southern element that has "invaded" the mountains. Of the two principal mountain species, Fraser's is easy to identify by the "ear lobes" at the base of the rather large leaves borne in a radial cluster.

Recreation Areas and Hiking Trails

MOCCASIN CREEK STATE PARK. [Fig. 27(12)] This is a small park, 32 acres, built on a flood-plain flat at the mouth of Moccasin Creek on the shore of Lake Burton. It is an excellent base of operations for area sightseeing, hiking and other recreational activities.

FACILITIES: *53 campsites, boat ramp and dock, wheelchair-accessible fishing pier, stream and lake fishing, lakeside picnic area, playground, open-air pavillion, trout hatchery, laundry facilities, comfort stations.*
DATES/HOURS: *Daily 7am-10 pm year round; office open 8am-5pm.*
Special Events: Daily interpretive programs Jun-Aug; annual special events include Lake Burton Fun Run, All About Mountain Trout and Lake Burton Arts and Crafts Festival.
DIRECTIONS: *Located 20 miles north of Clarkesville on GA 197 and 17 miles west of Clayton (take US 76 west to GA 197).*
ADDITIONAL INFORMATION: *Moccasin Creek State Park, Georgia Department of Natural Resources, Rt 1, Box 1634, Clarkesville, GA 30523. (404) 947-3194.*

NON-GAME WILDLIFE TRAIL. [Fig. 27(13)] 1.2-mile loop trail. Along the way are grassy fields, areas of old field pines—that is, white, Virginia and pitch pine—and old field scrub lacking a tree canopy. There is an extensive area of deciduous hardwoods with poplar, red oak and occasional sycamore. In this community along Moccasin Creek, alders dominate the creek bank along with dog hobbles and some American holly. Yellowroot, a mountain medicinal herb, occurs along the stream.

DIRECTIONS: *Trailhead is at the trout hatchery intake across the highway from the Moccasin Creek State Park entrance (see above).*

MOCCASIN CREEK TRAIL. [Fig. 27(13)] 6.2 miles. This trail follows Moccasin Creek, a beautiful trout stream with several waterfalls. It eventually passes several log roads which lead to FS Road 26-1 and to Addis Gap and the northern edge of the Tray Mountain Wilderness. A hardwood-rhododendron community with hemlock and white pine prevails along the creek. The canopy is mostly poplar, red oak, white pine, black birch and hemlock. Fraser's magnolia occurs. The beautiful high falls is about a one-hour walk from the trailhead.

DIRECTIONS: *The trailhead is the same as for the Non-Game Wildlife Trail, above.*

Guide To The North Georgia Mountains

Georgia Power Public Use Areas

(1) Jones Bridge Park
Hwy. 76 on Lake Burton
• Two sheltered picnic tables

(2) Timpson Cove Beach
Charlie Mountain Rd. on Lake Burton
• White sand beach • Picnic Area • Restrooms

(3) Murray Cove Boat Launch Area
Bridge Creek Rd. on Lake Burton
• Paved boat ramp for small and medium boats

(4) Lake Seed Boat Launch Area
Lake Rabun Rd. on Lake Seed
• Gravel boat ramp for small boats

(5) Lake Seed Campground
County Rd. on Lake Seed (follow signs)
• Wilderness campsites
• White sand beach • Picnic area
• Latrines • No water available

(6) Nacoochee Park
Lake Rabun Rd. on Tallulah River just below
Nacoochee Dam
• Picnic area • Restrooms

(7) Terrora Park and Education Center
Hwy 23/441 on Tallulah Lake
Camping Area
• Fifty campsites with electrical and water hook-
  ups, tables and grills
• Bath house with hot showers
• Playground • Pavilion

Park
• White sand beach with lifeguard in season
• Lighted tennis courts • Pavilion • Playground
• Picnic area • Restrooms • Fishing pier
• Nature trails and Tallulah Gorge overlook
• Playing field

Education Center
• Exhibits on electricity and North Georgia Hydro
  system
• Displays on mountain habitat, area history,
  pioneer culture and crafts
• Information on Georgia Power recreation areas

(8) Tallulah Point
Off Hwy 23/441 on hill overlooking Tallulah Gorge
(follow signs)
• Two sheltered picnic areas • Restrooms

(9) Tugalo Park
Off Hwy 23/441 below Tugalo Dam (follow signs)
• Primitive camping area • Restrooms
• Boat launch area

(10) Yonah Park
Ga. Hwy 184 to Yonah Dam Rd. on Lake Yonah
• Picnic area

0   3
Miles

Figure 27   TALLULAH BASIN RECREATION AREAS

RABUN BEACH RECREATION AREA AND HIKING TRAIL. [Fig. 27(14)] Located amidst lovely mountain scenery of 934-acre Lake Rabun, the hiking trail starts from camping area number two on Joe Branch and goes 0.5 mile to Panther Falls and 1.0 mile to Angel Falls. From late spring until July the trail travels through an outstanding display of flowering rhododendron.

FACILITIES: *Two camping areas on the opposite side of the road from the beach contain 80 campsites, restrooms, hiking, boating, fishing, swimming.*

DATES/HOURS: *7am-10pm Mon-Thu, 7am-11pm Fri-Sun, May 15-Nov 1.*

FEES: *$5 per campsite.*

DIRECTIONS: *Take US 23/441 north from Clarkesville for 14.4 miles or south from Clayton 9.6 miles to the National Forest, and Rabun Beach Recreation Area signs. Turn west on unnumbered county road and go 2.6 miles; turn left (south) on unnumbered road (old US 441) and go 4.8 miles.*

ADDITIONAL INFORMATION: *Rabun Beach Recreation Area, Chattahoochee National Forest, Tallulah Ranger District, Chechero/Savannah St., P.O. Box 438, Clayton, GA 30525. (404) 782-3320.*

MINNEHAHA TRAIL. [Fig. 27(14)] This 0.4-mile trail follows Fall Branch until it dead ends at 50-foot-high Minnehaha Falls.

DIRECTIONS: *From the Rabun Beach Recreation Area above, continue past the recreation area for 1.0 mile and turn left, crossing the river below Lake Seed Dam. Follow the left fork of the road for 1.7 miles to a sign marking the trail on the right side of the road.*

HIKING IN TALLULAH BASIN. The quartzite gorge made by the Tallulah River is the deepest single vertical cut in bedrock in the region, if not in the eastern United States. The gray-brown rock cliffs, pine-covered walls and numerous waterfalls all contribute to the gorge's year-round scenic quality. The marvelous vistas will appeal to photographers.

The gorge can be seen when looking south from the US 441 bridge atop the dam. Approximately 200 feet at this point, it gets deeper downriver. Much of the gorge can be seen from the rim or rim trails. The north rim trail begins in Terrora Park [Fig. 25(v)] and goes under the highway bridge to an overlook. The south rim trail begins at Tallulah Gorge Park.

Access to the gorge is limited, although several unmarked trails lead into it. Most of these trails are very steep and dangerous. The most accessible trail is found to the south of the Wallenda cable tower site [Fig. 26(64)] and leads south to the bottom. Another trail

begins inside the Tallulah Gorge Park [Fig. 26(65)]. Because of the
many dangers that exist in the gorge, check with Georgia Power's
Terrora Visitor Center before making a decision to enter the gorge.
They strongly recommend seeing a short video and reading a
brochure that explains the beauty and dangers of the gorge. Flash
flooding in the gorge could happen at any time *without warning*. If
a flash flood occurs, get to high ground immediately.

The rare persistent trillium and a wealth of other flora are
found in the gorge, as is the green salamander, a rare crevice-
dweller. The bird density is low, consisting mainly of vultures,
phoebes and swallows. Both the rare Carolina hemlock and table
mountain pine grow around the gorge rim. Carolina rhododendron is
unusually abundant, and this is one of the few areas where the rare
fringed polygala may be found.

Tallulah Falls School is planning a museum for Tallulah Gorge
Park.

FACILITIES: *A short (less than 0.25-mile) trail overlooking the gorge.*
DATES/HOURS: *Open every day Apr-Oct 10-5.*
FEES: *Adults $2, children $.75.*
DIRECTIONS: *The gorge is located south of the highway bridge and
immediately east of US 441 within the town limits of Tallulah Falls,
12 miles south of Clayton.*
ADDITIONAL INFORMATION: *Georgia Power Company, Tallulah Falls,
GA (404) 754-3161* (Visitor Center) or (404) 754-6036 (camping and
day use area).

PANTHER CREEK RECREATION AREA AND HIKING TRAIL. [Fig. 26
& 27(11)] Panther Creek originates on the southern slope of Stony
Mountain at an elevation of 2,440 feet, meanders down 940 feet
before crossing US 23 and 441 at the recreation area and empties
into the Tugaloo River, which forms the border between Georgia and
South Carolina. According to scientists who have studied the area,
the natural features of Panther Creek Gorge have changed little
during the past million years.

The six-mile Panther Creek hiking and nature trail [Fig. 26(11)],
marked with blue blazes, begins at the Panther Creek Recreation
Area. It winds through a forest of poplar, hemlock, white pine, oak,
hickory and red maple, with an occasional birch, as it follows the
steep, rocky bluffs of the creek. The trees, some of which are over
100 feet tall, provide shade in the summer and a display of colorful
foliage in the fall. There are many rock cliffs with mosses and ferns
growing in the moist crevices. In early spring trout lilies appear,
followed by violets and trillium. Trailing arbutus, dwarf iris and
gay-wings grow low to the ground. Spring flowering shrubs along
the trail include service berry, Carolina bells and horse sugar. There
are masses of mountain laurel blooming in May, and the white and
pink blossoms of the rhododendron are present well into June. The

Rainbow trout
(Onocorhynchus mykiss)

Native to the Sierras and mountains of the West Coast, rainbow were introduced into north Georgia by the legendary forest ranger Arthur Woody. More aggressive than the native brook trout, and an egg-eater, they have displaced the native "specks" from all but the tiniest headwater streams.

flowers of the dogwood and silver bell trees add to the beauty of the spring display.

The creek itself drops in a series of cascades. Little Panther Creek enters Panther Creek .6 mile before the stream turns sharply east at Mill Shoals, a former mill site [Fig. 26(69)]. Approximately 0.5 mile further, 3.6 miles from Panther Creek Recreation Area and 2.4 miles from the eastern end of the trail, the creek falls 60 to 70 feet into a pool [Fig. 26(70)]. The trail leads down to the pool where there is a grand view of the falling water. This waterfall is preceeded by an impressive High-Shoals Falls which could be mistaken for the more dramatic falls farther on. The trail ends at a dirt road near the point where Davidson Creek joins Panther Creek. The road continues for two miles to Lake Yonah Dam and Park. Do not plan to hike out and return to Panther Creek Recreation Area by road from Lake Yonah. It would be a very long walk.

The eastern, or lower, end of the trail is designated a Protected Botanical Area [Fig. 26(68)] by the U.S. Forest Service because of the richness and diversity of its plant life. This area is unique because it is within the Brevard Fault Zone. A relatively narrow band of limestone within the fault supports vegetation not commonly found in north Georgia. The soil allows calcium-loving plants, such as chinquapin oak to thrive here. The herbs, in particular, are remarkable.

Panther Creek Trail is recommended for day use only, since overnight camping areas are limited and water along the trail is not safe for drinking. The trail is moderately difficult to hike, with a few steep places. Hikers carrying heavy packs should be aware of the rocky overhangs and narrow trails.

Panther Creek, home to rainbow trout and redeye bass, is classified as a secondary trout stream. Fishing schedules are available on Georgia fishing licenses, which are renewable annually.

FACILITIES: *Recreation area, parking, restrooms, picnic tables with some shelters, hand pump for water, blazed hiking and nature trail.*
DATES/HOURS: *Trail open all year; recreation area closed in winter.*
DIRECTIONS: *Panther Creek Recreation area is 9 miles north of Clarkesville and 3.6 miles south of Tallulah Falls on US 23/441. A four-lane highway parallel to the existing one is scheduled to be completed by 1992.*
ADDITIONAL INFORMATION: *Panther Creek, U.S. Forest Service, Chattahoochee National Forest, Burton Road, Clarkesville, GA 30523. (404)754-6221.*

~TERRORA PARK AND VISITOR CENTER.

FACILITIES: *50 campsites with water and electrical hookups, restrooms, picnic area with shelters, rest areas, swimming beach, bathhouse with hot and cold showers, audio-visual displays about Georgia Power lake* *system.*

DATES/HOURS: *Open Wed-Sun.*
FEES: *$8 per tent, $9 per RV.*
DIRECTIONS: *Terrora Park is immediately north of the US 441 bridge over Tallulah Gorge in the town of Tallulah Falls.*
ADDITIONAL INFORMATION: *Georgia Power Company, Terrora Park, US 441, P.O. Box 9, Tallulah Falls, GA 30573. (404) 754-3276 (Visitor Center) or (404) 754-6036 (camping and day use area).*

~LAKE YONAH. [Fig. 27(15)] Lake Yonah, one of six lakes managed by Georgia Power Company, was formed when the Yonah Dam and Hydroelectric Plant were completed on the Tugalo River between Georgia and South Carolina in 1925. Yonah, meaning "big black bear" in Cherokee, is immediately south of Lake Tugalo and covers 325 acres. The land adjacent to the lake being very steep, there has been little timber harvested here. Happily, there remains an undisturbed heavy forest of pines and hardwoods. This area has a great diversity of plant life, including many wildflowers. Other than the common Georgia wildlife, including deer and turkey, there is an occasional bear. Private homes are built around the nine miles of shoreline, leaving the only public access to the lake at the boat ramps. The Lake Yonah boat ramp is paved and level. There is a small dock. The parking lot will hold approximately 15 cars and trailers. A dumpster is provided for trash. There are no restroom facilities.

The lake is popular year-round for canoeing and fishing for catfish and bass and in the summertime for waterskiing. Canoeists must use caution on the lake in warm weather because of the fast and constant ski traffic. The lake can be paddled easily in a day. A put-in spot to the right of the dam has many seasonal wildflowers and is good for picnicking.

~LAKE YONAH PARK. [Fig. 27(10), Fig. 26(66)] Located below the dam overlooking Tugaloo River, it has three picnic tables, trash cans and limited parking. The river banks are steep and overgrown, making access to the river difficult.

FACILITIES: *Picnic tables, parking, boat ramps, trash cans, dumpster, nature trail access.*
DIRECTIONS: *Yonah Dam road turns off GA 184 near its intersection with GA 17. Follow signs to Walker Creek boat ramp, Yonah boat ramp [Fig. 26(67)] and Lake Yonah Park [Fig. 26(66)].*
ADDITIONAL INFORMATION: *Georgia Power Company, Terrora Park, US Hwy 23/441, P.O. Box 9, Tallulah Falls, GA 30573. (404) 754-6036.*

MAP REFERENCES: *USGS 1:24,000 series: Tallulah Falls - Tugaloo Lake - Rainbow springs - Hightower Bald; Browns Guide, May 82*

Coweeta Creek and Betty Creek Valleys

~BETTY CREEK VALLEY. [Fig. 28(16)] This entrance to the eastern boundary of the Southern Nantahala Wilderness is one of the most beautiful valleys in north Georgia. Combining good hiking, scenic views and pleasant driving tours with the possibility of visits to the Hambidge Center or the Coweeta Hydrologic Laboratory, it will appeal to visitors with recreational, scientific or cultural interests.

Betty Creek Road [Fig. 28(16)] offers a scenic drive through this serene valley. The total distance from the turn-off at Dillard to the North Carolina state line where the pavement ends is about six miles. The continuation of the road (NC 1104) crosses Beasley Gap and descends Mulberry Creek [Fig. 28(21)] to a beautiful spring wildflower area which is accessible by car. It eventually comes out on US 441 south of Otto, NC.

~THE HAMBIDGE CENTER. [Fig. 28(19)] The creation of Mary Hambidge, a feminist, environmentalist and preserver of mountain culture who was 50 years ahead of her time. She helped her husband, Jay Hambidge, codify his ideas on classical design principles, which they labeled Dynamic Symmetry. Their work gained international recognition. Mary encouraged local crafts, particularly dyeing and weaving, done in the large loom room at the center. She perfected a range of vegetable dyes which has never been duplicated. She decorated President Truman's yacht, designed costumes for dancer Isadora Duncan and opened a successful shop on Madison Avenue in New York. Elliott Wigginton, who went on to found *Foxfire*, a hugely successful series of publications dedicated to the preservation of mountain culture, was a protege of hers. In later years she became reclusive.

Today the Hambidge Center, which consists of an office building, gallery, workshop, dining hall and a number of cabins on 600 picturesque acres, organizes workshops, seminars, and film and concert series. Approximately 20 different programs are offered during the months of May to October. In addition, each year the center awards 20 to 25 resident fellowships to encourage creative exploration and inner self-renewal.

The center is open daily Monday through Friday from 9 to 5. Visitors are asked to register in the office and are welcome to walk the center's nature trails. There is also a water-powered grist mill known as the Barker's Creek Mill, restored for the third time in 1988. It is usually open on Fridays and Saturdays for grinding grains brought by local residents.

DIRECTIONS: *On Betty Creek Road west of Dillard.*

Figure 28 COWEETA CREEK & BETTY CREEK VALLEYS

Witch hazel
Hammamelis virginiana

Witch hazel is fond of quite moist sites. It has the curious habit of blooming after its leaves have fallen, often in cold weather. Oil of witch hazel has scented a number of commercial liniments.

ADDITIONAL INFORMATION: *The Hambidge Center, P.O. Box 33, Rabun Gap, GA 30568. (404) 746-5718.*

~**PATTERSON GAP.** [Fig. 28(8)] The road to Patterson Gap (FS 32) [Fig. 28(17)] turns left off Betty Creek Road about 3.5 miles from US 441 and crosses a bridge. As one climbs a steep grade, off to the left is Patterson Creek Falls [Fig. 28(18)]. FS 32 passes through Moon Valley. After entering U.S Forest Service land, the road is steep but scenic through great coves of tulip poplar [Fig. 28(15)] which have come in after the death of the chestnut in the 1930's and following logging. Crossing Patterson Gap, one circles a cove hardwood forest [Fig. 28(35)], then descends along a pitch pine ridge [Fig. 28(9)]. Along the road banks grows the rare sweetfern. This road eventually joins Persimmon Road, which dead ends at US 76.

~**GRASSY RIDGE TRAIL.** [Fig. 28(11)] At Patterson Gap [Fig. 28(8)], a well-known trail goes up Grassy Ridge, forking off to the right to Till Ridge Cove [Fig. 28(10)], considered by many to be one of the finest botanical areas in the state. From over 1,000 trillium nodding their heads in the spring to dazzling displays of golden witch hazel blooms in late October, the cove offers a constant pageant of wildflowers. The left fork eventually crosses the west side of the ridge at Nichols' Gap [Fig. 28(34)] and encounters the Appalachian Trail at Carter's Gap [Fig. 28(12)]. Hikers along this trail can look up at Ridgepole Mountain [Fig. 28(13)] (5,007 feet), with its heath thickets out of which emerge some evergreens. South of Patterson Gap stands Wolf Knob [Fig. 28(33)] (3,329 feet). North-facing coves in this area have lush and interesting herb flora [Fig. 28(7)].

~**KEENER CREEK HIKING TRAIL.** [Fig. 28(5)] A nice trail goes up Keener Creek from the Wolf Fork Valley loop road past two waterfalls [Fig. 28(4)] in a gorge to the left, at or near the U.S. Forest Service boundary. Adventurous hikers equipped with topographic maps (the Dillard Quadrangle) will notice a large flat area at the head of Keener Creek which should be interesting botanically. This area can be reached from either Patterson Gap or up an old log road turning off the paved Wolf Fork Valley Road just east of the junction with the gravelled Blue Ridge Gap Road.

~**COWEETA HYDROLOGIC LABORATORY.** [Fig. 28(31)] The Coweeta Hydrologic Laboratory, site of a long-term ecological research program, is studying several watersheds for the effects of logging and other forest management practices on water yields and quality. Roadside signs indicate the experimental areas and explain the experiments. It is advisable to stop at the office to obtain a map of the area before beginning any exploration. The 14-mile driving tour takes approximately one hour.

DATES/HOURS: *The laboratory is open 7:30 to 4, Mon-Fri, closed holidays. The road to hiking trails, Pickens' Nose and Cherokee Cave is closed intermittently during periods of bad weather between Jan 1 and Mar 15.*
DIRECTIONS: *From Dillard, go north on US 441 4.3 miles to Coweeta Hydrologic Laboratory sign. Turn left and follow signs 2.9 miles to the parking lot.*

~DRIVE UP BALL CREEK [FIG. 28(37)] TO PICKENS' NOSE TRAIL HEAD [FIG. 28(26)]. This long and curvy climb leads first to Reynolds Gap [Fig. 28(36)]. Take the left fork at Reynolds Gap to the first place one can see down the slope both north and south of the road. From the pull-off [Fig. 28(25)] here, a short and fairly level trail leads south to the famed "Cherokee Cave," a huge overhanging ledge on the west side of Rockhouse Knob [Fig. 28(24)]. Mountain legend holds that a band of Cherokees hid out here to avoid being driven to Oklahoma during the Indian removal known as the Trail of Tears. Below is a veritable rock city [Fig. 28(23)] of gigantic boulders fractured and fallen from the cliff above. Growing on them are some plants characteristic of boulderfields—a vine-like gooseberry, for example. Further down the cove of Barkers Creek [Fig. 28(22)] is a rich area with spring seeps and abundant herbs such as turks cap lillies. This is a nice hike, but the lower end is private, so visitors should inquire.

The right fork at Reynolds Gap [Fig. 28(36)] leads to another gap [Fig. 28(26)] where parking is obvious on the right. The Pickens' Nose Trail [Fig. 28(30)] begins here on the left. It is a relatively gentle climb of less than a mile to the top [Fig. 28(29)]. The vegetation and views make it a very attractive hike. At 0.3 mile, watch for a short spur trail to a rock cliff on the left [Fig. 28(27)] with a great view to the east. The trail runs through northern red oak ridge forest but gradually changes more to rhododendron and shrubs. Watch for purple rhododendron and the rarer minniebush, *menziesia*, along with the common mountain laurel. At the Pickens' Nose Cliffs [Fig. 28(28)] is one of the best views in the eastern part of the wilderness as one gazes out over the vast Betty Creek Cove, 2,000 feet below, to Ridgepole and beyond. Outward Bound and others teach cliff climbing here. With care, exploration is possible down, around and under the cliffs. Plants that grow only on cliffs are found here. One, St. John's wort, is found only on high rock outcrops in the Southern Appalachians.

Albert Mountain [Fig. 28(32)] can be reached by continuing on FS with a short hike on the Appalachian Trail. It affords fine views.

MAP REFERENCES: *USGS 1:24,000 series: Prentiss - Dillard.*

Peregrine falcon
Falco peregrinus

Peregrines formerly nested in the cliffs and gorges of the Blue Ridge and northwest Georgia. They have even visited the "cliffs" of Atlanta's taller buildings and have used the Hurt Building, feeding on the pigeons that cross the park below. With controls on pesticides, these falcons are making a comeback.

Blue cohosh
Caulophyllum thalictroides

This characteristic plant of the deep mountain coves, unlike some of its cohorts such as baneberry and black cohosh, does not appear to occur in the northern Piedmont. It has blue berries which are poisonous.

Black Rock Mountain State Park

Black Rock Mountain State Park, named for its sheer cliffs [Fig. 29(1)] of dark granite, has the distinction of being Georgia's highest state park. It stretches over three miles along the Eastern Continental Divide, the spine of the Southern Blue Ridge Mountains. Containing six different peaks above 3,000 feet in elevation, it covers more than 1,500 acres. From its overlooks on a clear day, visitors may see mountaintop views extending for more than 80 miles. Among the areas of the Southern Appalachians visible are the Nantahala Mountains, the Cowee Range and—on especially clear days—the Great Smoky Mountains.

The park is noted for its many spring wildflowers, including several varieties of trillium, violets, bloodroot and flame azalea. In early summer, masses of mountain laurel and rhododendron are in bloom. In fall, leaves of oak, maple, sourwood and other deciduous trees and shrubs create a spectacular blaze of yellow, orange and red. Evergreens present a contrasting note. Goldenrod and other fall blooms add to the show. The most common natural environment in the park is a deciduous hardwood slope forest with red oaks dominant. Chestnut oaks in drier places and white oaks in certain areas lend diversity.

Animals in the park include gray squirrels, chipmunks, opossums, black bear, foxes, woodchucks, bobcats, skunks and occasional deer. There are wild turkey, ruffed grouse and, in season, many kinds of songbirds.

FACILITIES: *1,502 acres, 53 tent and trailer sites, 11 walk-in campsites, 10 rental cottages, playground, 2 picnic shelters, 17-acre lake and 10-mile trail system.*
DATES/HOURS: *Daily 7am-10pm year round; office open 8am-5pm.* Special Events: Spring wildflowers, May; overnight backpacking trip, fall.
DIRECTIONS: *In Mountain City, 3 miles north of Clayton via US 441.*
ADDITIONAL INFORMATION: *Black Rock Mountain State Park, Mountain City, GA 30562. (404) 746-2141.*

~TENNESSEE ROCK TRAIL. 2.2 miles. This trail passes through five different natural environments. The road west of the visitor center runs close to a ridgeline. At the Tennessee Rock Overlook there is much rock and the red oaks [Fig. 29(2)] are stunted and lichen-covered; about the only shrub is rosebay rhododendron. A little further along is the summit of Black Rock Mountain (3,640 feet), which is apparently just high enough to have on its north face a boulderfield [Fig. 29(3)] with some herbs, such as blue cohosh, indicative of moist, high elevations. Another plant of this type is the rarer and spectacular umbrella leaf. In the spring, fine wildflower

BLACK ROCK MOUNTAIN STATE PARK

Legend:
- ▲ Picnic Shelter
- ■ Cottage
- ◀ Comfort/Rest Station
- ⛺ Camping
- - - - Hiking Trail
- 🅿 Parking

To Wolffork Valley

Black Rock Lake

(Gravel)

Lookoff Mountain Overlook

Lookoff Mtn. el. 3162'

Backcountry

Marsen Knob el. 3205

Staff Residence

Scruggs Knob el. 3048'

James E. Edmonds Backcountry Trail (7.2 mi.)

To U.S. Route 441 Mountain City

Park Entrance

Greasy Creek

Gate

Taylor Creek

(Gravel)

TENNESSEE VALLEY DIVIDE

To German Valley

Staff Residence

Boundary Point Knob el. 3010'

Tennessee Rock Trail (2.2 mi.)

Tennessee Rock Overlook

Cowee Overlook

Ada-Hi Falls Trail (0.2 mi.)

Nantahala Overlook

C.S.

Tent and R.V.

Black Rock Mtn. el. 3640'

Playground

Black Rock Overlook

Trading Post

C.S.

C.S. Walk-In

Visitor Center & Rest Station

Cottage Area

Pioneer

0   2000
Feet

Adapted with permission from Georgia DNR

Figure 29   BLACK ROCK MOUNTAIN STATE PARK

displays are found here. The trees among the rocks are principally basswood and black birch. After leaf fall, clumps of intermediate wood fern and alum root are very visible. In summer the boulderfield is not visible from the trail, and the hiker must walk 150 feet to the lower edge of it at the second poplar cove (from either direction). Below the boulderfield is a poplar cove [Fig. 29(4)], one of three along the trail. Along the western edge of the park is an almost pure white-pine stand [Fig. 29(8)], the only one in the park. It probably seeded in after intensive logging of hardwoods.

~JAMES EDMONDS BACK COUNTRY TRAIL. 7.2 miles. Along this trail there are two patches of hemlock forest [Fig. 29(5)] and more extensive areas of red oak-rhododendron [Fig. 29(6)] in moist places, with mountain laurel replacing rhododendron in drier locations [Fig. 29(7)]. Where the rhododendron is thin, large patches of evergreen galax or "coltsfeet" are present.

~ADA-HI FALLS TRAIL. 0.2 mile. *Ada-Hi* is the Cherokee word for "forest." This hike starts out in the most common natural environment in the park—a deciduous hardwood-slope forest with red oaks dominant, chestnut oaks in drier places and white oaks in certain places. This phases into a red oak/rhododendron environment with huge patches of the evergreen galax in open places and ends in a cove of tulip poplars. Spring wildflowers can be seen along the trail; yellow root and rare grass of parnassus, along the streams. The cove of tulip poplars along the Ada-Hi trail was once heavily logged of hardwood timber [Fig. 29(17)].

Flame azalea
Rhododendron calendulaceum

This deciduous rhododendron with its showy yellow, orange or red blossoms gloriously dominates mountain forests in the spring, following the service berry. A common companion at high elevations is red oak-flame azalea.

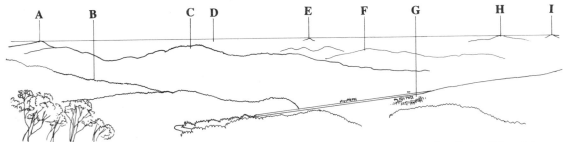

SOUTH VISTA
View from Black Rock Overlook

A - Rainy Mountain
B - Warwoman Valley
C - Screamer Mountain
D - South Carolina Piedmont
E - Pine Mountain
F - Stroud Mountain
G - City of Clayton
H - Cliff Mountain
I - Currahee Mountain

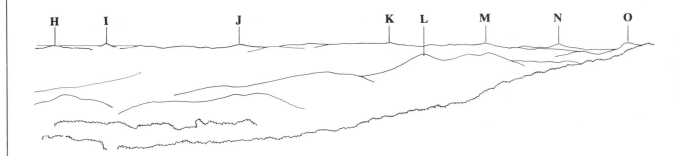

SOUTH VISTA (Continued)
View from Black Rock Overlook

H - Cliff Mountain
I - Currahee Mountain
J - Hickory Nut Mountain
K - Joe Mountain
L - Tiger Mountain
M - Oakey Mountain
N - Yonah Mountain
O - Glassy Mountain

The Georgia Conservancy

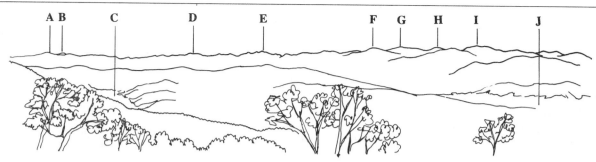

NORTH AND WEST VISTA
View from Tennessee Rock Overlook

A - Kelly Knob
B - Brasstown Bald
C - Germany Valley
D - Eagle Mountain
E - Hightower Bald

F - Dicks Knob
G - Little Bald
H - Standing Indian
I - Ridgepole Mountain
J - Wolffork Valley

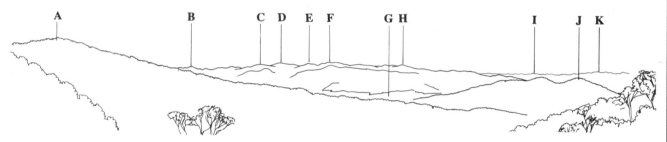

NORTHWEST VISTA
View from Nantahala Overlook

A - Black Rock Mountain, north summit
B - Hightower Bald
C - Dicks Knob
D - Little Bald
E - Standing Indian
F - Ridgepole Mountain

G - Wolffork Valley
H - Pickens Nose
I - Cowee Bald
J - Marsen Knob
K - Fishawk Mountain

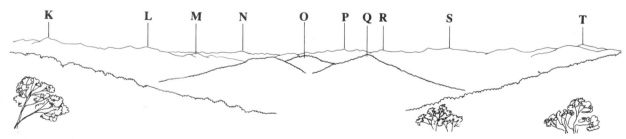

NORTHEAST VISTA
View from Cowee Overlook

K - Pickens Nose
L - Doubletop Mountain
M - Hannah Mountain
N - Cowee Bald
O - Lookoff Mountain

P - Fishawk Mountain
Q - Marsen Knob
R - Jones Knob
S - Scaly Mountain
T - Rabun Bald

~BEDROCK AND SOIL FORMATIONS. Black Rock provides a good look at some fundamental processes of nature involving bedrock and soil formations. At the trailhead parking area one may look closely at the cut bank and, as an experiment, even plunge a knife into its various layers. Most are soft. Seeping water, held by the leaf litter and soil above, has decomposed the hard bedrock. If there is enough iron in the rock the surface soil will be redder, as here. This decayed rock is called saprolite. If conditions are right it can decay 12 feet deep, in the process releasing about 22 different minerals needed by the plants and animals.

About nine feet up on the bank is a protruding group of harder rocks which refuse to decay rapidly. This is usually the source of broken rock, or "float," which one sees on the surface of the ground.

An entirely different situation is present at Tennessee Rock Overlook. The type of rock here does not weather deeply. It drains well and dries out rapidly. There is no red soil but rather a dark-brown forest soil which develops under rhododendron. The rocky top of this ridge suggests that it is a type of rock which resists decay. A similar hard quartzite rock is responsible for Tallulah Falls.

MAP REFERENCES: *Black Rock State Park Map.*

Rabun Bald

Rabun Bald (4,696 feet) [Fig. 30(11)] is the second-highest peak in Georgia; only Brasstown Bald (4,784 feet) is higher. The main ridgeline, which is indicated by the Bartram Trail on the map, is the Eastern Continental Divide, dividing waters draining northward into the Tennessee-Mississippi Gulf system from those draining southward to the Atlantic. Most of the streams of Rabun Bald drain via Warwoman Creek to the Chattooga, then to the Savannah and finally to the Atlantic.

The Rabun Bald area rates among Georgia's leading botanical sites; spring wildflowers are exceptional. Near the summit is a unique zone of dwarf oak heath (mainly scarlet oak and purple rhododendron). Look for striking red berries of mountain ash. In some places there is a thick ground cover of blueberries. Together with the Chattooga River to the southwest and the Cowee Mountains to the north, this country is large enough for deer, bear, wild boar and even mountain lion.

DIRECTIONS: *Take US 441 north from Clayton for 1 mile past Dillard; turn right onto GA 246 toward Highlands, NC; continue on 246 and NC 106 for 7 miles; turn right onto Hale Ridge Road (FS 7), which is beside the Scaly Post Office; go 2.1 miles and take the right fork (FS 7 goes left); go 1.3 miles and take a left fork on a steep dirt road toward Beegum Gap [Fig. 30(22)]; after 1.6 miles, park and walk 2 miles to Rabun Bald. There is an observation platform on the summit. Note the northern hardwood cove, boulderfield and wildflower area [Fig. 30(17)].*

~DRIVES, TRAILS AND POINTS OF INTEREST

WARWOMAN ROAD. A scenic drive which follows Warwoman Shear, a geologic "path" which provided Indians and early settlers in the region with their principal east-west trading route.

DIRECTIONS: *From US 441 in Clayton, go east at the light where US 76 turns left.*

WARWOMAN DELL. [Fig. 30(1)] This recreation area was developed in the 1930's by the Civilian Conservation Corps. Cuts of the old Black Mountain Railroad can be found here. This railroad was partially constructed but never operated before the Civil War. An interpretive trail with 25 numbered posts and an accompanying pamphlet identify many plants common to the region. Several rare ferns, including the walking fern, are found here.

FACILITIES: *Two picnic pavilions, outdoor restrooms with facilities for*

Garter snake
Thamnophis sirtalis

This is the snake most often encountered in terrestrial environments in the mountains at all elevations. It is fond of frogs and toads.

Figure 30 RABUN BALD

handicapped.
DATES/HOURS: *Open Memorial Day through Labor Day. Gate locked Fri and Sat at dark.*

BECKY BRANCH WATERFALL. [Fig. 30(15)] 0.25 mile from Warwoman Road.

TUKALUGEE CREEK ROAD [FIG. 30(2)] AND SARAH'S CREEK ROAD (FS 156) [FIG. 30(3)]. All-weather roads providing a 10-mile scenic loop drive. Gate closed Dec.-Mar.

DARNELL CREEK ROAD (FS 150). [Fig. 30(6)] All-weather road. Scenic drive.

OVERFLOW CREEK ROAD (FS 86). [Fig. 30(7)]

APPLE VALLEY. [Fig. 30(5)] Popular, dispersed camping-and-fishing area managed by the U.S. Forest Service. Sarah's Creek is heavily stocked with trout. Off GA 246.

SANDY FORD ROAD. [Fig. 30(18)] One of only two unpaved-road access points to the Chattooga River on the Georgia side (Earl's Ford, below, being the other). Good canoe put-in point for Section III of the river. Not a four-wheel drive road, but difficult in bad weather.

EARL'S FORD ROAD. [Fig. 30(19)] Old county road that once provided major access from South Carolina to Georgia by crossing the Chattooga River. It parallels and crosses Warwoman Road. Four-wheel drive is advisable.

ESTATOAH FALLS. [Fig. 30(14)] At GA 246.

SKY VALLEY. [Fig. 30(4)] Resort area with 18-hole golf course, pool, restaurant, condominiums, year-round and vacation homes. Lots for sale. Winter ski lift. Off GA 246.

THREE FORKS TRAIL. [Fig. 30(9)] 9.5 miles. The trail begins at the summit of Rabun Bald (4,696 feet) and ends at Three Forks on the West Fork of the Chattooga River. Steep descents. Also see *West Fork* section.

DIRECTIONS: *Hikers can also begin the trail from John Teague Gap. To start from there, take Warwoman Road east from Clayton for 16 miles to Overflow Creek Road (FS 86); turn left (northwest) and go 4 miles to John Teague Gap, where the trail crosses.*

BARTRAM TRAIL. [Fig. 30(12)] This National Recreational Trail stretches from the Georgia-North Carolina line over the summit of Rabun Bald to the Chattooga River. It is named for William Bartram, a naturalist who explored and wrote about this area in the 1770's.

DIRECTIONS: *Take US 441 north from Clayton for 1 mile past Dillard; turn right onto GA 246 toward Highlands, NC. Continue on 246 and NC 106 for 7 miles, then turn right onto Hale Ridge Road; go 2.1 miles, then take FS 7 for 1.1 miles.*

ALEX MOUNTAIN, FLINT KNOB TRAIL. [Fig. 30(10)]

DIRECTIONS: *From Flint Gap on the Bartram Trail, or take the Sky Valley exit from GA 246 and take either the Alex Mountain or Flint Knob forks.*

HOLCOMB CREEK TRAIL AND FALLS AND AMMONS CREEK FALLS. [Fig. 30(13)] 1.5-mile loop. Includes two waterfalls. Observation deck at Ammons Falls.

DIRECTIONS: *Take Warwoman Road east from Clayton for 10 miles. Turn left (north) on FS 7 (Hale Ridge Road), or south on Hale Ridge Road from NC 106, and go 9 miles.*

THE FLATS. [Fig. 30(8)] A remarkable high, flat area forming the western rim of the Highland Plateau. Formerly this was the location of a number of unique peat bogs. Among the rarest of mountain environments, these bogs occur at the heads of valleys where seeps and springs keep the soil consistently wet and produce rare plants such as bog laurel, swamp pink and cotton grass. Unfortunately, most of the bogs here have been drained or bulldozed.

DIRECTIONS: *See above.*

RAMEY FIELD. [Fig. 30(20)]

LAUREL SLICK. [Fig. 30(21)] Thick stands of rhododendron.

MAP REFERENCES: *USGS 1:24,000 series: Rabun Bald.*

The Chattooga River

The Chattooga River is the crown jewel of southern whitewater rivers and a symbol for wilderness river lovers throughout the United States and Canada. Its high rainfall, unusual geology (with many cliffs, gorges and waterfalls) and steep gradient place it in the "world class" category of rivers. Most remaining rivers of the Chattooga's quality are tucked away in western gorges or West Virginia Mountains. The river is arguably the area's prime single natural attraction, luring some 100,000 visitors a year for hiking, rafting, canoeing, kayaking, tubing, fishing, swimming or plain and simple river watching.

Headwaters of the Chattooga are in the Nantahala National Forest and private lands in North Carolina. Flowing southward out of North Carolina, they form approximately 40 river-miles of boundary between Georgia and South Carolina. The river drops from approximately 3,000 feet elevation at its headwaters to 950 feet at its termination into Lake Tugalo. It is under the control and protection of the Sumter National Forest in South Carolina, The Chattahoochee National Forest in Georgia and the Nantahala National Forest in North Carolina.

The names of the river's rapids and other landmarks bear witness to the area's early inhabitants. Indian names translated into English have become Sock'em Dog, Shoulder Bone and Cutting Bone Creek. Local settlers' humor shows in the names of two feeder creeks—Bad Creek and Worse Creek—both now covered by Lake Tugalo. Between those two streams is Sinking Mountain, named because of instability of the soil and underlying decayed rock.

The Chattooga was designated as a Wild and Scenic River by Congress in May of 1974. As a result, no motorized vehicles are allowed within a quarter-mile of its banks. In addition, man-made facilities are minimal, consisting primarily of maintained hiking trails. Primitive toilet facilities and water are available at camping areas. As a result of the minimal disturbance by man, the Chattooga and its corridor provide a clean, litter-free hiking or rafting experience. However, the growth in population in the mountain areas and resulting activities could pose a multifaceted danger to the river in the future.

~ACCESS TO RIVER CROSSINGS

HIGHWAY 76 BRIDGE. [Fig. 31&32(23)] Nine miles east of Clayton on US 76.

RUSSELL BRIDGE. [Fig. 34&35(25)] Follow Warwoman Road 15 miles east from Clayton, cross the West Fork of the Chattooga and go to the junction with Hwy 28. Turn right (south) on Hwy 28 and

Figure 31   LOWER CHATTOOGA/TUGALO LAKE

Figure 32   CHATTOOGA RIVER/U.S. 76 TO EARLS FORD

Figure   33   CHATTOOGA RIVER/EARLS FORD TO LONG BOTTOM FORD

Figure 34   CHATTOOGA RIVER/EAST FORK

go approximately 3 miles to the bridge.

BURRELL'S FORD BRIDGE. FS 646 begins 0.5 mile west of Russell Bridge. Follow FS 646 for approximately 5.5 miles to the bridge. See Ellicott Rock [Fig. 34&36(45)].

BULL PEN BRIDGE. Follow SC 107 south from the intersection of US 64 in Cashiers, NC. Turn west on Bull Pen Road and follow it to the bridge. See Highlands [Fig. 36&38(18)].

~CANOEING AND BOATING.

The Chattooga River is an outstanding whitewater experience that attracts boaters from all over the U.S. and Canada. While it is one of the finest recreational resources Georgia has to offer, it can be extremely unsafe -- even deadly -- for those who approach it unaware of its hazards. Many individuals, experienced as well as inexperienced boaters, have lost their lives in the river, particularly on Sections III and IV. A variety of books and maps details the river's boating pleasures and its dangers, and one or more of these resources should be consulted before attempting to navigate any section of the river. In addition, a number of outfitters provide canoeing and rafting expeditions on the Chattooga. No one should attempt Sections III and IV of the Chattooga without first going with an experienced guide. Both outfitters and reliable river guidebooks are listed in the appendix.

THE SECTION ABOVE GA 28, RUSSELL BRIDGE (THE EAST FORK). All boating is prohibited upstream of GA 28 bridge [Fig. 34&35(25)].

SECTION I (THE WEST FORK). The lower section from Overflow Creek Road Bridge to the junction with the east fork is a slow-moving, gentle stream suitable for the novice canoeist. (See West Fork section.)

SECTION II (FROM GA 28 TO EARL'S FORD). [Fig. 33(10)] One Class III rapid (Big Shoals) and other shelf-like rapids make Section II an excellent area for novice to intermediate whitewater boaters.

SECTION III (EARL'S FORD TO US 76 BRIDGE). [Fig. 31&32(23)] At this point the river becomes much more dangerous, requiring greater expertise in negotiating boulders, gorges and ledges. There are several Class III and IV rapids and one Class V at Bull Sluice, just above the take-out point near the US 76 bridge.

SECTION IV (FROM THE US 76 BRIDGE TO TUGALO LAKE). [Fig. 31(31)] The infamous Woodall Shoals, a Class IV rapid which has taken many lives, is located on this section a short distance below the bridge. From here on, the river narrows and concentrates into several Class IV and V rapids before entering Lake Tugalo where a 1.5-mile paddle across the lake to take out is required. Both Sections III and IV are dangerous and should be attempted only by experienced boaters.

~COMMERCIAL RAFTING TRIPS. Trips are available from local rafting companies in the area. Trips may last for one day or two, with an overnight camp-out available. Commercial operations usually run from late March through October, depending on stream flow and weather. For a listing of outfitters see the Appendix.

~HIKING TRAILS AND ACCESS POINTS

CHATTOOGA RIVER TRAIL. The southern end of the Chattooga River Trail begins in Georgia at the west end of US 76 bridge at the parking area and continues north for 10 miles, where it intersects and combines with the Bartram Trail. The combined trails continue another 10 miles to the GA 28 bridge, where the hiker must cross the bridge and pick up the trails on the South Carolina side. At a point 3.7 miles above the bridge, the Bartram Trail branches off to the east with the Foothills Trail, while the Chattooga River Trail joins with the Foothills Trail and parallels the river closely for another 6.7 miles to Burrell's Ford Campground and Burrell's Ford Road. One-half mile north of Burrell's Ford Road, the trail enters the Ellicott Rock Wilderness. Here the hiker must register. The Foothills Trail branches off to the east at this point and the trail to Ellicott Rock continues upstream for 2.1 miles, where it joins with the East Fork Trail, which continues 2.5 miles to Walhalla Fish Hatchery. The trail continues 1.7 miles upstream to Ellicott Rock where Georgia, North Carolina and South Carolina boundaries meet. Ellicott Rock can also be reached by foot from North Carolina (see Ellicott Rock). The only camping area with restroom and water facilities is the Burrell's Ford Campground. Other camping areas are primitive, and in some areas in the Ellicott Rock Wilderness camping is forbidden.

THE EAST FORK ABOVE BULL PEN ROAD. The upper Chattooga River harbors some of the river's most scenic and rugged stretches. Closed to boats, the area must be reached by foot. Major access points are Bullpen Road [Fig. 38(13)] and primitive roads off Whiteside Cove Road, both gravel roads accessible by car.

This section of the river is known for the steep, remote "Chattooga Cliffs" [Fig. 38(27)] and for a small gorge area called the

Upper Narrows. Both areas can be reached from the Bullpen Road Bridge [Fig. 36&38(18)] known locally as the "metal" or "government" bridge. It is recommended that the hiker have a car waiting at the bridge before beginning the walk upstream. There are two approach points are shown on the map (Highlands).

Along this stretch the Chattooga is narrow and wild. Further up-river is relatively flat, but the adjacent cliffs and overhangs provide constant interest. Here the rare Biltmore sedge, a northern clubmoss, and forests of giant mountain laurel up to 30 feet tall are present at the base of the cliffs. Further downstream one reaches the Upper Narrows, where the rushing water is compressed into a stream about six feet wide. Only the most skilled rock climber can maneuver through the gorge. For a safer route, it is recommended that the hiker walk the gorge's edge. Downstream from the Upper Narrows a loop trail is reached. This trail consists of a lower and upper section. The lower section affords good views of the boulder-strewn gorge which is found just upstream from the Bullpen Road Bridge. Car-sized boulders and unusual potholes are present, as well as several nice swimming pools.

Below the bridge the river is less scenic but still worth the visit. Two trails off Bullpen Road lead to Ellicott Rock.

The East Fork From GA 28, Russell Bridge To Burrell's Ford Bridge.

[Fig. 36(45)] Unlike some parts of the river, this section is relatively accessible. Old log roads up the East Fork and the splendid trail up the entire South Carolina side afford all degrees of hiking and fishing experiences (See Ellicott Rock map).

While the river itself is not constant white water, areas of it are breathtakingly wild and scenic. The area between the Big Bend [Fig. 34(43)] and Licklog Falls [Fig. 34(36)] is a challenge for the most intrepid fisherman, since there are no riverside trails. Crossing the river back and forth is essential and risky in winter and spring high water. The wild isolation of the Rock Gorge [Fig. 34(39)] and the magnificence of the Big Bend Falls [Fig. 34(42)] make it worthwhile. Prior to the construction of FS 646 (new Burrell's Ford Road), major accesses were at the Russell Bridge [Fig. 34&35(25)] and from SC 28 near Big Creek (the Old Burrell's Ford Road, seven miles of torturous mountain road). This was part of the "Mystery River" (see West Fork section), the area known for large brown trout. The river is open for fishing year round.

For easy hiking and fishing, the section of the Chattooga between Russell Bridge and Reed Creek [Fig. 34&35(28)] is hard to beat, for there is a trail (or log road) on either side. At the north side of the Russell Bridge one looks out over a marsh with ponds and wood-duck boxes. This was the old Whitmire place, formerly a fertile cornfield. When it was acquired by the Forest Service, beavers promptly dammed up Mose Branch, creating the marsh dominated by alder shrub, sedges and marsh grasses. One can go up the river by

Brook trout
Salvelinus fontinalis

Brook trout, along with lake trout, are classified as chars. The brook trout is our only native species and occupies every stream and rivulet except above significant waterfalls. They are colored like flowers, sides dotted with red spots surrounded by blue rings and with white-edged red fins. The flesh of chars is pink to orange in color.

climbing down the bridge riprap or more easily, but less speedily, by taking the first old road (gated) [Fig. 34&35(24)] that turns off west of the bridge. About a mile up this road (1.75 miles by river) one reaches some beautiful pools and camping places [Fig. 34&35(26)]. Further on there is an old field, called Reed Creek Bottoms, planted in loblolly pine [Fig. 34&35(27)], which is rare in the mountains unless planted. Here, one can turn up a trail on the west side of the field that leads up Reed Creek. Soon there will appear one of the most beautiful stands of white pine in north Georgia with abundant patches of club moss and pink lady slippers [Fig. 34&35(29)]. Farther on one enters Reed Creek Gorge [Fig. 34&35(30)]. There are no trails on this section. The cascades, falls and pools are extremely scenic and not too difficult to negotiate. With luck the visitor will see the highest of the falls, Reed Creek Falls [Fig. 34&35(31)] before a more tranquil section leading up to Persimmon Gap [Fig. 34&35(32)].

On the main river above Reed Creek there is more entrancing scenery, especially beginning at Lick Log Falls [Fig. 34(36)]. This area is most easily reached from the old Nicholson Ford Road [Fig. 34(34)]. Above this, around a long "square" bend, the road is fairly high above the river. The observant visitor may see signs of wild hogs rooting [Fig. 34(37)]. This is truly backcountry, in spite of the old log roads which soon will turn up the mountain, skipping the rock gorge entirely. On the approach to the gorge [Fig. 34(38)] one may see the beautiful mountain camellia, whose large white blossoms appear in late summer. This is a plant found in streamside zones and on most bluffs. It is difficult to negotiate the gorge [Fig. 34(39)], even with non-slip shoe soles. This can be a dangerous section. Towering cliffs appear, and the only way out is at least one mile upstream by wading and rock hopping. Where the main Chattooga River Trail on the South Carolina side comes down to the river after going high around the gorge, there is a waterfall with a beautiful falls and pool below [Fig. 34(40)]. Although unnamed, this falls and the section above it [Fig. 34(41)] are alone worth the trip. At the next huge pool upstream there is a trail [Fig. 34(41)] leading up to an east-west ridge with a road leading off to SC 107, the easiest access to the river above the rock gorge. Above this pool (and branch) is another 1.5-mile section which has no trail. The main trail cuts across a ridge and comes down just above Big Bend Falls [Fig. 34(42)]. A side trip down to the falls is worth the exertion. At the Big Bend [Fig. 34(43)], one will see pieces of truck axle sticking out of the rock, evidence of a former logging bridge. As unlikely as it may seem, trucks with light loads were able to haul logs up the steep ridge on the South Carolina side, now an access trail.

Further upstream the remaining several miles of river up the "stairs" [Fig. 34(44)] are a pleasant riverside hike and quite beautiful, with more whitewater and fewer huge pools than above Burrell's

Ford Bridge.

~SECTIONS II, III AND IV ACCESS POINTS. These sections of
the Chattooga accommodate those who enjoy the thrills of whitewater
boating or watching others negotiate dangerous rapids. On the
Georgia side of the river, a good hiking trail, the Chattooga River
Trail later joined by the Bartram Trail, parallels the river between the
US 76 and SC 28 bridges. Below 76 there are no trails and the
gorge is navigable only by floating. Most of the locations listed
below are access points along the river. At normal water levels,
Section III is a good Class III run. At low water, outfitters avoid
Section III and run Section IV, which extends from the US 76 bridge
downriver to Lake Tugalo.

Three outfitters -- Southeastern Expeditions, Wildwater Limited
and Nantahala Outdoor Center, all carefully regulated by the federal
government -- conduct raft trips lasting from a half day to two days.
Their locations are shown on the map, and addresses and phone
numbers are listed in the appendix.

RUSSELL BRIDGE, LONG BOTTOM FORD PUT-INS. On SC 28 1.25
miles south of the Russell Bridge is a parking and put-in area [Fig.
33(4)]. One-half mile below there a dirt road turns off south to
Long Bottom Ford [Fig. 33(6)], where a low-water bridge and ford
was the major river crossing for the early settlers around Pine
Mountain on the west fork. Boaters can put in there. Most cars can
travel the road.

SOUTH CAROLINA ACCESS TO EARL'S FORD AND SANDY FORD.
Downstream, Earl's Ford is the next point of access. At Mountain
Rest about 3.75 miles turn right (south) on 196 and go 3.25 miles to
a four-way stop at Whetstone; turn right (west) and go off pavement
at 1.75 miles on a good gravel road for 1.25 miles. There [Fig.
32&33(7)] is a camp specially designed to accommodate horses and
horse trailers, and from it radiate horse trails that explore the area.
If one turns left here on road 721A, in 1.25 miles the river corridor
is reached, and a trail leads 0.25 mile to the river. This is the
Sandy Ford access [Fig. 32&33(9)] from the South Carolina side.
Continuing straight on Whetstone Road one mile past the horse
camp, one reaches a parking area and trail to Earl's Ford [Fig.
32&33(8)].

GEORGIA ACCESS TO EARL'S FORD AND SANDY FORD. Georgia
has access to both Earl's Ford and Sandy Ford, but the roads in are
long, sometimes muddy and are not used by the commercial
outfitters. The Georgia Earl's Ford Road access [Fig. 32&33(10)]
can be reached by ordinary car, except that in high water Warwoman
Creek [Fig. 32&33(11)] cannot be forded. It is possible to drive,

with care, to Sandy Ford. In both cases, roads go to the river's edge, unlike those in South Carolina.

On the Georgia side at Sandy Ford [Fig. 32&33(14)] is a beautiful high waterfall on Dick's Creek. Take the Bartram Trail north [Fig. 32&33(12)] about 0.5 mile past the Dick's Creek Bridge to a viewing platform constructed by the U.S. Forest Service [Fig. 32&33(13)].

FALLS CREEK ACCESS. The next access is best approached off US 76. Two miles east of the 76 bridge turn left (north) onto the Chattooga Ridge Road (FS 196), the first paved road to the left. Go two miles, take the gravel road (FS 722) [Fig. 32(15)] left (west). At the second fork (two miles), the right hand fork (FS 723) goes to an access point [Fig. 32(16)] with a very steep trail to the river (0.25 mile). The left fork (FS 769) leads to a less steep but longer trail [Fig. 32(17)]. There are two lovely waterfalls on Falls Creek [Fig. 32(18)] and [Fig. 32(19)].

THRIFT'S FERRY. The next access is at Thrift's Ferry [Fig. 32(20)], reached by a gravel road (P795) which turns north about one mile east of the US 76 Bridge.

US 76 SHOULDER ACCESS. Further downriver, there is a special short access trail (parking is on US 76 shoulder) [Fig. 31&32(21)] where some outfitters put in for short runs over Bull Sluice [Fig. 31&32(22)].

BULL SLUICE TRAILS. There are two trails upriver to Bull Sluice, at high water levels a very dangerous, roaring Class V rapid. Some visitors choose to walk up the better trail on the east (SC) bank [Fig. 31&32(23)] from the 76 Bridge parking area to watch the rafters come through the sluice. Photographers often prefer to walk up the west bank (GA) trail [Fig. 31&32(24)], which is less well maintained but offers better views of the falls from below. (This is not the Chattooga River Trail. One has to walk too far on the CRT to reach Bull Sluice, while this trail is a short hike.)

WOODALL SHOALS. A beautiful rapid for picnicking and swimming is Woodall Shoals [Fig. 31(25)]. Rated a Class IV rapid, it is considered to be the most dangerous on the river. Given proper water levels it can be run by or with professionals, but normally it should be portaged. Visitors should be content to explore below the rapid. On the east side of Woodall Shoals is one of the best places in north Georgia to see how Blue Ridge Mountain rocks have been metamorphosed by heat and pressure, as compared to the sedimentary or "layer cake" type mountains of the Cumberland Plateau in the northwestern part of the state. In fact, this site is said to be the

"Rosetta Stone" for the interpretation of the changes that have taken place in the rocks of the Eastern Blue Ridge. Most of the rock at Woodall Shoals is a gneiss with black mica, but in it are dark bands and lumps of calcium-rich amphibolite, which furnishes good nutrition for nearby plant communities. Fresh rock is exposed here, courtesy of Mr. Woodall who apparently dynamited the west side of the river several decades ago so his logs would not be trapped by the rapids along the east bank. Woodall Shoals is reached by turning right (south) 2.5 miles east of the US 76 bridge, and again right at the first gravel road to the right. It is about two miles to the parking and camping areas. Note that camping is prohibited here within the Wild and Scenic corridor.

LONG CREEK FALLS. Below Woodall Shoals there is a beautiful falls [Fig. 31(26)] on Long Creek where most rafts stop for a swim and photographs. It can also be reached by a trail [Fig. 31(27)]. Turn south off US 76 4.5 miles east of the 76 Bridge. After turning at Long Creek, go 2.5 miles, turn right (west) on 758 and go 1.25 miles; turn left onto a gravel road, which in 1.5 miles becomes a jeep road until the trailhead is reached. This is the Long Creek Road.

'POSSUM CREEK FALLS. The 'Possum Creek Falls [Fig. 31(28)] is reached by a 1.5-mile trail which turns south in a bend [Fig. 31(29)] 0.5 mile off the paved road at Battle Creek, the same access to Long Creek Road.

TUGALO LAKE ROAD. The last access road on the SC side is off this same paved road about 4 miles south of US 76. Turn right (west) onto the gravel Tugalo Lake Road [Fig. 31(30)]. Be cautious in wet weather. This is the road used by busses to pick up rafters who have made the Section IV trip [Fig. 31(31)]. Length is 3.5 miles.

LICK LOG. Coming down the river on the Georgia side below Sandy Ford is the Lick Log access road [Fig. 32(32)]. It is reached by turning south off Warwoman Road at the Antioch Church turnoff to Sandy Ford, bearing left at the first fork (0.5 mile), then bearing right at the second fork (about 0.25 mile). Then take the next left-hand road (FS 9). (See Rabun Bald section for road access from Warwoman Road). These are gravel roads suitable for all vehicles.

FS 9 APPROACH. Another Georgia approach is off US 76 east from Clayton, 2.8 miles past The Willows. Turn north (left) on gravel road [Fig. 32(34)], go 3.5 miles, take FS 9 [Fig. 32(32)] east (right) 3.8 miles to a gate. An old road [Fig. 32(35)] goes down a ridge to the river.

SUTTON HOLE ROAD. About 0.75 mile west of the US 76 Bridge a gravel road (290) turns south [Fig. 31&32(37)]. Within 0.5 mile the short Sutton Hole Road (290A) [Fig. 31&32(36)] goes down to the river corridor, where the outfitters overnight their customers on two-day trips [Fig. 31&32(38)]. This is a jeep or pick-up truck road, not for ordinary cars.

WOLF CREEK ROAD. The Wolf Creek Road [Fig. 31(39)] requires about a 1-mile walk to the river. To reach it, turn right (east) off US 441, 4 miles north of Tallulah Falls Bridge, onto the second paved road to the right. Keep straight for about 3 miles (the road turns to gravel). Turn right (east) at the Wolf Creek Church sign (Road 515). This is an interesting area. From above the church along Wolf Creek, the strange, introduced Japanese paper plant grows wild [Fig. 31(40)]. Botanical groups often visit this site to see it. Further down Wolf Creek below the church are at least a dozen beaver dams [Fig. 31(41)]. A jeep can go down to within one mile of the Chattooga (stay on the right hand road). This road leads to two potentially exciting areas which have not been much explored nor apparently logged. The gorge of Cliff Creek [Fig. 31(42)] and lower Stekoa Creek (refer to Rainey Mountain Quad topographic map) are excellent places to explore.

CAMP CREEK ROAD. [Fig. 31(44)] One of the most exciting access points to the Chattooga. It is the first paved road to the east, north of the Tallulah Falls Bridge on US 441. It soon becomes gravel. About two miles from the highway is a fork. It is about four miles to the river corridor if the visitor stays on the good gravel road (Rd 511) [Fig. 31(45)]. Drive with care; busses carrying rafters or logging trucks also use the road. There is an old road down to the river's edge [Fig. 31(46)]. Walking downstream one soon comes to the first of a series of Class V rapids [Fig. 31(47)] with names like "Corkscrew," "Jawbone" and "Sock'em Dog." In good weather it is quite a show to watch river runners go through this white water. A ford at or near the mouth of Camp Creek was evidently the main old settlers' route to South Carolina, a wagon road down which herds of hogs were reportedly driven to market.

Back about a mile from the terminus of 511, a jeep road (511 B) [Fig. 31(48)] turns north, terminating on a ridge [Fig. 31(49)]. A trail drops down 0.75 mile to the Raven Rock Pool [Fig. 31(50)], a grand, scenic place to have lunch, fish and watch the rafters go by.

The main Camp Creek Road (511) continues south [Fig. 31(44)] and is paved nearly to a fork; it then turns left (east) [Fig. 31(51)] on road 73 (74 continues on to come out at Terrora Park on Tallulah Falls Lake). It is about two miles to the Camp Creek Church. Just west of it is a ridge which has yielded rock crystals [Fig. 31(52)] which also occur on a rocky knob several miles to the west [Fig. 31(53)]. On these rocky ridges and southward around the Tallulah Gorge the dominant pine is often the rare table mountain pine, with cones so prickly that it can hardly be handled. One can park past the Camp Creek Church [Fig. 31(54)]. A jeep can go only another 0.5 mile; then one takes a trail. In this area, as in the area southward around Tallulah Gorge, the dominant heath is Carolina rhododendron, which has a purple bloom, as well as abundant azalea. At the terminus of the trail [Fig. 31(55)] one will be able to gaze off into the gorge of the Chattooga. This is the fabled "Sinking Mountain," where the visitor who stands long enough in one spot can feel the ground giving way underfoot. Bulldozers left overnight have been known to sink a foot or two. An Indian myth attributes this to a race of spirit people or "little people" who mined beneath the mountain, which is now caving in on their tunnels.

MAP REFERENCES: *USGS 1:24,000 series: Cashiers - Highlands - Satolah - Tamassee - Rainy Mountain.*
USFS special maps: Chattooga River Corridor Map.

West Fork

~THE WEST FORK OF THE CHATTOOGA RIVER. From Three Forks to its junction with the East Fork. The West Fork of the Chattooga River begins at Three Forks, the intersection of three creeks -- Holcomb, Overflow and Big Creek. From there the West Fork flows six or seven miles to the southeast to meet with the East Fork. The entire West Fork, plus one mile upstream along Overflow Creek, is included within the boundaries of the Chattooga National Wild and Scenic River.

The upper portion of the West Fork is one of the most beautiful river sights in Georgia -- a river of low falls and deep green pools hemmed in by bluffs and steep forested slopes. From Overflow Creek Road bridge down to the junction with the East Fork, the river is relatively calm with long, deep pools ideal for lazy floating or swimming. Fine picnic and strolling sites are accessible and reached by road.

This is a country of beautiful but unknown waterfalls. One is on Overflow just above Three Forks and there are three on Big Creek; the middle one is outstanding. It is along the West Fork's headwaters that the last remnants of the old splash dam logging system can be seen. The old Burrell's Ford road offered the only former access to the Chattooga's east fork which, in the 1940's was discovered to be Georgia's famed "mystery river." Large brown trout kept turning up but no one would reveal their source until it was found that the inaccessibility of both the east and west forks had protected a remarkable fishery resource. The west fork is also an area rich in mining lore. The ultrabasic deposits along the lower river below Pine Mountain have yielded asbestos and soapstone and was the site of Georgia's most famous corundum mine at Laurel Creek. Most maps show that Laurel Creek, Reed Creek and Warwoman Valley form one of north Georgia's most remarkable geologic features, a straight line or lineament, the "Warwoman shear," that continues to control topography as far west as Tray Mountain. After float logging divested the West Fork of much of its hardwood timber, white pine seeded in and by 1950 was abundant and was subsequently harvested, this time by log roads.

DIRECTIONS: *From US 441 in Clayton where US 76 turns west, turn east onto paved Warwoman Road; once on Warwoman, turn right (not hard right) at the stop sign; proceed past the Georgia Power building; follow Warwoman Road for about 14 miles to the intersection with Overflow Creek Road (FS 86). From Highlands, NC, take NC 28 south to the intersection of Warwoman Road; turn right onto Overflow Creek Road (FS 86). Beaver dams can be seen below the road.*

Figure 35 WEST FORK CHATTOOGA RIVER
202

Carolina rhododendron
Rhododendron minus

Its leaves closely resemble mountain laurel, but its flowers do not. Its purplish blooms come after mountain laurel has flowered. You can identify it best by the smooth bark, unlike the lightly furrowed and shreddy bark of the mountain laurel. Carolina rhododendron is very common in the vicinity of Tallulah Falls and Panther Creek.

~JOHN TEAGUE GAP [FIG. 35(2)] AND THREE FORKS HIKING TRAIL. [Fig. 35(2)] While the Three Forks Trail originates on Rabun Bald (see Rabun Bald), it is most often hiked from John Teague Gap. From there it gently descends through a forest typical for the area—oak-hickory slope forest with scattered patches of white pines. At 0.7 mile the path crosses the blue-blazed boundary of the Chattooga National Wild and Scenic River. Three-tenths mile further it dips to a three-way intersection with an old jeep road. Here the Three Forks Trail, occasionally blazed with white diamonds, turns left and heads downhill following the road to a slab of bedrock overlooking a cascade on Holcomb Creek. This is the end of the designated trail. The remainder of the route down this gorge is on the north side of Holcomb Creek (cross the creek) down a ravine with pot-holed rocks and falls that reach all the way to Three Forks (about 0.25 mile). It is not difficult bushwhacking, but one must pick a path through hemlock-rhododendron heath which, along with white pine, forms the bulk of the streamside zone of vegetation.

~FISHERMAN'S TRAIL. [Fig. 35(3)] The trail passes rock shelters and cliffs harboring colonies of wood rats.

DIRECTIONS: *Upstream on north side of West Fork from where FS 86 crosses West Fork.*

~OLD SPLASH DAM REMNANTS. [Fig. 35(4)] Around the turn of the century, loggers in this area built what were termed "splash dams" across creeks like Holcomb and Overflow. Cut logs were dragged down to the creeks and backed up behind the dam. At a prearranged signal, dams on several creeks were broken at one time, sending water and logs raging down the stream. Called "float logging," this method was used to harvest many of the slope forests, including streamside hemlocks. Logs from the West Fork were destined for Madison, S.C.

DIRECTIONS: *About 0.25 mile below where Billingsley Creek Road crosses Holcomb Creek. Cross the bridge and go down the north side of the creek.*

~BILLINGSLEY CREEK ROAD. [Fig. 35(5)] Built by the Forest Service so that Overflow Creek watershed could be logged.

~TRAIL AND LOG ROAD. [Fig. 35(6)] Joins with Blue Valley and Clear Creek road system.

~THREE FORKS. [Fig. 35(7)] The intersection of Holcomb Creek, Overflow Creek and Big Creek divides the forest landscape into four neat quadrants and rewards determined hikers with the light, sound and color of one of the most delightful scenes in Georgia. Other than by the Three Forks Trail route (#2 above), Three Forks can be reached via NC 28. See below.

~OVERFLOW FALLS. [Fig. 35(8)] Waterfall about 0.5 mile above Three Forks.

~LOWER BIG CREEK FALLS. [Fig. 35(9)] Waterfall on Big Creek [Fig. 35(10)] and Upper Falls on Big Creek [Fig. 35(11)]. Old log road [Fig. 35(12)] provides a good hike to Big Creek.

~FALLS ON UPPER BIG CREEK. [Fig. 35(13)]

~HIGH FALLS ON UPPER BIG CREEK. [Fig. 35(14)]

DIRECTIONS: *Proceed on Hwy 28 to Satolah, Georgia, at the bridge over Big Creek. Just north of the bridge, turn off and park on the west side of the highway. Find a forest service log road which crosses a little branch immediately and follow this easy graded road all the way to Three Forks. The middle and upper Big Creek Falls can be found either by walking the creek or by their roar. The lower Big Creek Falls is a rugged series of cascades that plummets all the way to Three Forks and is only for hardy adventurers.*

~OLD BURRELL'S FORD ROAD. [Fig. 34&35(15)] In the 1940's reports filtered out of the north Georgia mountains of giant brown trout from a "mystery river." Eventually, it was discovered that the mystery river was the Chattooga above Burrell's Ford, reached from Georgia only by the Old Burrell's Ford Road (FS 121), which turns east off NC 28.

~BUZZARD'S ROCK CLIFFS. [Fig. 35(16)] Hanging Rock Cliffs [Fig. 35(17)] and Cedar Cliff [Fig. 35(18)]. These are a series of high cliffs reached only by bushwhacking. On Cedar Cliffs is found Georgia's only location for sand myrtle. These cliffs are adorned with a picturesque spike moss, which forms thick, photogenic mats with twisted, hairlike spines. On Cedar Cliff Mountain is a Rock Shelter [Fig. 35(19)] containing evidence of both goats and the rare wood rat.

~HEDDON CREEK FALLS. [Fig. 35(20)] On Heddon Creek Road. Accessible only by four-wheel drive. Just beyond the falls is a flat swampy area, the site of a shrub bog.

DIRECTIONS: *Take FS 121 east off Hwy 28 about 2 miles south of Big Creek Bridge. About 4 miles down FS 121 the road fords Heddon Creek. To reach the falls, turn left up the creek.*

~LAUREL CREEK CORUNDUM MINE. [Fig. 34&35(21)] Georgia's most famous corundum mine, unworked since 1894 when a huge block of peridotite fell, closing the tunnels. In addition to corundum, which is the second hardest mineral (only diamond is harder) and is used in the manufacture of abrasives for grinding and smoothing, the mine produced excellent specimens of blue and red corundum, though seldom of ruby and sapphire quality. The peridotite outcrop covers several hundred acres including two rough, barren hills. The private owners of the land at the road terminus have not objected to hikers and parking. The trail can also be reached at the opposite end from Persimmon Gap on the New Burrell's Ford Road (FS 646).

DIRECTIONS: *Laurel Creek is the first creek crossed going south from the junction of Warwoman Road and Hwy 28. After crossing the creek (about 1 mile), turn east.*

~PERSIMMON GAP TRAILHEAD. [Fig. 34&35(22)]

~DAM RUINS. [Fig. 34&35(23)] Water was dammed to power a turbine which turned machinery for milling asbestos ore. The ore came from a mine just across the river on Dockins' Mountain. A nearby soapstone deposit at Adline Branch [Fig. 34&35(24)] was cut into blocks with crosscut saws and used to build the blacksmith forge at the Laurel Creek Corundum Mine, and to line local fireplaces.

MAP REFERENCES: *USGS 1:24,000 series: Satolah - Tamassee.*

Ellicott Rock Wilderness Area

~ELLICOTT ROCK. A 9,012-acre tract of unspoiled mountain land which surrounds the point where Georgia, North Carolina and South Carolina come together. The first boundary, a small scenic area, was identified and established in 1966. It and a much larger area were made a part of the national wilderness system in 1975 and thus became fully protected by guidelines of the 1960 National Wilderness Protection Act.

This primitive land is isolated and well-protected, allowing a near-wilderness experience within its rocky, mountainous terrain.

The Wild and Scenic Chattooga River flows through the wilderness, cascading from 2,381 feet to 2,100 feet within its boundaries. Fork Mountain, 3,294 feet above sea level, is the second highest point in South Carolina. This wilderness has several unique plant communities, a number of rare and endangered plants growing alongside the trails, evergreen forests with dense understory of mountain laurel, streamside rhododendron which defies human penetration, and a diverse population of large and small animal life including many fish.

Hiking is the only method available for exploring the interior of Ellicott Rock Wilderness. The automobile-access roads merely provide a way to get to the trailheads. No horses, bicycles or motorized vehicles are permitted. Camping is allowed within the wilderness. Campsites must be over 0.25 mile from an approach road and 50 feet from a stream or maintained trail.

~TRAILS

CHATTOOGA RIVER TRAIL. [Fig. 34&36(46)] This portion of the Chattooga River Trail within the wilderness is 3.4 miles of old Indian trail. It runs beside the east bank of the Chattooga River from a Burrell's Ford trailhead near the river to an intersection with the East Fork Trail (1.5 miles), then to Ellicott Rock (1.6 miles) [Fig. 36&38(30)] to join Bad Creek Trail [Fig. 36&38(26)] and Ellicott Rock Trail [Fig. 36&38(28)] (0.3 mile). The trail is a moderately easy climb through patches of rhododendron and old-growth stands of hemlock, white pine and mixed hardwood. Bad Creek is easily crossed during low water but may have to be waded when water is high.

DIRECTIONS: *To reach the trailhead from the intersection of US 64 and NC 107 in Cashiers go south on NC 107 to Burrell's Ford Road, FS 708; turn right (west) and proceed to the trailhead near the river.*

ELLICOTT ROCK TRAIL. [Fig. 36&38(28)] See trail information in Highlands section.

Figure 36   CHATTOOGA RIVER/ELLICOTT ROCK WILDERNESS

BAD CREEK TRAIL. [Fig. 36&38(26)] See trail information in Highlands section.

SLOAN BRIDGE TRAIL. [Fig. 36,38&39(60)] This is a moderately difficult trail in good condition. From Sloan Bridge picnic area [Fig. 36,38&39(61)], it joins Bad Creek Trail (6.3 miles), then proceeds to Ellicott Rock (1.4 miles). Sloan Bridge Trail is perhaps best used for overnight camping after leaving a shuttle at some other trailhead, such as the Walhalla Fish Hatchery [Fig. 36(47)].

Also called Fork Mountain Trail, it crosses SC 107 and approaches the wilderness from the east. The trail ascends and descends, steeply at times. It climbs to near the top of Fork Mountain and falls to streamside, where it passes opulent woodland flora. Ornithologists find the trail of interest because of the diversity of species related to altitude and flora. Hawks and eagles are often seen in this most remote area of the wilderness.

DIRECTIONS: *To reach the trailhead from the intersection of US 64 and NC 107 in Cashiers, go south on NC 107 to about 0.75 mile south of the NC/SC border. Ample parking is available at Sloan Bridge Trailhead north of the picnic area.*

EAST FORK TRAIL. [Fig. 36(62)] Sometimes called the Fish Hatchery Trail, this path immediately enters the wilderness and runs downstream alongside the East Fork of the Chattooga for 2.5 miles until it intersects the Chattooga River Trail. The renowned "Forty Thousand Dollar Bridge " which spans the mouth of the East Fork is located here. To reach Ellicott Rock, follow the river upstream 1.7 miles.

Many water-carved rocks, cascades and deep pools in the Chattooga combine with the streamside hemlock and white pine forest to make this a particularly appealing area. There is a stand of old-growth hemlock preserved near the hatchery. The trail is marked with black blazes, and the round trip of about 8.1 miles is easily covered on a full-day hike.

DIRECTIONS: *To reach the trailhead from the intersection of US 64 and NC 107 in Cashiers, go south on NC 107; turn right on the road to the Walhalla Fish Hatchery [Fig. 36(47)]. The trailhead is at the parking area of the Chattooga Picnic Area, next to the hatchery.*

FOOTHILLS TRAIL. [Fig. 34,36&38(63)] 6.6 miles. This is a long, well-marked and well-maintained South Carolina trail. It approaches the Ellicott Rock Wilderness Area across the road from Burrell's Ford Campground parking area [Fig. 34&36(45)] and skirts the southeastern boundary of the wilderness to leave the area at Sloan Bridge picnic area on SC 107. Unlike the other trails in this section, it does not penetrate the interior of the wilderness. After leaving the Burrell's Ford parking area, the trail climbs Medlin Mountain, passes the Fish Hatchery Road (3.3 miles) on the Chattooga Ridge escarpment and proceeds to the Sloan's Bridge picnic area (3.3 miles). The Medlin Mountain climb is moderately difficult, but other areas of the trail are traveled with ease. The trail has segments which may be chosen for day hikes, overnight camping or extended visits along the wilderness border and/or into the Chattooga River corridor. This is especially true when the Foothills Trail is connected to other trails.

DIRECTIONS: *To reach the Burrell's Ford trailhead from the intersection of US 64 and NC 107 in Cashiers, go south approximately 13.5 miles on 107 and turn right on Burrell's Ford Road; go to the parking area and trailhead.*
To reach the place where the trail crosses Fish Hatchery Road from the intersection of US 64 and NC 107 in Cashiers, go south on NC 107 approximately 12 miles and turn right on Fish Hatchery Road; go to the trail crossing.
To reach the Sloan Bridge trailhead from the intersection of US 64 and NC 107 in Cashiers, go south on NC 107 approximately 10 miles to the Sloan Bridge picnic area.

~SPOON AUGER FALLS. [Fig. 34&36(65)] These picturesque, cascading falls can be visited by taking an easy loop trail starting across from the entrance to Burrell's Ford Campground parking lot [Fig. 34&36(45)]. The trail climbs gradually through lovely hardwoods and rhododendron for about 0.5 mile to the falls, crosses the creek and continues on about 1.7 miles until it interconnects with the Chattooga River Trail [Fig. 34&36(46)]. Returning to the parking lot via the Chattooga River Trail and Burrell's Ford Road is a walk of about 1.5 miles.

~KING'S CREEK FALLS. [Fig. 34&36(64)] Located on a beautiful mountain stream surrounded by dense hardwoods and an undergrowth of hemlock and rhododendron. At the falls, water can be seen freely falling for approximately 80 feet into a picturesque pool. The falls are located about 0.5 mile from the Burrell's Ford Campground parking lot [Fig. 34&36(45)]. They are easily reached on a loop trail starting at the display board on the east side of the parking lot. The trail crosses King's Creek and follows the creek upstream about 300 yards to the base of the falls. One can then backtrack 0.7 mile to the parking lot, continue downstream 0.5 mile to the campground or go down the loop trail to its intersection with the Chattooga River Trail. The return to the parking lot on the Chattooga River Trail is about two miles.

MAP REFERENCES: *USGS 1:24,000 series: Tammassee - Satolah -*

Highland - Cashiers - Ellicott Rock ; special maps: USFS Chattooga Corridor map.

EAST VISTA
View from Satulah Mountain

A - Richland Balsam
B - Balsam Range
C - Whiteside Mountain
D - Rocky Mountain
E - High Hampton Inn
F - Chimney Top
G - Toxaway
H - Blackrock
I - Sassafras (N.C)
J - Chattooga Cliffs

K - Terrapin
L - Sassafras (S.C)
M - Pinacle Knob
N - Ellicott
O - Glade
P - Gorge of Chattooga
Q - Blue Ridge Escarpment
R - Buzzard Cliffs
S - Big Stakey (S.C)

SOUTH VISTA
View from Satulah Mountain

AA - Big Stakey
BB - Big Creek
CC - Queen
DD - Three Forks W
EE - Hale Ridge
FF - Clear Creek
GG - Rainey
HH - Rabun Bald

WEST AND NORTH VISTA
View from Satulah Mountain

A - Rabun Bald
B - Osage
C - Wolfknob
D - Ridgepole
E - Little Scaly (The Mountain)
F - Scaly
G - Brushy Face
H - Albert
I - Wallace Gap
J - Fork
K - Nantahalas

L - Jones
M - Dog
N - Big Fishawk
O - Great Smokies
P - Keener
Q - Rich
R - Cowee Bald
S - Flat
T - Plott Balsams
U - Satulah

Mountain pepperbush
Clethra acuminata

This large shrub or small tree has attractive flowers. It prefers moist sites with lots of light. It is outstanding along the Satulah Mountain trail (Highlands sector). According to mountain lore, the dried fruits have been used as a condiment.

Highlands, N.C. Area

Central to this remarkable and highly scenic area is an unusually high (4,000-foot) plateau on the southern edge of the Blue Ridge. Unique in the Southern Appalachians are numerous mountains in this area with steep granite cliffs which create imposing scenery. These cliffs may be seen from US 64 and, indeed, throughout the area; but they are best observed from the tops of two remarkable mountains, Whiteside and Satulah. Both of these summits are reached by short, easy trails.

The cliffs and rock outcrops are botanical treasure houses showcasing the southernmost distribution of numerous rock-loving plants which need a combination of altitude, bare rock and high rainfall to survive. These cliffs are excellent places to see peregrine falcons, ravens and wintering golden eagles.

This region encompasses the headwaters of the famed Chattooga River and is the major northern access to the Ellicott Rock Wilderness. Streams such as the Cullasaja fall off the plateau in steep gorges. Waterfalls are frequent. Vistas of the Rabun Bald country and Blue Valley, now an experimental forest, are visible from US 64.

~WHITESIDE MOUNTAIN. [Fig. 38(19)] An outstanding example of the isolated, cliff-sided mountains characteristic of the Highlands-Cashiers area. Its summit offers fine views from a high ridgetop amidst the beauty and solitude of the forest. To the north the visitor can see Devil's Pulpit, a huge rock outcropping, and the headwaters of the Chattooga River. To the south are Whiteside Cove and a long view back into Georgia.

Whiteside Mountain is a magnificent and popular spot for eagle hacking, hang gliding and technical rock climbing. The mountain was known by the Indians as "the sitting-down place" because they camped there when traveling through the area. Evidence indicates that Spanish explorers also visited the mountain as they passed through this part of the country.

The U.S. Forest Service acquired Whiteside in 1974. The old road is now closed to motorized vehicles. The visitor can hike part or all of the two-mile loop trail to the 4,893-foot summit for a view of the valley floor, lying 2,100 feet below the surrounding mountains. The Whiteside Mountain Trail is designated a National Recreation Trail and is a component of the National Trail System.

Both the north and south faces of Whiteside contain sheer cliffs ranging from 400 to 750 feet in height. These cliffs were formed from metamorphic rock commonly called whiteside granite. This rock, a gneiss, contains a high content of feldspar, quartz and mica, along with such minerals as pyrite and rare monazite. Due to the weathering and drying effects of wind and sunlight, the cliffs on the

Figure 37   SCALY MTN./HIGHLANDS

Figure 38   HIGHLANDS/WHITESIDES

south side have little vegetation. Their blue-grey hue is the natural rock color. The very noticeable white streaks that decorate this side are veins of feldspar and quartz.

The north face, which receives less sunlight and more moisture, has a darker appearance, due to the mosses and lichens that are able to grow in this more-favorable environment.

Two distinct plant communities are present on Whiteside. First is the forest where oaks -- particularly northern red oak -- are dominant. Also commonly found in the forest are Fraser's magnolia, black birch, yellow birch, striped maple and witch hazel. Before the chestnut blight in the early 1900's destroyed all of the large chestnut trees, there was a concentration of chestnut here. There is an abundance of chestnut sprouts in the area, but they seldom reach more than three inches in diameter before dying.

The second community exists in the rock outcrops along the cliffs' edges and along trails. An abundance of flowering and non-flowering plants and shrubs grows here -- some rare, all beautiful. The common shrubs include rosebay rhododendron, mountain laurel and flame azalea. Common smaller plants include false lily of the valley, several species of trillium, summer bluets and wild strawberry.

FACILITIES: *Parking lot, two primitive toilets.*
DIRECTIONS: *From downtown Highlands go east on US 64 for 5.5 miles to Whiteside Mountain Road sign; turn right on paved road NC 1600 and go 0.6 mile; bear left at Wild Cat Ridge Road sign and go 0.35 mile; turn left into gravel parking lot.*

~SATULAH MOUNTAIN. [Fig. 37(21)] The summit of Satulah (4,543 feet) is classified as a heath bald. From here the visitor can view the mountains of three states.

Ascending the trail, one first encounters a forest comprised of northern red oak, white oak and chestnut oak. At the first switchback there begins a remarkable stand of mountain pepperbush overhanging the trail. Both chinquapin and witch hazel are common shrubs here. Soon hikers pass into a stunted, virgin oak forest. At the trail fork, go right. As one approaches the summit, the forest becomes heath (rhododendron) with stunted white oak. At the summit are scattered, dwarfed white oak, some 200 years old. This is a zone with dwarfed pitch pine where a 200-year-old tree may be only 10 inches in diameter. The first purple rhododendron is encountered along with the first pines. Chinquapin is abundant.

The summit provides the best look at unusual plants growing only on bare granite rock so characteristic of the cliffs of this area and extending into Georgia only on similar cliffs along the Chattooga headwaters. One of the most fascinating, the twisted hair spike moss, forms large, thick mats on the upper cliffs. Another, sand myrtle, grows only at the outer edge of the ground cover extending

Large flowered trillium
Trillium grandiflorum

The large white flowers are held erect above the three leaves which are characteristic of trilliums. Where soils are basic, this trillium is often found in dense colonies.

onto the rocks. A juniper forms low-spreading, wind-pruned growth. Exploring the summit, one can find curious potholes, the basement of a former firetower and patches of soil forming in moist depressions in the naked rock. Normally on other outcrops, the niche of the pitch pine would be filled by the rarer table mountain pine, and any hemlocks would be the rare Carolina hemlock. In the spring the evergreen heaths on these balds present unequalled wildflower displays. The mountain summit is protected and offered for public use and education by the Satulah Summit and Ravenel Park, Inc.

DIRECTIONS: *From downtown Highlands, turn south on Hwy 28 and proceed up Fourth Ave to Satulah Road, which begins at Calico Cottage Restaurant. Follow the Satulah Summit signs, bearing right at a fork, about 0.5 mile to the end of the pavement and continue 0.3 mile to a small parking area (five-car maximum) at a gated driveway. The trail is the ungated, rocky roadbed to the left.*

~THE MOUNTAIN (LITTLE SCALY). [Fig. 37(4)] A short but narrow road leads to the summit, which is privately owned and affiliated with the Unitarian Church. It is an excellent example of a rock bald with an unusual forest of ancient, "krummholz" (wind-sheared) white oak, along with evergreen heath. A viewing tower is present. This is one of the very few instances in which one can drive to the summit of a granite dome.

DIRECTIONS: *About midway between Highlands and Scaly Mountain on the south side of US 64, a sign designates The Mountain.*

~THE OLD TIFFANY SAPPHIRE MINE. In the Highlands/Cashiers area and eastward, corundum deposits have yielded many sapphires of gem quality. One community near US 64 is in fact named Sapphire. Some old mines are quite close to the highway. The trail to the mine is 1.5 miles long and fairly steep.

DIRECTIONS: *Follow the Blue Valley Road (FS 79) 6 miles west of Hwy 28 to the trailhead [Fig. 37(24)]. At a broken culvert in the west fork of Overflow Creek, cross the creek and take the right-hand trail [Fig. 37(25)], which was once used to drive livestock up to the grazing grounds in the "Flats" between Scaly Mountain and Rabun Bald.*

~THE HIGHLANDS NATURE CENTER. The center offers daily programs for children and adults, including lectures, nature classes, tours of the botanical gardens and outings. The center offers exhibits on local archeology, geology and biology, including live salamanders, snakes and fish. Fresh wildflower arrangements are available to help visitors identify local plants. Next door is the Appalachian

Ringneck snake
(Diadophis punctata)

Usually only a foot long, this beneficial little black snake with a yellow neck ring eats bugs and worms. It lives under logs and rocks and may, on occasion, enter mountain houses.

Environmental Art Center, where one may enroll in classes in nature and landscape photography.

DATES/HOURS: *Open Jun-Labor Day; 10-5 Mon-Fri, 12-5 Sat.*
DIRECTIONS: *On Horse Cove Road [Fig. 38(12)], an extension of East Main St in Highlands.*
ADDITIONAL INFORMATION: *The Highlands Nature Center, (704) 526-2623.*

~THE HIGHLANDS BIOLOGICAL STATION. Founded in 1929, the Highlands Biological Station hosts about 20 scientists and students annually for research in the field of biology of the Southern Appalachians. On 20 acres, it maintains a rhododendron trail as well as one of the finest wildflower "gardens" in the Appalachians. The garden is a series of loop trails through the forest, with plants labeled along the way.

DIRECTIONS: *Either park at the nature center (above) and walk around back of it -or- drive around (Sixth St. off Horse Cove Rd., turn right at sign) to where the trails actually start at the parking area of the biological station.*

~HORSE COVE ROAD [FIG. 38(12)] AND BULL PEN ROAD [FIG. 38(13)]. This very scenic drive is a major entrance to the Ellicott Rock Wilderness from the north.

In Highlands, East Main Street becomes Horse Cove Road shortly before the nature center. Follow this winding paved road into beautiful Horse Cove. As one enters the cove, Wilson Gap Road is on the right. Approximately 200 feet up the road on the right is the path to a giant poplar, the second largest in North Carolina and one of the three largest in the country. There is a direction sign to the tree. Continue on Horse Cove Road to the fork at the end of the pavement. The right fork is Bull Pen Road, a beautiful one-lane gravel road that is something of a hiking trail for cars. Bull Pen Road crosses the Chattooga on an iron bridge. By the bridge is a good place to stop and view the river. The water has worn basins in the rocks from the size of a thumb print to larger than washtubs.

About 1.25 miles along Bull Pen Road, before reaching Ammons Branch Campground, is an unmarked single-lane gravel road [Fig. 38(66)] that connects FS 121 to Heddon Creek Road. However, it is not recommended as a drive, even with 4-wheel drive vehicles. It closely parallels the western boundary of the Ellicott Rock Wilderness.

From Bull Pen Road there is access to Chattooga River Cliffs Trail [Fig. 38(27)], Chattooga Loop Trail, The Chattooga Wild and Scenic River, Bad Creek Trail [Fig. 36(26)], Ellicott Rock Trail [Fig. 36(28)] and Ammons Branch Campground [Fig. 36&38(18)]. The

Common blue violet
Viola papilionacea

road returns to NC 107 south of Cashiers.

The left fork from Horse Cove Road is Whiteside Cove Road. A fine view from the bottom of Whiteside Mountain can be found in Whiteside Cove. This road also returns to NC 107.

~CULLASAJA RIVER GORGE. [Fig. 37(5)] US 64 runs between Highlands and Franklin, North Carolina, following the gorge cut by the Cullasaja River through the granite mountain and passing a number of waterfalls and scenic areas.

~BRIDAL VEIL FALLS. [Fig. 37(11)] This falls cascades from a height of 120 feet over the highway, 1.2 miles west of Highlands. Basswood and yellow birch trees, characteristic of northern hardwood forests, are found in the vicinity.

~DRY FALLS RECREATION SITE. [Fig. 37(10)] 2.1 miles from Highlands. There is plenty of parking, and the short trail down the cliff to the 75-foot falls is well-marked. Those who do not mind getting a bit wet can walk under the falls to view the gorge. Mountain laurel is abundant.

In the area around both Bridal Veil and Dry Falls, visitors will see Fraser's magnolia, white pine, eastern hemlock and red maple along with dog-hobble, rosebay rhododendron and wild hydrangea. These falls nurture some extremely rare ferns.

~VANHOOK GLADE CAMPGROUND. [Fig. 37(6)] About 4.3 miles west of Highlands (elevation 3,300 feet). The campground is open from about mid-May until late October, depending on the weather. Each of the 21 quiet, secluded, small campsites has a parking space, grill/fireplace, table and tent pad. A small- to medium-size trailer will fit the parking space; no RV's are allowed. A volunteer host is on site to answer questions. No group larger than family-size is permitted to camp. There are five water spigots and a flush toilet. The area is 1.5 miles from Cliffside Lake by either road or trail.

~CLIFFSIDE LAKE RECREATION AREA. [Fig. 37(7)] 4.4 miles west of Highlands and 1.5 miles off US 64, Cliffside is open year-round, but no water is available from the end of October until mid-May. There are 11 campsites, picnic tables and shelters, a bathhouse with cold showers and flush toilets and a clifftop vista shelter. There are no facilities for trailers. Cliffside Lake provides good trout fishing and a swimming beach. There are six marked hiking trails in the area ranging from 0.5 mile to 1.5 miles in length, including a loop trail around the lake. White pine and eastern hemlock trees, rhododendron, blackberry and mountain laurel grow in the campground.

~LOWER CULLASAJA FALLS. 8 miles west of Highlands, this falls cascades about 250 feet. It is unmarked, but there is a pull-over area in which to park and view the falls. The trees in this area include tulip poplar, yellow birch, red oak and chestnut oak. Also present is grape, Virginia creeper and wild hydrangea.

~GLEN FALLS (BLUE VALLEY). [Fig. 37(22)] A gravel, one-lane, forest service road approximately 1.5 miles southwest of Highlands on the south side of NC 106 leads to Glen Falls. Follow this road about a mile to the parking area and a sign for Glen Falls Scenic Area. It is a short 0.5-mile walk to the falls. Glen Falls is a series of three falls, approximately 60 feet each, on the east fork of Overflow Creek. A steep one-mile trail with steps and places to rest along it goes down to the bottom of the falls, where the view is better. Be cautious, as the trail has washed away in some places. The trail continues down into Blue Valley Campground (primitive). Blueberries and rhododendron grow in the area. Glen Falls offers a magnificent vista over northeastern Georgia and northwestern South Carolina, the Chattooga River valley.

~HIKING TRAILS IN THE HIGHLANDS AREA.

ELLICOTT ROCK TRAIL. [Fig. 36(28)] About 3.75 miles. One of the oldest trails in the area, Ellicott Rock Trail runs from the trailhead to the surveyor's rock marking the intersection of Georgia, North Carolina and South Carolina. It follows an old road bed for over two miles, makes a left turn at a fork and descends to the Ellicott Rock Wilderness and the Chattooga River corridor. It then climbs steeply, crosses the Chattooga River and joins the Chattooga River Trail and Bad Creek Trail. Ellicott Rock is downstream on the far bank, inscribed with a simple "NC" [Fig. 36(30)]. The rock which most people find is actually Commissioner's Rock—the true intersection of the three states. It is located 10 feet downstream from Ellicott Rock and inscribed *LAT 35 AD 1813 NC SC*. Both rocks were named for surveyors who marked state boundaries. The return hike is more difficult than going in; the climb requires two hours or more.

DIRECTIONS: *Follow the directions to Bull Pen Road (above). Go on this road past a primitive campground and look for a sign on the right marked FS 441-F, which leads to a parking area. The trail starts on this old road bed.*

BAD CREEK TRAIL. [Fig. 36(26)] Similar in terrain to the Ellicott Rock Trail (above). This trail follows an old road bed for about 0.75 mile to where an old road, now blocked off, led down to Bad Creek. The main trail continues with gentle ascents and descents for

1.5 miles, where it intersects the Sloan Bridge Trail. It then continues down steeply, with switchbacks for 1.5 miles to the river level. Here it joins the Ellicott Rock Trail and Chattooga River Trail. Ellicott Rock is one-eighth mile down stream.

DIRECTIONS: *The head of the Bad Creek Trail is about 3 miles east of the Bull Pen Road Bridge. The old Forest Service Road, 441-F, is closed, providing unlimited parking available about 50 yards away across Fowler Creek Bridge. A trailhead marker is to be erected to replace the present Ellicott Rock Wilderness boundary sign.*

YELLOW MOUNTAIN TRAIL. [Fig. 37(23)] About 9.4 miles, round-trip. The longest trail in the Highlands area leaves Cole Mountain Gap (4,200 feet) and traverses two peaks—Cole Mountain (4,600 feet) and Shortoff Mountain (5,000 feet)—and ends with a 360-degree panoramic view on Yellow Mountain (5,127 feet). The gneissic, oak ridge forest is dominated by white oak (formerly mixed with chestnut) with unusually abundant serviceberry as a sub-canopy. Offering trailside snacks in late summer and fall are two abundant heaths, deerberry and buckberry. In April to June there are floral displays. Masses of hayscented and New York fern offer pleasing vistas.

DIRECTIONS: *From the junction of US 64 and NC 28 in Highlands, go east on US 64 for 2.6 miles to Cole Mountain Road, also called Buck Creek Road; turn left at the Shortoff Baptist Church sign; go 2.2 miles to Cole Gap and park on the left side of the road. Trail sign is to the right.*

~CAMPGROUNDS AND RECREATION AREAS.

AMMONS BRANCH CAMPGROUND. [Fig. 36&38(18)] Located on the right about 1.5 miles from the fork at the beginning of Bull Pen Road (see above), marked with a Forest Service sign. This little-used, small campground may not be accessible by car after heavy rains. The only water supply is from streams and must be boiled or treated. There are three picnic tables, a grill and a pit toilet. A connector trail leaves from the campground, parallels Bull Pen Road and joins the Ellicott Rock Trail about .2 mile from its head on Bull Pen Road, one mile west of the bridge. There is limited parking at the trailhead.

BLUE VALLEY PRIMITIVE CAMPING AREA. [Fig. 37(29)] Go 6 miles south of Highlands on NC 28, turn right (west) on a gravel road into Blue Valley and then go 3 miles. There is a pit toilet. The water supply is from streams and should be boiled or treated before using. This camp area is recommended for groups. The

Highlands Ranger District Office of the U.S Forest Service has descriptions and maps of hiking trails and waterfalls in the area, as well as brochures on wildflowers and on Whiteside Mountain. This literature would add to the enjoyment of a visit to the area. The office is on US 64, east of Highlands.

ADDITIONAL INFORMATION: *Highlands Ranger District, U.S. Forest Service, Rt. 2, Box 385, Highlands, NC 28741. (704) 526-3766.*

MAP REFERENCES: *USGS 1:24,000 series: Highlands.*

Escarpment Gorges

At the southern edge of the Blue Ridge Mountains the terrain suddenly plunges in a steep escarpment to the Piedmont, over a thousand feet below. In this area rivers form deep gorges and dramatic waterfalls—some near roads and easily seen, others requiring hikes of varying lengths over rugged terrain.

~WHITEWATER FALLS. [Fig. 39(1)] At 411 feet, this is the highest waterfall in the eastern United States. A five-minute walk on a paved path takes visitors to an overlook with a dramatic view of the falls.

To the right, about 100 steps down the gorge, is another excellent view. This is also a good place to see the rock-loving Carolina hemlock. Along the trail, just as it descends from the overlook, large colonies of the uncommon faded trillium may be found blooming in early May. The trail descends to Whitewater River in the bottom of the gorge. A spur trail goes north up the Whitewater River to the base of the falls. There Gleason's white trillium occurs. The rare green salamander is known to inhabit crevices below the falls.

To the left of the overlook, the visitor can follow the Foothills Trail (see below), which passes through this point to the head of the falls about a half mile away.

FACILITIES: *Parking area, picnic area, chemical toilet, bulletin board with trail information, paved path to overlook.*
DIRECTIONS: *From the intersection of US 64 and NC 281 (Bohaynee Road [Fig. 39(2)]), go south on 281. From I-85 north take SC 11, Cherokee Scenic Highway, north to SC 130/171; turn left and go to the entrance of Whitewater Falls picnic area (SC 130/171 becomes NC 281). Note that NC 281, or Bohaynee Road, crosses Horsepasture, Thompson and Whitewater Rivers on the edge of the escarpment.*

~HORSEPASTURE RIVER. [Fig. 39(3)] Includes Drift Falls, Turtleback Falls, Rainbow Falls, Stairstep Falls and Windy Falls [Fig. 39(4)]. These are a series of dramatic waterfalls along Horsepasture River, which has been designated a Wild and Scenic River.

DIRECTIONS: *To reach Horsepasture River [Fig. 39(3)] from the intersection of US 64 and NC 107, go east on 64 and turn right (south) on NC 281, Bohaynee Road; go about 2.2 miles to a small off-road parking area just north of the bridge over Horsepasture River. Several paths and rough roads follow the river downstream and do not consolidate into one identifiable trail until below the first waterfall, Drift Falls. In the summertime this falls becomes a thrilling*

Figure 39 ESCARPMENT GORGES

waterslide for adventurous daredevils. A quarter- to a half-mile downstream from Drift Falls is Turtleback Falls, where the river turns sharply right. Another quarter mile beyond that is Rainbow Falls, which drops a stunning 150 feet over darkened, resistant Cashiers gneiss. A broad spray zone supports interesting bog and seepage area plants. The white water against the dark rock, and the blast of spray, make a trip to Rainbow well worth the short hike. Continue past Rainbow Falls another 0.5 mile to a campsite by a stream. Cross the stream at the right end of the campsite and follow the trail up the hill several hundred yards to a path that goes down the ridge to the river. Take the path to the river where there is another campsite. To the left of the campsite is a trail following the river downstream. Hike along it to see the aptly named Stairstep Falls. Backtrack to the main trail on the ridge and then turn right and continue walking old primitive roads. At each possible turn, go to the right. After about 2 miles, come to the top of Windy Falls [Fig. 39(4)]. Here the Horsepasture is a roaring, windy, rushing, boulder-strewn river in a remote gorge. Some boulders at the top of the falls are the size of small cabins. Only Whitewater Falls [Fig. 39(1)] equals Windy Falls in scenic beauty. Do not try to reach the bottom of Windy Falls from the top. It is simply too treacherous. Instead, on a separate overnight trip, follow the Horsepasture River upstream from the Foothills Trail to the base of the falls. It is a three-to-four-hour hike, well worth the time. Windy Falls may also be reached from the bottom by way of a primitive road from Rosman using a four-wheel-drive vehicle.

Caution: This is extremely rugged and dangerous country. Do not walk or wade close to the rim of any falls. Rainbow Falls alone has claimed a number of lives.

~TOXAWAY DAM. [Fig. 39(5)] This is the best place in all of Appalachia to see how vulnerably thin and shallow mountain soil is, and to witness the fragility of the mountain soils and vegetation. As recounted in *The Floods of 1916* by the Southern Railway Company, on July 5 and 6, 1916, a tropical cyclone came inland from the Gulf of Mexico, reaching the western Carolinas around the 8th. A second storm came in from the Atlantic, and there were tremendous rains on the 15th and 16th in the same area. The French Broad River was four feet, or flood stage, on the morning of the 15th. It had come down from 8.8 feet on the 11th. But with the new rains on the 15th, the river rose to 13.5 feet at 8:00 a.m. on the 16th of July. By 9:00 a.m. on the same day, the river rose to 18.6 feet. At 10:00 a.m. the bridge on which the height of the river was measured was washed away. The crest of the flood was estimated to be 21 feet. It was this rain that washed away the dam at Lake Toxaway in 1916 and sent waters rushing down 16 miles of the Toxaway River Gorge. The dam was not rebuilt until 1960. The force of the flood removed all vegetation from the streamside zone, leaving a remarkable scene of exposed bedrock clearly evident to the visitor today. The dam creating Lake Toxaway is just on the north side of the US 64 bridge over the Toxaway River [Fig. 39(5)].

~SLOAN BRIDGE HIKING TRAIL. To Whitewater Falls via the Foothills Trail. At the Sloan Bridge picnic area [Fig. 36,38&39(61)] the Foothills Trail [Fig. 36,38&39(63)] goes south towards the Fish Hatchery Road and east to Whitewater Falls, while another trail goes west to Ellicott Rock (see Ellicott Rock section). The Foothills Trail to Whitewater Falls provides an interesting and different approach to the falls. This well-marked trail is only moderately difficult, 4.4 miles each way. Approaching the top of Whitewater Falls from upstream gives the hiker a fine view of the South Carolina Piedmont and the gorge. One could hike another 0.3 mile to the picnic area in the parking lot.

FACILITIES: *Picnic tables, a chemical toilet, parking.*
DIRECTIONS: *The beginning point for the hike, the Sloan Bridge picnic area, is on NC 107 about 0.2 mile north of SC 413.*

~FOOTHILLS TRAIL. To Thompson River Gorge [Fig. 39(6)]. About five miles one way. From the Whitewater Falls overlook [Fig. 39(1)] (see directions above), descend into the gorge to the river and walk the Foothills Trail to Thompson River Gorge and the bridge crossing it. The trail follows Whitewater River downstream for about 1.6 miles. It then crosses over ridges and follows old roads for part of the way to Thompson River. Look for wild bergamot and several small falls. There is an especially nice slide just off the trail to the left about 10 yards before the trail makes a sharp right turn from an old road to descend into Thompson River Gorge. The rushing water, huge boulders and steep-sided gorge provide a sense of remoteness from civilization seldom found. Some adventurous hikers may wish to rockhop upriver to Thompson High Falls, one of the most beautiful falls in the Escarpment Gorge region. Allow two or more hours for this trip.

This is also one of the few areas where *shortia* or *oconee bells*, can be seen. According to Duncan and Foote, *Wildflowers of the Southeastern United States*, this flower is found in only seven counties in Georgia, South Carolina and North Carolina.

On the other side of Whitewater River, a nature trail is marked at the point where the Foothills Trail leaves the river at 1.6 miles. Old trail books by Allen de Hart describe a cable bridge which crosses the river to the nature trail. The bridge is not there now, and the river may be too high to ford. The Duke Power folder also describes a road to this area with a parking lot and access to lower Whitewater Falls. This access to the lower falls, however, is blocked by the Duke Power Bad Creek Reservoir Project. One can hike to

Oconee bells
Shortia galacifolia

One of our rarest plants, shortia occurs only in the escarpment gorges from Toxaway River west to possibly the Chattooga watershed where there is at least one possible natural colony. Shortia was found by Michaux in 1788, then "lost" and rediscovered in 1877 north of Lake Jocassee.

the top of the lower falls, but it is not reccommended, it requires scrambling on unmarked fishermen's paths.

~BACKPACKING ALONG THE FOOTHILLS TRAIL. One of the best ways to understand and learn about the Escarpment Gorges would be to backpack the Foothills Trail from Whitewater Falls to Toxaway River boat-access or to US 178 at Laurel Valley. One could set up two cars, one at Whitewater Falls picnic area (see directions above) and the other at Laurel Valley. The distance would be 32.7 miles one-way along the Foothills Trail. The hiker would visit the gorges of the Whitewater River, Thompson River, Bear Camp Creek, Horsepasture River and Toxaway River.

DIRECTIONS: *For driving to Whitewater River picnic area, see above. To leave a car or set up a shuttle at Laurel Valley, contact Hugh or Carol Nourse (404) 353-8222.*
ADDITIONAL INFORMATION: *For a brochure on the Foothills Trail, contact Duke Power Company Project Recreation, P.O. Box 33189, Charlotte, NC., (704) 373-8032; or the Foothills Trail Conference, P.O. Box 3041, Greenville, SC 29602.*

~SILVER RUN FALLS. [Fig. 39(7)] Silver Run is one of the creeks merging into Whitewater River to create Whitewater Falls. The falls drops 30 feet into a marvelous open pool with its own beach. Sitting on a rock in this pool, one would imagine it to be very far from the road.

DIRECTIONS: *To reach the falls from the junction of US 64 and NC 107, go south 4 miles on 107. There will be a dirt parking area on the left side of the road. There are two such areas along this stretch; the one with the telephone pole is the correct one. The trail to Silver Run Falls starts by the pole and is an easy graded trail for 0.14 mile.*

MAP REFERENCES: *USGS 1:24,000 series: Cashiers - Reid. Other maps: Duke Power Company Foothills Trail Brochure; Forest Service handout map with falls marked.*

The Georgia Conservancy

Figure 40   COWEE GEM REGION

©1990 THE GEORGIA CONSERVANCY, INC.

0   Miles   2

Cowee Gem Region

During the late 1800's, corundum—a mineral second in hardness only to diamond—was mined extensively in north Georgia and North Carolina. Corundum was valuable in the manufacture of abrasives such as sandpaper. Impurities in the mineral also resulted in gem-quality sapphires and rubies, which were sometimes found during the course of mining corundum ore. In fact, the mineralized zone running northeast and southwest through Georgia and North Carolina was second only to the Mogok region of Burma as a source of high-quality rubies and sapphires. After the discovery that, with plentiful electricity, aluminum oxide could be artificially fused to make corundum, the commercial mining operations quickly closed down, and the economics of gemstone mining never made it a viable industry in the area. Presently, Thailand seems to be the main source of gem-quality rubies and sapphires. In more recent years, serious rock hounds and those just simply curious have discovered that the Cowee gem region and a number of locations around Franklin, North Carolina, still produce valuable gems, primarily for the tourist market.

Most mines in Macon County are placer or gravel deposits. The gems weather out of decomposing bedrock higher in the watershed and are washed down by streams. Most of the gem mines furnish equipment, shovels, screens and running water to wash the gravel. Either there is a flat fee, or one pays for the gravel processed.

~FRANKLIN GEM AND MINERAL MUSEUM. [Fig. 40(1)] Located in the 15-year-old brick jail, the museum displays a variety of Macon County minerals, including a 48-pound corundum crystal. This is a good first stop on a visit to the area to become familiar with the appearance of the minerals and gems mined nearby.

DATES/HOURS: *Open May 1-Oct 31.*
DIRECTIONS: *Located on Phillips St. in Franklin, NC.*

~MINING OPERATIONS. [Fig. 40(*)] A number of these mines lie along Caler's Fork [Fig. 40(3)] on Cowee Creek [Fig. 40(2)]. Many of these mines, as well as others in the area, have native gems such as rubies, sapphires and garnets. Some also sell "enriched" gravel by the bucket, meaning that exotic (and inexpensive) stones from all over the world have been added to the raw material.

FACILITIES: *Facilities vary at each mining location, but most have restrooms, picnic and play areas; some have campsites with showers; most provide assistance in learning how to search for gems.*
DATES/HOURS: *Most mines are open from 8 or 9 in the morning until 5 or so in the evening, six or seven days a week. Season is generally*

from Apr through Oct.

DIRECTIONS: *Go 6 miles north of Franklin on NC 28; turn right at West's Mill [Fig. 40(2)]; take the first road south, then the first road east (1340) and follow that as it becomes 1341 and eventually 1343 along Caler Fork. Watch for signs.*

~CORUNDUM HILL. [Fig. 40(4)] This is a famous corundum mine which has yielded some fine gems, including sapphires in orchid, green, yellow, pink and blue, as well as 587- and 760-caret rubies. This deposit is associated with the ultrabasic rocks serpentine and dunite, as is the corundum at the Buck Creek olivine pine barrens.

DIRECTIONS: *Just north of US 64, about 5.5 miles east of the 441/64 interchange in Franklin, NC.*

~MINCEY MINE. [Fig. 40(5)] This is another well-known deposit of unusual bronze sapphires which "star." No equipment is furnished here.

DIRECTIONS: *Go 2.4 miles east of the US 441/64 interchange on US 64, turning left just before the first bridge and proceeding 5.8 miles to Ellijay. Inquire.*

~MASON MOUNTAIN. [Fig. 40(7)] The Franklin area is also noted for the occurrence of a splendid rose-pink variety of pyrope garnet called "rhodolite," first discovered on Mason Mountain. One can visit the Mason Mountain Rhodolite Mine or screen or pan for garnets in the gravels of Mason's Branch, Cowee Creek and Caler Fork. With luck, amateur miners might recover a piece of ruby or sapphire corundum. Mason Mountain is just south of Caler's fork. Watch for signs.

~OTHER MINES. A look at the map will indicate the stunning number of old or active mines in the area around Franklin (mine symbols). All are not gem mines. Some are giant open cuts where mica or other minerals were mined [Fig. 40(6)]. This particular mine has enormous amounts of almost pure-white quartz. Unfortunately there are no good maps to the location of Macon County mines, nor is there information as to what is or was mined at particular sites. A few mines are no longer on revised 7.5-minute topographical maps. Inquiring of local residents seems to be one of the most productive means of finding interesting localities.

~NIKWASI INDIAN MOUND. [Fig. 40(1)] The Franklin area is rich in Indian history and pre-history. Practically in the center of Franklin is an Indian mound on the south bank of the Little Tennessee River at the bridge.

Near West's Mill there is a marker on Hwy 28 showing the location of the major Indian communities of Cowee [Fig. 40(8)] on the flood plain of the Little Tennessee River. Explorer and naturalist William Bartram passed through the Franklin area in the late 1700's.

MAP REFERENCES: *USGS 1:24,000 series: Greens Creek - Alarka - Franklin - Corbin Knob (NC).*

Long Trails

Three long trails -- the Appalachian, the Benton MacKaye and the Bartram -- provide hikers with an opportunity to cover long distances entirely by foot. In addition, by combining these three trails with the Foothills Trail in South Carolina, the resourceful hiker could travel between 360 to 400 miles across some of the most varied and dramatic scenery in the Southeast.

The Appalachain Trail

The Appalachian National Scenic Trail is a wilderness footpath that winds over 2,100 miles along the crest of the Appalachian Mountains. It runs through fourteen eastern states, stretching from Springer Mountain in Georgia to Mount Katahdin in Maine. The "AT," as it is called, is known throughout the world, each year attracting hikers from many different countries.

The trail began over 60 years ago with a "grand vision" articulated in 1921 by Benton MacKaye—forester, regional planner and conservationist. MacKaye, now known as the "Father of the Appalachian Trail," proposed a "long trail over the full length of the Appalachian skyline, from the highest peak in the North to the highest peak in the South." His proposal, not just a detailed trail plan, envisioned the long trail as an escape for people in the crowded cities of the Eastern Seaboard, a place for regeneration of the human spirit through what he termed "harmony with primeval influences." The work on the trail was to be done primarily by volunteers. Trail enthusiasts, some of whom had also suggested a "grand trunk" trail along the Appalachian ridges, were galvanized into action by MacKaye and his inspiring article. The establishment of the Appalachian Trail was to be the culmination of many years of their hopes and dreams. Early hiking clubs in New England and New York had laid the foundations for this new trail; parts of their existing trails were used to form the first sections of the AT. In 1925 the Appalachian Trail Conference was formed as a confederation of clubs which were to build and maintain the trail.

In the South little was known of the mountain areas, and a trail route was chosen largely from maps. In 1929 Roy Ozmer, a Georgian and accomplished woodsman, was chosen to scout the entire trail from Virginia through Georgia. Once a route was decided upon, volunteers were recruited, maintenance clubs were formed and, in some places, with the help of U.S. Forest Service and Civilian Conservation Corps crews, the trail was built. The last section to be completed was in Maine in 1937.

The trail in Georgia was completed in 1931, through the combined efforts of members of the newly-organized Georgia Appalachian Trail Club and the U.S. Forest Service. The original southern terminus of

Figure 41   LONG TRAILS

the trail was Mt. Oglethorpe, near Tate, but development and chicken farming on private land between Amicalola Falls and Mt. Oglethorpe intruded on the wilderness experience of hikers, forcing the terminus to be moved in 1958 to Springer Mountain.

In 1968 Congress authorized the AT as the first "National Scenic Trail;" in 1978 it appropriated funds to acquire lands along the route to protect the trail from encroaching development. Maintenance of the trail rests with the Appalachian Trail Conference (ATC). In 1984, the Secretary of Interior signed a delegation agreement with ATC assigning to it unprecedented responsibilities for operations, development, monitoring and maintenance of the trail. Volunteers in AT clubs carry out these duties.

The Georgia portion of the AT extends some 75.6 miles through primitive areas of the Chattahoochee National Forest. Although rising at times to elevations of over 4,400 feet, the trail is mostly along ridges at elevations around 3,000 feet. Ascents and descents are sometimes steep but often rewarded by grand views from rocky outcrops and open summits.

Most of the AT goes through deciduous hardwood forest—largely hickory, oak and poplar. Rainfall is heavy and frequent, especially in the spring; ridges are often snow-capped or ice-covered in the winter. Mid-April through mid-May is the peak wildflower season. Flowers found along the trail include trillium, bloodroot, mayapple, bluets, wild azalea and sometimes pink and yellow lady slippers. In June many sections are covered with flowering rhododendron and mountain laurel. The heavy rains ensure lush vegetation during the summer months; ferns are found in abundance all along the trail. The last two weeks of October are usually the best time to find autumn colors at their height. In winter when the leaves are off the trees, the trail offers ever-present scenic vistas of the surrounding countryside and of the mountains of the north and west.

The Georgia portion of the trail is managed and maintained by the Georgia Appalachian Trail Club, through a cooperative agreement with the U.S. Forest Service, Chattahoochee National Forest. Members of the club may be found on the trail almost every weekend cutting weeds, clearing blowdowns, painting blazes, repairing shelters, reconstructing portions of the trail or participating in recreational hikes.

The trail's southern terminus is located atop remote Springer Mountain, near FS 42. Since this area is difficult to reach by automobile, an 8.5-mile approach trail begins at Amicalola Falls State Park on GA 52. Mountains along the trail with outstanding scenic views include Big Cedar Mountain, Blood, Cowrock, Rocky and Tray. One of the many side trails leads from Chattahoochee Gap to the highest point in Georgia, Brasstown Bald. The trail passes through three of Georgia's wilderness areas: Raven Cliffs Wilderness between Neel's Gap and Tesnatee Gap, Tray Mountain Wilderness between Tray Gap and Addis Gap and the Southern

Nantahala Wilderness north of Dick's Creek Gap. Bly Gap on the Georgia/North Carolina border is the northern end of the AT in Georgia.

The trail is marked throughout its length with rectangular white blazes and is generally easy to follow. Double blazes indicate caution, usually meaning a turn in the trail. Side trails and trails to water are blue-blazed; signs are placed at road crossings, shelters and other important intersections.

There are 11 shelters on the Georgia AT, placed more or less at intervals permitting easy day hikes. All but one of these shelters are three-sided, open-front types with floors. Springs are reasonably close by. The exception is the stone, two-room structure atop Blood Mountain. It has four sides, a fireplace, windows and a sleeping platform. There is no water on top of Blood Mountain.

~REACHING THE TRAIL. There is no public transportation to the AT in Georgia. The trail can be reached via the six main highways which traverse the mountains; usually the trail crosses at the highway's highest point, where a large hiking trail sign should be visible. Ample parking is available.

~ROAD CROSSINGS. Approximate Distances from the Nearest Town, and Distance by Trail to the Next Paved Road Crossing:

AMICALOLA FALLS STATE PARK APPROACH TRAIL ON GA 52. *15 miles west of Dahlonega, 15 miles northwest of Dawsonville, 20 miles east of Ellijay. 28.8 miles by AT to Woody Gap.*

WOODY GAP ON GA 60. *15 miles north of Dahlonega. 11.3 miles by AT to Neel's Gap.*

NEEL'S GAP ON US 129/19. *15 miles south of Blairsville, 19 miles northwest of Cleveland, 22 miles north of Dahlonega. 5.7 miles by AT to Tesnatee Gap, 6.6 miles to Hog Pen Gap.*

TESNATEE GAP AND HOG PEN GAP ON GA 348. (RICHARD RUSSELL SCENIC HIGHWAY). *12 miles northwest of Helen, 15 miles southeast of Blairsville. 14.9 miles by AT from Tesnatee Gap to Unicoi Gap, 14 miles from Hog Pen Gap to Unicoi Gap.*

UNICOI GAP ON GA 75. *10 miles north of Helen, 14 miles south of Hiawassee. 16.6 miles by AT to Dick's Creek Gap.*

DICK'S CREEK GAP ON US 76. *11 miles east of Hiawassee, 18 miles west of Clayton. 8.7 miles by AT to Bly Gap on North Carolina border (no road access).*

NOTE: The approach to Springer Mountain by automobile involves traveling on rough, unpaved Forest Service roads. One such road, FS 42, which runs from the town of Suches (enter from GA 60 next to Tritt's Store, 1.6 miles north on highway from Woody Gap) provides access to several points along the trail passing through Gooch Gap, Cooper Gap, Hightower Gap and Springer Mountain. It also connects with FS 58 to Three Forks.

~SUGGESTED DAY HIKES

SPRINGER MOUNTAIN-THREE FORKS AREA. *Highlights are views from a rocky outcrop atop Springer Mountain, southern terminus of the AT; the magnificent stand of virgin hemlock along Stover Creek; and three beautiful mountain streams which converge at Three Forks. From Springer Mountain both the AT and the Benton MacKaye Trail (marked by diamond-shaped white blazes) lead by different routes to Three Forks, intersecting twice to form either two five-mile loop trails or one 10-mile figure-eight loop trail. Access to Springer Mountain is on unpaved FS 42 and to Three Forks, on unpaved FS 58. Both are moderate climbs.*

BIG CEDAR MOUNTAIN. *Views from rocky overlook; two-mile round-trip hike north on AT from Woody Gap.*

BLOOD MOUNTAIN. *Grand views from rocky summit and rock outcrops below summit; 4.2-mile round trip to top; south on AT from Neel's Gap; 1,300-foot climb.*

LAKE WINFIELD SCOTT LOOP. *Blue-blazed trail leads from the west side of the camping area one mile to Jarrard Gap on the AT and from the east side 2.2 miles to Slaughter Gap on the AT. By following the AT between Jarrard and Slaughter Gaps, one can make a loop hike. An additional 2.2-mile round-trip hike can be made from Slaughter Gap to the summit of Blood Mountain.*

NEEL'S GAP TO TESNATEE GAP. *5.7 miles one-wa,y or 11.4 miles round-trip hike along ridge trail, with viewpoints from Levelland, Turkey Pen and Cowrock Mountains. At Neel's Gap the trail passes through the archway between two buildings at Walasi-Yi Inn, a hiking/craft store; moderate climbs.*

WILDCAT MOUNTAIN. *Viewpoints on summit and on top of ridge out blue-blazed side-trail. One-mile round trip to summit plus one-mile round trip on blue-blazed trail; south on AT from Hog Pen Gap; easy/moderate climb.*

ROCKY MOUNTAIN LOOP. *Six-mile loop or three-mile round trip to summit; north on trail from Unicoi Gap. Fine views lie southward along the summit trail. For loop hike, continue along summit on AT; descend 1.3 miles to Indian Grave Gap; turn left (north) on forest road following blue blaze for approximately one mile; turn left off road into woods and follow blue blaze back to junction with AT (approximately 1 mile); 1,200 foot climb.*

TRAY MOUNTAIN. *Views from an open, rocky summit. 10.8-mile round trip north on trail from Unicoi Gap; or one-mile round trip north on trail from Tray Gap on FS 79 (access from GA 75, two miles north of Helen or two miles north of Unicoi Gap).*

~Trail Descriptions

APPROACH: AMICALOLA FALLS STATE PARK. *From visitor center, trail goes 8.5 miles north to summit of Springer Mountain. Frosty Mountain at mile 4.8 of approach trail; Nimblewill Gap at mile 6.2 of approach trail*

00.0 MILE. *Springer Mt. (3,782 feet). Southern terminus of the AT. Plaque on rock, mailbox with register on nearby tree. Mount Katahdin in Maine is 2,100 miles north via the white-blazed trail.*

00.2 MILE. *Springer Mt. shelter with seasonal spring. Located down side trail to right of AT, 02.5 Miles. Stover Creek shelter with all-season stream nearby. Located to left of AT, down old logging road.*

05.0 MILES. *Long Creek Falls.*

07.7 MILES. *Hawk Mt. shelter; water from nearby stream.*

08.2 MILES. *Hightower Gap (gravel FS Rd 42).*

16.7 MILES. *Gooch Gap shelter to right; good spring 0.2 mile south on AT.*

20.3 MILES. *Woody Gap (paved GA 60); parking.*

21.3 MILES. *Big Cedar Mountain; good rock ledges and views.*

29.5 MILES. *Blood Mountain (4,461 feet); highest point on the Georgia AT. Fine views are afforded on clear days. Blood Mt.*

shelter is located on the summit. Closest water is in Slaughter Gap, one mile and 660-foot descent south on AT.

31.6 MILES. *Neel's Gap (paved US 19); parking at Byron Reese, north on highway.*

32.9 MILES. *Levelland Mt.; views to right and left.*

35.2 MILES. *Wolf Laurel Top; views to right in clearing.*

36.5 MILES. *Cowrock Mt.; views on rocks via side trail to right.*

37.3 MILES. *Tesnatee Gap on GA 348, Russell Scenic Hwy.; parking.*

38.0 MILES. *Wildcat Mt.; views. Side trail leads right 1.1 miles to Whitley Gap shelter with dependable spring.*

38.2 MILES. *Hogpen Gap on GA 348; parking.*

42.6 MILES. *Low Gap shelter, right via side trail into cove; spring and stream nearby.*

47.6 MILES. *Chattahoochee Gap with spring, right via side trail, being the headwaters of the Chattahoochee River. 49.4 miles. Site of former Rocky Knob shelter, recently torn down. New shelter 0.5 mile north on trail; spring downhill below old shelter site.*

50.0 MILES. *Blue Mt. shelter via side trail to left; spring on AT just before turnoff to shelter.*

52.2 MILES. *Unicoi Gap (paved GA 75); parking.*

57.6 MILES. *Tray Mt. (4,430 feet); outstanding views from summit. On descent going north, obscure trail to right leads out an arm to pinnacle.*

58.1 MILES. *Tray Mt. shelter left via side trail; good spring behind and down from shelter.*

63.4 MILES. *Addis Gap shelter to right, 0.3 mile down old fire road; stream in front of shelter.*

63.8 MILES. *Dick's Creek Gap (paved US 76); picnic tables; seasonal stream.*

73.1 MILES.   *Plum Orchard Gap shelter located to the right of the gap down side trail. Spring near shelter, but better spring down ravine to left of AT.*

77.5 MILES.   *Bly Gap; the Georgia/North Carolina state line. There is no road access to this gap except by four-wheel-drive vehicles. The gap is often missed by hikers because as one comes from the south, the gap is climbed into instead of descended into. Hikers have arrived when there is a gnarled tree to the right and a sweeping vista to the left.*

80.7 MILES.   *Muskrat shelter in North Carolina to right; stream and privy next to shelter.*

The Benton MacKaye Trail

On October 14, 1989, many volunteers, along with a number of U.S Forest Service employees with whom they had worked jointly on the endeavor, celebrated the opening of the Georgia section of the interesting and diverse Benton MacKaye (pronounced Mac-eye) Trail (BMT). From its beginning at Springer Mountain, the trail's distance covers 78.6 miles to the border of Tennessee in the Cohutta Wilderness. The trail should eventually wind through Tennessee and North Carolina, forming a 250-mile loop with the Appalachian Trail and providing an alternative long-distance footpath in the Southeast.

Named for Benton MacKaye, the "Father of the Appalachian Trail" (see above), this trail grew out of the need to develop an alternative to the popular Appalachian Trail and also to develop a trail that more closely adhered to MacKaye's original trail plan—a plan that envisioned a path reaching to the Cohuttas in the north-central portion of Georgia.

Although the trail is new, volunteers have already documented much of the variety along its path. Two beautiful waterfalls, Long Creek Falls and Fall Branch, are scenic attractions. Atop Rhodes Mountain in the winter, one is afforded a 360-degree view of the surrounding countryside. A striking man-made attraction is the suspension bridge across the beautiful Toccoa River. The terrain varies: from laurel-and-rhododendron-covered walks along creeks to timbered land to ridgetop pathways to walks through thick forests. There are areas with quick access to major highways through Georgia, as well as quite remote areas within and south of the Cohutta Wilderness. There is a 26-mile stretch of trail with only two road crossings.

The BMT is blazed with an off-white diamond symbol. The blazes are located at an approximate interval of 200 feet. There may be other blazes present, such as the white vertical two-by-six-inch stripe of the AT or the two-by-six-inch vertical blue blaze of the Duncan Ridge Trail. These blazes are present only along the first 20 miles of the BMT and will not be seen west of Rhodes Mountain. See below for other trail blazes in the Rich Mountain area and in the Cohutta Wilderness area.

ADDITIONAL INFORMATION: *Write the Benton MacKaye Trail Association, P.O. Box 53271, Atlanta, GA 30355-1271.*

~WALKING THE BENTON MACKAYE TRAIL

SECTION 1: SPRINGER MOUNTAIN [FIG. 41(1)] TO THREE FORKS [FIG. 41(2)]. *5.8 miles, south to north. Easy. This section essentially traverses the pre-1977 corridor of the AT. It is well-constructed, well-blazed and relatively easy. Access roads are FS 42 and FS 58 (Noontootla Creek Road).*

SECTION 2: THREE FORKS [FIG. 41(2)] TO GA HWY 60 [FIG. 41(3)]. *11.4 miles, south to north. Moderate. This section is contiguous in part with the AT and entirely with the Duncan Ridge Trail. It is moderate in difficulty and is essentially an overnight hike. Highlights of this section are the dramatic Forest Service suspension bridge over the Toccoa River and the newly-created wildlife opening where many animals and plants may be readily seen. Access roads are FS 58 and GA Hwy 60.*

SECTION 3: GA HWY 60 [FIG. 41(3)] TO SKEENAH GAP [FIG. 41(4)]. *5.7 miles, south to north. Difficult. This section is the most strenuous part of the BMT. The view from the top, however, after the character-building climb up the south face of Wallhalah Mountain, is worth the effort. Note that at Rhodes Mountain the Duncan Ridge Trail turns east-northeast, while the Benton MacKaye Trail regains its own identity and proceeds westward. Access roads are GA Hwy 60 and Skeenah Gap Road.*

SECTION 4: SKEENAH GAP [FIG. 41(4)] TO WILSCOT GAP [FIG. 41(5)]. *5.3 miles, east to west. Moderate. An up-and-down hike through general forest area. This is a very nice day-hike, especially in winter, with views of the adjacent ridges and pastoral valleys. Access roads are Skeenah Gap Road and GA Hwy 60 at Wilscot Gap.*

SECTION 5: WILSCOT GAP [FIG. 41(5)] TO SHALLOWFORD BRIDGE [FIG. 41(6)]. *7.1 miles, east to west. Moderate. The most difficult part of this hike is the initial climb up Tipton Mountain. After this, the trail undulates over Brawley Mountain and Garland Mountain before descending to the beautiful Toccoa River. The climbs will challenge, and the beauty of the forest is rewarding. Access is by GA 60 and adjacent FS road, Dial Road and Aska Road. The number of access points allows for shorter hikes if desired.*

SECTION 6: SHALLOWFORD BRIDGE [FIG. 41(6)] TO GA HWY 5 [FIG. 41(7)]. *11.4 miles, east to west. Moderate. This is an obvious overnight trek, but may be shortened to a very pleasant day hike by skipping 3.2 miles of road walk on the eastern end and 1.6 miles of road walk on the western end, taking only the 6.6-mile trail from Fall Branch to Laurel Creek. This section provides many sites atop Rocky and/or Davenport Mountains or Scroggin Knob to stop, rest and enjoy the views. Fall Branch Falls is a highlight right at the start, and the view from Scroggin Knob near the end of the hike is also pleasurable. It is here, climbing Rocky Mountain, that the BMT begins to follow the western arm of the Blue Ridge. White square blazes designating the contiguous Rich Mountain Trail will also be seen here. The BMT will follow this ridge to its current terminus at the Georgia-Tennessee state line at Double Spring Gap. Access to the forested portion is via Stanley Gap Road, 3.2 miles west of where it and Aska Road intersect, and the Weaver Creek Road at its southwest end at the USFS boundary line.*

SECTION 7: GA HWY 5 [FIG. 41(7)] TO BUSH HEAD GAP [FIG. 41(8)]. *6.6 miles, east to west. Easy. This is a road walk along the public roads of Gilmer County. The scenery ranges from mobile homes to second-home developments to farm dwellings. Roads include Gilmer County Road 187, Boardtown Road and the Bush Head Gap Road.*

SECTION 8: BUSH HEAD GAP [FIG. 41(8)] TO DYER GAP [FIG. 41(9)]. *12.6 miles, north to south and south to north. Moderate. A long day-hike or a very pleasant overnight trip, this part of the BMT is located entirely along the Tennessee Valley Divide. This is general forest land and many activities of the multi-use forest, such as logging, will be seen here. Road access is by the Bush Head Gap Road and FS 64 south of Watson Gap at the northern end.*

SECTION 9: DYER GAP [FIG. 41(9)] TO WATSON GAP [FIG. 41(10)]. *4.5 miles, south to north. Easy. A very short segment of the BMT, this footpath traverses riverside, forest timber management activity areas and climbs a mountain with views of the Cohutta Wilderness before returning to the trailhead. Road access is by FS 64 at Dyer Gap and the old State Route 2 at Watson Gap.*

SECTION 10: WATSON GAP [FIG. 41(10)] TO DOUBLE SPRING GAP [FIG. 41(11)]. *8.5 miles, south to north. Moderate. This section along the high ridge is located primarily within the Cohutta Wilderness boundary. It is minimally blazed and semi-primitive in construction. The BMT is contiguous with the Hemptop Trail north of Dally Gap. The blazing changes once again, but the former Forest Service road provides an easily-followed path. Road access is at Watson Gap. Double Spring Gap is at the Georgia-Tennessee state line in the middle of the wilderness. A trail here leads north.*

The Bartram Trail

William Bartram was a native Philadelphian from a prominent family boasting kinship with Benjamin Franklin. In his early 30's, while unsuccessfully managing a plantation in northern Florida, Bartram became enamored with the Southern wilderness—a fascination which was to launch him on a career that would lead to worldwide fame. An instinctive naturalist and explorer, he roamed through Georgia, Florida, South Carolina and Alabama and as far west as Louisiana from 1773 until 1776, studying and drawing the plants and animals of the region. His voluminous illustrated journals of those trips serve as the basis for the Bartram Trail, a portion of which now winds through the north Georgia mountains.

Map Sources

The enjoyment and usefulness of this guidebook will be greatly enhanced by the employment of maps in conjunction with the text. A vast amount of information is available from the following sources.

Topographical Maps of All States

Powers Elevation Co., Inc., *Post Office Box 440889, Aurora, CO 80044 (800) 824-2550. All USGS topos: $3.75 for 1:24,000, $6.00 for 1:100,000, plus postage and handling charge from $2 to $10 per order. Visa, Mastercard and American Express accepted. Allow five to ten days.*

Timely Discount Topos, Inc., *9769 West 119th Drive, Suite 9, Broomfield, CO 80020. (800) 821-7609. All USGS topos: $3.50 for 1:24,000, $5.50 for 1:100,000, plus postage and $1 handling charge per order. Checks only. Allow five to ten days.*

The U.S. Geological Survey, *Map sales, Box 25286, Denver, CO 80225. (303) 236-7477. Call 1-800-USA MAPS first for a free index with order form. Cost: $2.50 for 1:24,000, $4 for 1:100,000. Allow six to eight weeks.*

Topographical Maps of Georgia

Enpro Engineering Reprographics, *1800 Peachtree St., Suite 210, Atlanta, GA 30309. (404) 355-8520. Cost: $3 for 1:24,000, $4.50 for 1:100,000, plus postage and $1.89 if maps are rolled rather than folded. Allow five to eight days.*

The Georgia Geological Survey, *Agriculture Bldg., Room 406A, 19 Martin Luther King Jr. Dr. SW, Atlanta, GA 30334. (404) 656-3214.* Cost: $2.50 for 1:24,000; $4.00 for 1:100,000 plus 5% sales tax and postage. Allow three to five days.

Topographical Maps of Western North Carolina and Towns County and Rabun County, Georgia

Macon County Supply Company, *190 Depot St., Franklin, NC 28734. (704) 524-4428. Cost: $3.75 for 1:24,000. Raised relief maps of GA, NC, SC and TN. $14.95 for 1:125,000.*

THE GEORGIA CONSERVANCY

State Park Maps

The Georgia Department of Natural Resources, *Parks, Recreation and Historic Sites Division, Floyd Tower East, 205 Butler Street SE, Suite 1362, Atlanta, GA 30334 (404) 331-5187. To make reservations, call the appropriate park at the number listed in Appendix B.*

Forest Service Maps

The U.S. Department of Agriculture, *Forest Service, Southern Region, Suite 850, 1720 Peachtree Road NW, Atlanta, GA 30367-9102 (404) 347-2384 or, in limited quantities, from USFS ranger stations throughout Georgia. Cost: free, $2, $5. Maps used for this guidebook included The Cherokee National Forest, The Appalachian Trail, The Chattahoochee National Forest, The Chattooga National Wild and Scenic River, The Cohutta Wilderness, The Nantahala Wilderness, and The Southern Nantahala Wilderness and Standing Indian Basin.*

TVA Maps of Lakes Blue Ridge, Chatuge and Nottely

The Tennessee Valley Authority, *Maps and Surveys Dept., 101 Haney Bldg., 311 Broad St., Chattanooga, TN 37402-2801 (615) 751-6277. Cost: $.75 or $1.50 plus a handing/mailing charge of $1 or 10% for orders over $50.*

Army Engineers' Lake Maps of Carter's Lake and Lake Allatoona

The U.S. Army Corps of Engineers, *Public Affairs Office, 30 Pryor Street SW, Atlanta, GA 30303 (404) 331-6715.*

State Highway Maps and County Roadmaps

Alabama Highway Department, *1409 Coliseum Blvd, Rm. R-103, Montgomery, AL 36130 (205) 261-6071.*

Georgia Department of Transportation, *Map Sales Division, 2 Capitol Square, Atlanta, GA 30334 (404) 656-5336.*

North Carolina Department of Transportation, *Map Sales Division, Location and Survey Unit, P.O. Box 25201, Raleigh, NC 27611 (919) 733-7600.*

South Carolina Highway Department, *Map Sales Division, P.O. Box 191, Columbia, S.C. 29202 (803) 737-1501.*

Tennessee Department of Transportation, *Map Sales Office, Suite 1000 James K. Polk Building, 505 Deaderick Street, Nashville, TN 37219-5538 (615) 741-2195.*

Note: Information on road conditions in Georgia is available from the Georgia Department of Transportation at (404) 656-5267.

State Parks

Mountain Area Parks

Georgia's state parks are operated by the Parks, Recreation and Historic Sites Division, Georgia Department of Natural Resources, Floyd Tower East, Suite 1352, 205 Butler St. SE, Atlanta, GA 30334. The following state parks are in the mountain region covered by this guidebook.

Amicalola Falls, *Star Route, Dawsonville, GA 305341 (404) 265-2885.*

Black Rock Mountain, *Mountain City, GA 30562 (404) 746-2141.*

Cloudland Canyon, *Route 2, Box 150, Rising Fawn, GA 30738 (404) 657-4050.*

Fort Mountain, *Route 7, Box 1K, Chatsworth, GA 30705, (404) 695-2621.*

James H. "Sloppy" Floyd, *Route 1, Summerville, GA 30747 (404) 857-5211.*

Moccasin Creek, *Route 1, Lake Burton, GA 30523 (404) 947-3194.*

Red Top Mountain, *Cartersville, Ga 30120 (404) 974-5184.*

Unicoi, *P.O.Box 849, Helen, GA 30545 (404) 878-3366.*

Vogel, *Route 1, Box 1230, Blairsville, GA 30512 (404) 745-2628.*

Georgia's state parks offer excellent opportunities to enjoy a variety of natural environments. There is much to see and do including hiking, swimming, camping, fishing, boating and picnicking.

All state parks in the Georgia mountains offer tent and trailer camping, and all but two ("Sloppy" Floyd and Moccasin Creek) offer cottages for rent. Day use picnicking is not allowed in the camping areas. No fees are charged for fishing in park lakes, rivers and streams, but a valid Georgia fishing license is required of all residents 16 or older. Non-residents must have a valid, non-resident license. Trout stamps are required for fishing in streams. Canoes, fishing boats and boats with motors are available for rent at many state parks.

Campgrounds

Campgrounds are open from 7 am to 10 pm and require registration and payment of a fee before setting up camp. Permits to set up camp should be obtained by 8 pm; checkout deadline is 3 pm. Arrivals at campsite after hours will be asked to pay the following morning.

Camping rigs plus two boat trailers and one pup tent are allowed on each site. Park campgrounds have picnic tables with benches, electrical hook-ups, water faucets, charcoal grills, playground equipment, garbage pick-up and restrooms with hot and cold water, showers and lavatories. Some have sanitary dumping stations, coin-operated laundromats, public telephones and refreshment vending machines. Maximum occupancy of any particular site is 14 days. Campers under 18 must be accompanied by a responsible adult.

Organized groups are expected to use group campsites or pioneer camping areas rather than individual, developed tent and trailer camping areas. No RV's are allowed in these areas.

Group camps, available only to groups with a camp director or official supervising committee, offer sleeping quarters, kitchen, dining-assembly room, craft shops, activity field and swimming area.

Reservations for stays of two days or more can be made up to 30 days in advance by calling the numbers listed below. There is a small non-refundable registration fee. Mastercard and Visa are honored for all camping fees.

Cottages

All cottages in the state parks are fully equipped with stoves and refrigerators, necessary cooking and serving equipment, linens and blankets. All are heated; most are air-conditioned. Maximum period of occupancy is 14 days.

Check-in time for cottages is between 4 and 10 pm; check-out time is 11 am. No pets are allowed in cottages and there are no kennnels available. The cottages are not available to organized groups.

Cottage reservations are accepted no more than 11 months in advance. For June 1 to Labor Day, reservations made more than 30 days in advance must be for a minimum of one week--otherwise, and during the remainder of the year, for two nights. A minimum 72-hour cancellation notice is required for a refund. There is a $10 per unit cancellation fee.

Outfitters, Guides, and Suppliers

The following is a listing of some of the outfitters providing specialized equipment and/or guided expeditions in the Georgia mountains and beyond.

Back Country Adventures. *Sales and rental of backpacking, camping and mountain biking equipment. Guided backpacking and mountain bicycling trips in north Georgia and North Carolina. Rt. 2, Box 2242-A, Persimmon Rd., Clayton, GA 30525 (404) 782-6489.*

Bargain Barn. *Sales of hunting, fishing, archery, camping and backpacking equipment. Hwy. 53, P.O. Box B, Jasper, GA 30143 (404) 735-3340.*

Blue Ridge Mountain Sports. *Sales of backpacking, camping, canoeing and kayaking equipment and rental of backpacking and camping equipment. Lenox Square Mall, 3393 Peachtree Road NE, Atlanta, GA 30326 (404) 266-8372.*

Call Of The Wild. *Sales of backpacking, camping, canoeing, fly fishing and rock climbing equipment and rental of backpacking and camping equipment. 425 Market Place, Roswell, GA 30075 (404) 992-5400.*

Chattooga Whitewater Shop. *Sales and rental of canoeing, kayaking and rafting equipment. Instruction in canoeing, kayaking and rafting. Shuttle service on the Chattooga River. Cost: $10.00 - $30.00. US 76, Long Creek, SC 29658 (803) 647-9083.*

Georgia Outdoors. *Sales and rental of canoeing, fishing, backpacking and camping equipment. 6518 Roswell Rd., Sandy Springs, GA 30324 (404) 256-4040.*

Go With The Flow. *Sales of canoeing, kayaking and windsurfing equipment and sales and rental of windsurfing equipment. 4 Elizabeth Way, Roswell, GA 30075 (404) 992-3200.*

High Country Outfitters, Inc. *Sales of rock climbing equipment and sales and rental of backpacking, camping, canoeing and kayaking equipment. Location 1: 595 Piedmont Ave., NE, Atlanta, GA 30308 (404) 892-0909; Location 2: 1349 Cumberland Mall, Atlanta, GA 30339 (404) 434-7578; Location 3: 4400 Ashford Dunwoody Rd., 1412 Perimeter Mall, Atlanta, GA 30346 (404) 391-9657; Location 4: The Mall at Green Hills, 2168 Abbott Martin Rd., Nashville, TN 37215 (615) 383-1007.*

The History Store. *Sales of maps and books on southern Appalchia, official US geological surveys, topography maps, guide books and field guides. 114 North Park St., P.O. Box 358, Dahlonega, GA 30535 (404) 864-7225.*

Mountain Crossing. *Sales of camping and backpacking equipment. Route 1 Box 1240, Blairsville, GA 30512 (404) 745-6095.*

Mountain Crossing at Walasi-Yi Center. *Sales of backpacking and camping gear, specializing in long distance trips. Operation of seasonal hostel (March 1 - May 31) on Appalachian Trail. Advice and information on local trails and campsites. Hwy. 129, Rt. 1, Box 1240, Balirsville, GA 30512 (404) 745-6095.*

Mountaintown Outdoor Expeditions. *Sales and rental of canoeing, kayaking, camping, backpacking, and mountain biking equipment. P.O. Box 86, Ellijay, GA 30540 (404) 635-2524.*

Mountain Ventures. *Sales of camping, backpacking, rock climbing, caving and canoeing equipment and rental of camping and backpacking equipment. 3040 N.Decatur Rd., Scottdale (Decatur) GA 30079 (404) 299-5254.*

Nantahala Outdoor Center. *Sales of paddling, bicycling, backpacking, rock climbing and camping equipment and rental of canoeing, kayaking and rafting equipment. Instruction in canoeing, kayaking, backpacking and rock climbing. Guided raft trips on the Chattooga, Nantahala, Ocoee, French Broad and Nolichucky Rivers. Adventure travel expeditions to many destinations within and outside the U.S. U.S. 19 West, Box 41, Bryson City, NC 28713 (704) 488-2175.*

Outback Outfitters & Bikes. *Sales of mountain bikes and accessories, backpacking and camping equipment and apparel. 1125 Euclid Ave. NE, Atlanta, GA 30307 (404) 688-4878.*

REI. *A consumer cooperative offering sales of camping, backpacking, climbing, boating and skiing equipment and mountain bikes. Comprehensive rental department. 1800 NE Expressway, Atlanta, GA 30320 (Intersection of Clairmont and I-85) (404) 633-6508.*

Rock Creek Outfitters. *Sales of rock climbing, camping, backpacking, canoeing and kayaking equipment and rental of backpacks and tents. 4825 Hixson Pike, Chattanooga, TN 37443 (615) 877-6256.*

Smoky Mountain Sports. *Sales and rental of canoeing, kayaking, backpacking and camping equipment. 1226 Clairmont Road, Decatur, GA 30030 (404) 325-5295.*

Southeastern Expeditions. *Guided raft trips on the Chattooga and Ocoee Rivers. 1955 Cliff Valley Way, Suite 220, Atlanta, GA 30329 (404) 329-0433.*

Wilderness Southeast. *Nonprofit outdoor school offering adventure trips throughout the Southeast and to the Virgin Islands and Costa Rica. 711 Sandtown Road, Savannah, GA 31410 (912) 355-8008.*

The Wildewood Outpost. *Sales and rental of canoeing and rafting equipment. P.O Box 119, Helen, GA 30545 (404) 865-4451.*

Wildwater Ltd. Outdoor Adventures. *Guided raft trips on the Chattooga and Ocoee Rivers. Long Creek, SC 29658 (803) 647-9587.*

Wolfcreek Wilderness. *Nonprofit outdoor school offering leadership training and instruction in backpacking, canoeing and rock climbing. Rt. 1 Box 1190, Blairsville, GA 30512 (404) 745-5553.*

Books and References

The following books and booklets will help to illuminate the botany, geology, geography, commerce and culture of the Georgia mountains.

A Directory to North Carolina's Natural Areas *by Charles E. Roe, NC Natural Heritage Foundation, 1987, 1988 (second printing).*

Appalachian Whitewater, Volume 1 The Southern Mountains *by Bob Sehlinger, Don Otey, Bob Benner, William Nealy and Bob Lantz, Menasha Ridge Press, Birmingham, AL 1986.*

The Atlas of Georgia *by Thomas W. Hodler and Howard A. Schretter, The University of Georgia, Athens, Ga 1986.*

Foxfire *series edited by Eliot Wigginton, Anchor Press/Doubleday, Garden City, NY 1975.*

The Hiking Trails of North Georgia *by Tim Homan, Peachtree Publishers, Ltd., Atlanta, GA 1987.*

Inns of the Southern Mountains *by Patricia L. Hudson, EPM Publications, McLean, VA 1985.*

Mountain Getaways *by Rusty Hoffland, On the Road Publishing, Atlanta, GA 1988.*

Mountain Singer, The Life and The Legacy of Byron Herbert Reece *by Raymond A. Cook, Cherokee Publishing Company, Atlanta, GA 1980.*

The Natural Environments of Georgia *by Charles H. Wharton, Georgia Department of Natural Resources, Atlanta, GA 1978.*

North Carolina Hiking Trails, *Second edition by Allen de Hart, Appalachian Mountain Club Books, Boston, MA 1988.*

Northern Georgia Canoeing *by Bob Sehlinger and Don Otey, Menasha Ridge Press, Birmingham, AL 1980.*

Trees of the Southeastern United States *by Wilbur H. Duncan and Mirion B. Duncan, The University of Georgia Press, Athens, GA 1988.*

Wildflowers of the Southeastern United States *by Wilbur H. Duncan and Leonard E. Foote, The University of Georgia Press, Athens, GA 1975.*

Special Events, Fairs and Festivals

Attendance at a select few annual events in the mountains would give the reader a good insight into mountain history, culture and people. Following are some of the best of these events. Dates are subject to change.

Annual Harvest Sale, *Crafts and antiques show in Blue Ridge in October (404) 632-5680.*

Clarkesville Fall Festival, *Arts and crafts show, Georgia 115 east of Clarkesville in October (800) 822-0316.*

Dahlonega Blue Grass Festival, *at Blackburn Park on Old State Rd. 9E, 7 miles west of Dahlonega in June (404) 864-3721.*

Fall Harvest Festival, *Country music, arts and crafts at Fairgrounds in Hiawassee in October (404) 896-4191.*

Fasching Karnival, *In Helen in December and January (404) 878-2521.*

Georgia Apple Festival, *Crafts show in Ellijay in October (404) 635-7400.*

Georgia Mountain Fair, *12 days of crafts exhibits and entertainment at fairgrounds in Hiawassee in August (404) 896-4191.*

Harvest Festival, *Arts and crafts at farmer's market on U.S. 441 in Dillard (404) 782-4812.*

Helen to the Atlantic Hot-Air Balloon Race, *In June (404) 878-2521.*

Helen's Oktoberfest, *German food, beverage and entertainment in Helen in October (404) 878-2521.*

Mountain Maffick, *Arts and crafts festival, Hwy. 441 south of Clayton in May and October (404) 782-5246.*

New Echota/Cherokee Fall Festival, *Festival of Cherokee Indian culture, on GA 225, 3 miles east of Calhoun in October (404) 629-8151.*

Prater's Mill Country Fair, *Arts and crafts festival, Ga. Hwy. 2, 10 miles north of Dalton in May and October (404) 259-5765.*

The Reach of Song, *An Appalachian drama presenting the Georgia mountains through the life and words of native poet Byron Herbert Reece; in Hiawassee in June and July (404) 536-3431.*

Sorghum Festival, *in Blairsville in October (404) 745-5789.*

Spring Country Music Festival, *At fairgrounds in Hiawassee in May (404) 896-4191.*

Conservation and Outdoor Organizations

All of the following are non-profit organizations dedicated to the enjoyment and/or preservation of nature's bounty in the Georgia mountains and beyond.

Atlanta Audubon Society, *Box 29217, Atlanta, GA 30359 (404) 364-9479. Conservation and environmental education, including bird study. Monthly programs on environmental concerns. News hotline concerning programs and bird sightings.*

Atlanta Whitewater Club, *P.O. Box 33, Clarkston, GA 30021.*

Benton MacKaye Trail Association, *P.O. Box 53271, Atlanta, GA 30355. Enjoyment and maintenance of the Benton MacKaye Trail. Monthly hikes and trail maintenance along sections of the trail.*

The Dogwood City Grotto, *1865 Ridgewood Dr. NE, Atlanta, GA 30307. Atlanta chapter of the National Speleological Society. Cave protection, conservation and exploration. Monthly outings to explore caves in the Southeast.*

Forest Watch, *1819 Peachtree Road NE, Suite 714, Atlanta, GA 30309. (404) 876-2900. Protection of national forests and the preservation of their biodiversity. Annual workshops and frequent field trips to monitor road building and timbering on national forest land.*

Friends of the Mountains, *Box 368, Clayton, GA 30525. Preservation and enjoyment of the Southern Appalachian Mountain environment. Quarterly business meetings and conservation fair each spring. Monthly outings to natural areas in north Georgia and western North Carolina.*

Georgia Appalachian Trail Club, Inc., *P.O. Box 654, Atlanta, GA 30301. Maintenance of the Appalachian Trail and approach trails in Georgia. Weekly hikes and outings. Monthly trail maintenance.*

Georgia Botanical Society, *7575 Rico Road, Palmetto, GA 30268. Furthering the appreciation of wildflowers. Monthly or semi-monthly outings throughout Georgia and contiguous states.*

Georgia Canoeing Association, *P.O. Box 7023, Atlanta, GA 30305. River enjoyment and conservation. Training programs and weekly paddling trips in Georgia and contigious states.*

Guide To The North Georgia Mountains

THE GEORGIA CONSERVANCY

The Georgia Conservancy, Inc., *781 Marietta Street NW, Suite B100, Atlanta, GA 30318.* (404) 876-2900. *711 Sandtown Road, Savannah, GA 31410 (912) 897-6462. Protection of Georgia's environment and the encouragement of responsible stewardship of our vital natural resources. Annual conference, naturalist trips and chapter activities.*

Georgia Ornithological Society, *P.O. Box 1278, Cartersville, GA 30120. Furthering education about and understanding of birds. Semi-annual statewide meetings for field study, fellowship and information exchange.*

Georgia Wildlife Federation, *1936 Iris Drive, Conyers, GA 30207* (404) 929-3350. *Wise use and conservation of wildlife and its habitat.*

Ens And Outs, *Unitarian Universalist Congregation of Atlanta, 1911 Cliff Valley Way NE, Atlanta, GA 30329. Preservation and enjoyment of nature. Weekly outings to a variety of destinations throughout the state.*

The Nature Conservancy, *1401 Peachtree St. NE, Suite 136, Atlanta, GA 30309.* (404) 873-6946. *Preservation of rare and endangered species and natural communities through protection of the ecosystems that sustain them. Annual general membership meetings and field trips throughout the year.*

North Carolina Bartram Trail Society, *Route 3, Box 406, Sylva, NC 28779. Development, maintenance and enjoyment of the Bartram Trail.*

The Sierra Club, Georgia Chapter, *P.O. Box 46751, Atlanta, GA 30346. Exploration, enjoyment and preservation of the nation's forests, waters, wildlife and wilderness. Seven chapters throughout Georgia with monthly meetings and frequent outings to locations throughout the Southeast.*

Trout Unlimited, Georgia Council, *5074 Odins Way, Marietta, GA 30067. Protection, preservation and enhancement of cold water fisheries.*

The Wilderness Society, *1819 Peachtree Road NE, Suite 714, Atlanta, GA 30309.* (404) 355-1783. *Protection of natural areas on our federal lands, including national forests, national parks and national wildlife refuges. Helps coordinate activities of the citizen group, Forest Watch.*

262

Safety in the Mountains

The mountains of Georgia invite you outdoors. Their cool glades, interesting trails, diverse wildlife, rushing streams, lush vegetation and scenic vistas attract both the casual visitor and the hearty explorer. This is as it should be, and the reader is encouraged to use this guide as a companion when venturing into Georgia's exciting mountain wonderland.

We also urge users to be cautious and prepare for the unexpected. In a few minutes, what was a pleasant hike in the warm summer sun, can become a test of endurance in a cold, heat-sapping, hypothermia inducing rain storm. Or, you can experience the feeling that comes from being "temporarily disoriented" in a strange area without map or compass. Or, the even more serious feeling that comes from being alone and injured on an out-of-the-way trail.

Recognizing and preparing for these possibilities will help the visitor to cope with minor inconveniences or major emergencies.

The Georgia Conservancy recommends that you not travel alone on any but the most heavily used trails, and certainly not on long hikes or overnight trips.

There are a few essentials that should always accompany you when enjoying outings in the mountains. A day pack is sufficient to carry most of them. Prepare your own list to your comfort level, but the essentials should include:

Water - Carry one or more unbreakable bottles of fresh water. You might also wish to carry a simple water treatment system for emergency field treatment.

Food - Carry enough for the time you expect to be out, plus extra for the unexpected. Include quick energy items such as trail mix (gorp) and candies.

Compass and Map - If without a map, use the compass to walk in a straight line in the direction of a known landmark, such as a road. A good map allows exploration of areas you might not otherwise attempt. Learn how to use the compass and become familiar with your map before setting off.

First Aid - At a minimum, carry a basic first aid kit containing, bandages, tape, aspirin, moleskin, disinfectant/antiseptic, analgesic tablets, small mirror and any personal medicines. If allergic to insect stings, etc., be prepared for them. Familiarity with first aid, stabilizing broken bones, controlling bleeding, recognizing and treating hyperthermia, etc. can be reassuring to you and members of your party. A small investment of time and money in a first aid course can provide that reassurance.

Carry sunscreen, lip protection, sunglasses, etc. as appropriate to the season and conditions.

Flashlight - A good idea even on day outings. Carry extra bulb and batteries.

Pocket Knife - A sturdy, multi-purpose knife is recommended.

Waterproof Matches and/or Lighter - Combined with a small amount of combustible materials, one can light a fire for signaling and warmth. Keep materials in a waterproof container.

Space Blanket - A compact, light-weight material with a reflective side. Helps to hold in body heat. Can be used as a lean-to in emergencies. Also carry 20-30 ft. of twine and several baby diaper pins (useful for all sorts of emergencies and minor repairs).

Clothing and Rainwear - Always prepare for the possibility of sudden rain and wind storms. Depending on the season, anything from a cheap plastic poncho to the latest in protective clothing. At the minimum, a lightweight water repellant windbreaker is recommended.

Always carry a pair of gloves (wool or pile recommended), and a hat.

Most experts recommend dressing in "layers" of clothing suitable to weather conditions. Carry extra clothing in a waterproof container, perhaps a large plastic freezer bag.

GLOSSARY OF COMMON PLANT NAMES
USED IN THE GUIDE BOOK

Alabama snow-wreath	*Neviusia alabamensis*
Alum root	*Heuchera villosa*
Arbutus, trailing	*Epigaea repens*
Ash, blue	*Sorbus americanum*
Ash, mountain	*Sorbus americana*
Azalea, flame	*Rhododendron claendulaceum*
Azalea, pinxterflower	*Rhododendron nudiflorum*
Basswood	*Tilia heterophylla*
Beech	*Fagus grandiflora*
Biltmore Sedge	*Carex sp.*
Birch, black	*Betula lenta*
Birch, sweet	*Betula lenta*
Birch, yellow	*Betula lutea*
Black locust	*Rabinia pseudo-acacia*
Black walnut	*Juglans nigra*
Bloodroot	*Sanguinaria canadensis*
Blue cohosh	*Caulophyllum thalictroides*
Blue Ridge St. John's wort	*Hypericum buckleyi*
Bluebell, Virginia	*Mertensia virginica*
Blueberries, hi-bush and low-bush	*Vaccinium sp.*
Bluestem grass	*Andropogon sp.*
Bluets	*Houstonia sp.*
Buckeye	*Aesculus octandra*
Buttercups, mountain	*Ranunculus sp.*
Camellia, mountain	*Stewartia ovata*
Carolina bells	*Halesia carolina*
Cedar, red	*Juniperus virginiana*
Cherry, black	*Prunus serotina*
Chestnut, American	*Castanea dentata*
Chokeberry	*Sorbus melanocarpa*
Cinquefoil	*Potentilla sp.*
Colombo	*Swertia carolinensis*
Cotton-grass	*Eriophorum virgincum*
Cucumber tree	*Magnolia acuminata*
Deerberry	*Vaccinium sp.*
Dog-hobble	*Leucothoe axilaris* or *recurva*
Dogwood	*Cornus florida*
Dogwood, alternate-leaf	*Cornus alternifolia*
Dropseed, prairie	*Sporobolus sp.*
Dutchman's breeches	*Dicentra cucullaria*

THE GEORGIA CONSERVANCY

Elderberry	*Sambucus pubens*
False lily of the valley	*Maianthemum canadense*
Fern, bracken	*Pteridium aquilinum*
Fern, Christmas	*Polystichum acrostichoides*
Fern, cinnamon	*Osmunda cinnamonea*
Fern, hayscented	*Dennstaedtia punctilobula*
Fern, log	*Dryopteris celsa*
Fern, marginal wood	*Dryopteris marginalis*
Fern, New York	*Thelypteris noveboracensis*
Fern, rock cap	*Polypodium virginianum*
Fern, walking	*Asplenium rhizophyllum*
Fir, Fraser's	*Abies fraseri*
Fleabane	*Erigeron philadelphicus*
Galax	*Galax aphylla*
Gay-wings	*Polygala pavcifolia*
Gentian, fringed	*Gentiana crinita*
Ginger, wild	*Hexastylis sp.*
Ginseng	*Panex quinquefolius*
Goldenrod	*Solidago sp.*
Gooseberry	*Ribes sp.*
Grass of parnassus	*Parnassia asarifolia*
Harbinger of spring	*Erigenia bulbosa*
Hawthorne	*Crataegus sp.*
Hazelnut, beaked	*Borylus cornuta*
Hellebore	*Veratrum viride*
Hemlock, Carolina	*Tsuga caroliniana*
Hemlock, Eastern	*Tsuga canadensis*
Hickory	*Carya sp.*
Holly	*Ilex opaca*
Hop hornbeam	*Ostrya virginiana*
Horse sugar	*Symplocos tinctoria*
Horsetail	*Equisetum sp.*
Hyacinth, wild	*Camissia seilloides*
Hydrangea, wild	*Hydrangea arborescens*
Iris	*Iris cristata* and *Iris verna*
Japanese knotweed	*Polygonum sp.*
Japanese paper plant	*Edgeworthia papyrifera*
Kudzu	*Pueraria lobata*
Lady slipper, pink	*Cypripedium acaule*
Lady slipper, yellow	*Cypripedium calceolus*

Laurel, bog	*Kalmia augustifolia*
Laurel, mountain	*Kalmia latifolia*
Lily, turk's cap	*Lillium superbum*
Lily of the valley	*Convallaria majalis*
Locust	*Robinia sp.*
Lovegrass, weeping	*Eragrostis sp.*
Magnolia	*Magnolia sp.*
Magnolia, Fraser's	*Magnolia fraseri*
Maple	*Acre sp.*
Maple, mountain	*Acer spicatum*
Maple, red	*Acer rubrum*
Maple, striped	*Acer pensylvanicum*
Maple, sugar	*Acer saccharum*
Mayapple	*Podophyllum peltatum*
Minniebush	*Kalmia angustifolia*
Mock-orange, hairy	*Philadelphus hirsuta*
Monkshood	*Aconitum sp.*
Moss, primitive club	*Lycopodium sp.*
Moss, reindeer	*Cladonia sp.*
Moss, sphagnum	*Sphagnum sp.*
Nettle, hedge	*Stachys nuttallii*
Oak, chestnut	*Quercus prinus*
Oak, chinquapin	*Quercus prinoides*
Oak, Northern red	*Quercus rubra*
Oak, scarlet	*Quercus coccinea*
Oak, white	*Quercus alba*
Oconee bells	*Shortia galacifolia*
Orchid, purple fringed	*Habenaria psycodes*
Orchis, showy	*Orchis spectabilis*
Oxalis	*Oxalis acetosella*
Pepperbush, mountain	*Clettora acuminata*
Pine, Eastern white	*Pinus strobus*
Pine, loblolly	*Pinus taeda*
Pine, pitch	*Pinus ridgida*
Pine, short leaf	*Pinus echinata*
Pine, table mountain	*Pinus pungens*
Pine, Virginia	*Pinus virginiana*
Pine, white	*Pinus strobus*
Polygala, fringed	*Polygala paucifolia*
Poplar, tulip or yellow	*Liriodendron tulipifera*
Poppy, celandine	*Stylophorum diphyllum*
Pussy-toes	*Antennaria sp.*
Ramp (wild mountain onion)	*Allium tricoccum*

267

Raspberry, mountain	*Rubus odoratus*
Rhododendron, Carolina	*Rhododendron minus*
Rhododendron, catawba	*Rhododendron catawbiense*
Rhododendron, rosebay	*Rhododendron maximum*
Rosy twisted stalk	*Streptopus roseus*
Sand myrtle	*Leiophyllum buxifolium*
Saxifrage	*Saxifraga sp.*
Serviceberry	*Amelanchier arborea*
Silverbell	*Halesia carolina*
Smoketree	*Cotinus obovatus*
Solomon's seal	*Polygonatum biflorum*
Sourwood	*Oxydendron aboreum*
Spike moss	*Lycopodium selago* or *porophilum*
Spike moss, rock	*Selaginella ruprestris*
Spike moss, twisted-hair	*Selaginella tortipila*
Spikenard	*Aralia racemosa*
Spurge, nodding	*Peltrandra procumbrens*
Strawberry, bush	*Euonymus atropurpureus*
Strawberry, wild	*Potentilla tridentata*
Swamp pink	*Helonias bullata*
Toothwort	*Dentaria diphylla*
Trillium, faded	*Trillium sp.*
Trillium, Gleason's white	*Trillium simile*
Trillium, lanceleaf	*Trillium lancefolium*
Trillium, persistent	*Trillium persistens*
Twinleaf	*Jeffersonia diphylla*
Umbrella leaf	*Diphylleia cymosa*
Viburnum	*Viburnum alnitolium*
Violets	*Viola sp.*
Virginia creeper	*Parthenocissus quinquefolia*
Watercress	*Nastaurtium officinale*
Wild bergamot	*Monarda fistulosa*
Willow, dwarf	*Salix humilis*
Witch hazel	*Hamamelis virginia*
Wolfsmilk	*Euphorbia purpurea*
Yellowwood	*Cladrastris lutea*
Yellowroot	*Xanthorhiza simplicissima*

NOTE: *sp.* = species, either not known specifically or several different ones represented.

Index

The Georgia Conservancy

THE GEORGIA CONSERVANCY

SPONSORS

The Georgia Conservancy gratefully acknowledges the following sponsors who made the publication of this guidebook possible:

Georgia Department of Natural Resources

Georgia Power Company

Nell H. Jones

Thomas D. Perrie

Charles and Deen Day Smith

Charles A. Smithgall

Charles H. Wharton

The Georgia Conservancy

The Georgia Conservancy is an independent, nonprofit organization of citizens, community groups and businesses dedicated to protecting Georgia's environment and encouraging responsible stewardship of vital natural resources. In pursuing this mission, The Georgia Conservancy works to ensure a balance between environmental concerns and the demands of social and economic progress.

Since its founding in 1967, The Georgia Conservancy has built a solid reputation for its reasoned, pragmatic approach to environmental problem-solving and its well-practiced ability to build consensus on difficult and complex issues. Through education and advocacy, The Georgia Conservancy plays a key role in developing public policy and enhancing environmental quality. Achievements include the designation of Cumberland Island as a National Seashore, protection of the Cohutta Mountains and Okefenokee Swamp as Wilderness Areas, creation of the Chattahoochee River National Recreation Area, initiation of state growth management policies, development of a national forest management plan, and protection of coastal marshes, sand dunes and freshwater wetlands.

As Georgia continues its unprecedented growth, the pressures on our environment increase. The Georgia Conservancy is committed to its leadership role as the state's primary resource for environmental information and advocacy. The Guide to the North Georgia Mountains, like its companion book, A Guide to the Georgia Coast, celebrates our magnificent natural heritage and is a testament to the compelling need to protect it for present and future generations.

Georgia Conservancy Membership Benefits

When you join The Georgia Conservancy, you join thousands of citizens who have decided to act positively for environmental quality. Basic membership benefits include:

* *Action alerts about important environmental issues*
* *Georgia Conservancy decal*
* *Opportunities to identify, research and address environmental issues*
* *Weekend adventures and monthly naturalist day trips*
* *Annual environmental conference*
* *Chapter activities where available*
* *Representation with local and national environmental decision makers*
* *Personal satisfaction in making a positive difference for Georgia's natural environment.*

Special membership benefits are available to members at Sustaining, Donor and Cambium levels.

Make the Natural Decision.
Join The Georgia Conservancy.

Yes, I/we would like to join The Georgia Conservancy and safeguard Georgia's natural beauty. Enclosed is a tax deductible contribution of:

$1,000 Gold Cambium	$40 Family/Dual
$ 500 Silver Cambium	$40 Nonprofit organization
$ 250 Bronze Cambium	$25 Individual
$ 100 Donor	$15 Retiree
$ 70 Sustaining	$15 Student

I/We would like to give a gift membership at the level marked above to the following. The acknowledgement should read:

From_____

Name_____

Address_____

City_____

Telephone (work)_____(home)_____

Please make your check payable to The Georgia Conservancy. Mail to 781 Marietta St., Atlanta, GA 30318.

٢١